Classic
JUNIOR LEAGUE®
COOKBOOK COLLECTION

THE GASPARILLA COOKBOOK

Compiled

by

THE JUNIOR LEAGUE

of

TAMPA

1961

WITH ILLUSTRATIONS by *LAMAR SPARKMAN*

Favorite Recipes® Press

Copyright © 2011 by
Favorite Recipes® Press
an imprint of

FRP. INC

a wholly owned subsidiary of Southwestern
P.O. Box 305142
Nashville, Tennessee 37230
1-800-358-0560

The Gasparilla Cookbook
Copyright © 1961 by The Junior League of Tampa, Inc.

Published and Distributed by FRP, Inc., under license granted by
The Junior League of Tampa, Inc.

Executive Editor: Sheila Thomas
Project Editor: Tanis Westbrook
Classic Junior League Cookbook Collection Cover Design: Starletta Polster

Library of Congress Control Number: 2011924421
ISBN: 978-0-87197-553-9

Manufactured in the United States of America

One of the criteria to be considered for the Classic Junior League Cookbook
Collection is the original publication date; the cookbook must be at
least 25 years old. As a result of the length of time in print, some titles have
gone through revisions and updates; others have been intentionally
left in their original context in order to preserve the integrity and authenticity
of the publication. This printing has been taken from the most recent
edition. We hope you enjoy this American icon.

For more than 70 years, Junior League cookbooks have been sought out and collected by both novice and seasoned home cooks. Turned to again and again for their tried-and-true recipes, these cookbooks are a testament to the Junior League volunteers who dedicate themselves to improving the quality of life within their communities. These treasured cookbooks have played a significant role both in raising funds to help fulfill the organizations' missions and by documenting and preserving regional culinary traditions.

Favorite Recipes® Press, a longtime friend and partner of the Association of Junior Leagues International, is proud to present the *Classic Junior League Cookbook Collection*. The inaugural collection is comprised of six Junior League cookbooks that define all that is *Classic;* each serves as a standard of excellence and is considered an authentic and authoritative work on the foods and traditions of its region.

Enjoy,

Sheila Thomas

Executive Editor
Favorite Recipes Press

Acknowledgements

It is a simple matter to decide to publish a cookbook.

It is another matter to finance it, to name it, to devise a suitable theme and a make-up to carry it, to illustrate it, to collect the recipes for it (which must then be sorted, checked, revised, tested and catalogued), to print it, to proofread it, to index it, to copyright it, to bind it, to cover it, and to publicize it. This is not simple.

But it has been done, and for this accomplishment we are indebted to:

Deedee Gray

who supervised every phase of the operation as Cookbook Chairman in addition to her painstaking work as Editor.

Patricia Morgan

who, as Co-Editor, wrote the narrative theme of the book and supervised the layout.

Annie Laurie Saxton

who reviewed over 2,000 recipes (with the help of Shirley Savage and Kay Hampton) before the final selections were made, and then revised hundreds of recipes to conform to standard.

Byron Crowder

who, as Promotion Chairman, made of the book a seeming reality long before it was a fact, and who was instrumental in securing the art work.

Carlton Wilder

who managed to use a fierce pirate on the same dust jacket with delicious food and make of it a beautiful and believable picture.

Lamar Sparkman

who combined an inborn love of the region with his creative ability to illustrate the theme so aptly.

Gloria Sparkman

Lamar's devoted wife who was chief proofreader as well as the artist's inspiration.

Mary Singleton

who laboriously cross-indexed the book's recipes in addition to proofreading.

Margaret Davis and
Marguerite Nettles

who (with the help of Mary Audrey Blake) spent hundreds of hours typing
id checking the manuscript.

Dottie Sue Crowell

who contacted famous restaurants in the area and obtained from them their
iost prized recipes.

Sue McNevin

who checked and revised recipes as well as researching background material
or the Junior League story on the dust jacket. Also active on the original
ommittee were Jean Harris, Jane Hewit, Martha Sue Logan and Ruth
[cMullen.

Winkie Howell and
Mary Sue Frank

who spent a year laying the groundwork for a book of this type including
etailed plans for financing it.

Ye Mystic Krewe of Gasparilla

who let us use their name and endorsed the project in the interest of the
ommunity.

Henry Quednau,
L. Robert Frank and
Ann McDuffie

who served as unpaid professional advisors when and wherever we needed
hem.

Tampa Electric Leisure House

where Miss Julia B. Sanders and Mrs. Betsy Byrnes supervised the testing
f recipes free of charge.

All The Good Cooks

who parted with their favorite recipes, especially those who prepared dishes
or cookbook promotion parties where Nonita Henson proved her skill as
Iospitality Chairman.

The Headquarters Committee

who bravely delayed their building plans so that their funds might be used
o launch the cookbook.

Chris Dingman

who conceived the idea of a Gasparilla cookbook and whose advice made
t possible.

Hillsboro Printing & Lithographing Company

whose personnel translated an effort into this accomplishment.

J. L. T.

Invasion Day

Introduction

A friend of ours once went to a famous restaurant in New Orleans and asked the waiter to suggest a meal that was new and different.

"Ah!" he smiled, "Madame should try the most delicious Le Filet De Pompano En Papillote, a delicate fish baked in a paper bag."

"Oh, we have that at home," replied the customer. "What else would you suggest?"

"Then, perhaps Madame would like Le Filet De Truite Amandine, an elegant combination of trout with an almond sauce."

"We have that at home," said Madame.

"Le Coeur De Filet De Boeuf Marchand De Vin?"

"That too."

"Langouste Thermidor?"

"Also."

With an incredulous air the waiter regarded his customer. "But, Madame," he cried, "where are you from?"

"Tampa, Florida," replied our friend and settled for a savory bowl of gumbo, one dish she could not get at home.

For those of you who, like the waiter, have never heard of Tampa this book has been compiled. Where the spine of Florida, the Ridge District, begins its gentle slope westward to the Gulf of Mexico there lies a town at the head of a beautiful bay, unlike any other town in Florida. This is Tampa, named by the Caloosa Indians long before the advent of the Spanish Conquistadors. This is Tampa which has been occupied in turn by Spanish treasure seekers, missionaries, pirates, U. S. troops garrisoned here during the Seminole Indian Wars, a French Count who was the head surgeon of Napoleon's Navy, pioneers from southern states, pioneers from northern states, Union troops, Confederate troops, Cuban cigar makers from Key West, troops in the Spanish-American War, Tin Can tourists, wealthy tourists, real estate speculators, Air Corps personnel in World War II, and last of all an influx of permanent residents who have made this the fastest growing area in Florida.

The bays and inlets of this Gulf Coast were once the hiding place of pirates who preyed on shipping in the Caribbean and the Gulf of Mexico. The last of these was Jose Gaspar, a lieutenant in the Spanish Navy, who seized his ship in 1783 and sailed to Florida where he spent over thirty years in a bloody career of piracy. He changed the name of his ship to GASPARILLA and named his base of operations Gasparilla Island. When he was 65 years old, he decided to retire to the life of a gentleman in South America with his millions in stolen treasure, and he and his band of cutthroats set sail. However, they made the mistake of trying to seize one more rich prize, a camouflaged U.S. Navy ship, and the GASPARILLA was badly riddled in the battle. Rather than submit to capture, Gaspar wrapped a length of anchor chain about his waist and leaped into the sea. His legend lives on in tales of treasure buried along the Gulf Coast as well as in the annual Gasparilla Invasion which takes place in Tampa yearly during the month of February. The week-long festival begins with an actual invasion of the city by Ye Mystic Krewe of Gasparilla aboard their full-rigged pirate ship. This is an unparalleled sight. The ship sails up the bay and into the Hillsborough River with guns and cannons blazing, accompanied by a flotilla of pleasure boats out to join in the fun. The members of the Krewe are costumed as pirates to such an extent that they are unrecognizable as the business and professional men they are the rest of the year. From the moment the mayor of Tampa surrenders the keys of the city, carnival reigns, through the Invasion Parade, the Coronation Ball where a new King and Queen of Gasparilla are crowned, a torchlight parade in the Latin section called Ybor City, and a host of social events which last until the final night of the festival when the pirates board ship once more and sail away down the bay. Tampa is nationally famous for its Gasparilla festivities not only because it's a fabulous spectacle but because the presence of so many visitors has spread the fame of the city's Spanish Restaurants.

In 1885 due to labor troubles in the cigar industry in Key West, Vicente Martinez Ybor came to Tampa where he established his factory and built the town of Ybor City for his workers. At the same time the cigar-making firm of Sanchez & Haya built a plant in the newly-platted town. Through the years it became a city within a city, the Latin Quarter of Tampa. From modest beginnings as coffee shops for the cigar workers, there evolved the Spanish restaurants of today which are unequalled for their variety and excellence of food. One restaurant has a dining room designed to resemble a Spanish courtyard, another has a splashing fountain; one has strolling guitar players, another has tiles depicting the story of Don Quixote in sequence around the walls; all have murals of scenes from Andalusia and the Basque country, all have snowy napery and water goblets in the jewel colors of cathedral windows, and all have Spanish waiters with old world manners. Each has still its coffee shop apart from the main dining rooms where the natives of Ybor City gather to discuss politics and drink the strong black Cuban coffee. All are famous for their Cuban sandwiches and soups which are more than a meal. And here are served the elegant dishes which the waiter in New Orleans recommended, but their names are spoken in lilting Castilian with a roll and a flourish.

Tampa is the hub of the region industrially, but more important for our purposes it's the hub of good food. Great cattle enterprises lie to the south and east, 22 miles down the coast of Tampa Bay is the farming community of Ruskin known as the salad bowl of the nation, across the bay to the west are the Gulf Beaches where seafood is king, all the area is citrus country at any point of the compass, and 28 miles northwest there is a Greek community called Tarpon Springs where the customs, the language, and the recipes are straight from the isles of the Aegean. The natives of this little town came to Tarpon Springs many years ago from Greece to harvest the sponges which are found in the Gulf of Mexico. Curio shops line the docks on the Anclote River where the sponge fleet ties up, but the Greek food affords the visitor's greatest enjoyment. In a dining room and lounge decorated with Grecian war masks, maps of the world as Homer knew it, models of ancient Greek warships, and the hull of a primitive sponge boat, one may feast on Greek salad which is fashioned as carefully as a mosaic and just as beautiful to behold. This alone would be worth the trip, but you may also have lamb prepared in strange and delicious ways, scarlet stone crab claws, the meat of which is too delicate to describe, or your choice of seafood, followed by honey-and-almond confections. Tampans can and do find a wonderful meal in any direction. All the good restaurants serve succulent steaks, there are several fine Chinese restaurants, there is even a good French restaurant west across Tampa Bay.

The notion that all Florida is palm trees, sand, and bathing beauties is false. So is the idea of Florida as a vast interior of sleepy cracker towns with pigs and chickens running the roads, or a steady diet of greasy fried chicken with blackened string beans. Florida is sun and sand, yes, but it is also cool lakes, ancient oaks, and lacy cypress trees, big cities, beautiful farms, and citrus groves covering rolling hills like tufted bedspreads. Florida is lush ranchland, crystal springs, dogwood and maple trees, people from everywhere and all walks of life who came to see, got sand in their shoes, and had to return. Tampa is a composite of all of it.

It's a bountiful land. We wish all could see for themselves. But if that is impossible, then we in our small way, will try to bring it to you. The food of a land tells the life of its people, and we would like to share our good life with everyone. Here is our offering. May it bring you pleasure as we have known it.

THE JUNIOR LEAGUE OF TAMPA

X

ILLUSTRATIONS
by Lamar Sparkman

Table of Contents

Brand names are given only when absolutely necessary.

XII

Kissing don't last: cookery do!

George Meredith, *The Ordeal of Richard Feverel*

CHAPTER I

Appetizers and Dips

At no time during the year is the cosmopolitan nature of Tampa more evident than at Gasparilla. All over the city visitors from far and near join with the native populace in celebrating this joyous midwinter festival. Under skies as blue as a robin's egg the participants set out with picnic hampers to watch the pirate invasion of the city from grassy spots on the banks of the sparkling bay or from the decks of pleasure boats. Later in the day there will be cocktail parties where the company is good, and the hors d'oeuvres bring to the occasion a touch of Latin flavor which is typical also of the city.

As the backgrounds of Tampa's citizens are varied, so are the foods. One finds the usual canapés and cocktail spreads interspersed with such delicacies as Bollitos or Guacamole. Bollitos are a Spanish appetizer made from ground dried black-eyed peas, flavored highly with garlic, formed into small balls, and fried in deep fat until they are a crusty, crunchy gold. Waiters bearing trays of these piping hot tidbits often get the feeling they are being followed. Many a guest has foregone dinner after a cocktail party because he was replete with Bollitos.

Guacamole is a creamy dip, the color of chartreuse, made from the incomparable Florida avocado pear. In the older sections of town there is a towering glossy-leaved avocado tree in every backyard, and when the fruit is ripe there is occasion for rejoicing. Neighbors appear mysteriously on the premises with a look of hope in their eyes. Is it possible the family has more pears than they can eat right away? The smooth rich meat of the avocado is a feast served with just salt and pepper, oil and vinegar, but there are many other ways to utilize this fruit which is truly more like a vegetable. Guacamole is a Spanish way of preparing the mashed avocado meat with spices, lemon, onion, and mayonnaise for a party snack which is a regional favorite.

Appetizers

WHOLE BEEF TENDERLOIN FOR HORS D'OEUVRES

1 whole beef tenderloin
Bacon
1 5-ounce bottle A-1 sauce
¼ pound butter

1 7-ounce can mushroom buttons, undrained
1 loaf Cuban bread or French bread (Cuban preferred)

Preheat oven to 400°. Lay several strips of bacon over the tenderloin; place on rack in roasting pan and bake uncovered for 15 to 25 minutes total time (15 minutes for rare to 25 minutes for well done or use meat thermometer). While meat is cooking heat to boiling the A-1 sauce, butter, mushrooms and juice. Cut Cuban bread into bite-size pieces.

To serve, place meat while hot on platter. Have bread on separate tray beside chafing dish containing sauce. Slice bite-size pieces of meat very thin, dip in sauce, place on piece of Cuban bread and eat as small open-faced sandwich. Serves 10 or 12. Four tenderloins will serve about 50 with double the sauce.

MRS. W. E. SUMNER

BOLLITOS-LA FLORIDA

1 pound dry black-eyed peas
2 cloves garlic

1 teaspoon salt

Soak peas overnight. In the morning slip the skins from the peas. (This is done by rubbing the peas between the hands.) Wash and drain. Grind peas and garlic fine until almost a paste. Add salt. Beat until the consistency of cake batter, then chill. Drop from a tablespoon into deep fat heated to 350°. Brown and serve hot.

JAMES E. WALL, JR.

PÂTÉ OF CHICKEN ALMOND

1 cup chicken, minced fine
¼ cup butter
1 tablespoon sherry

¼ cup chopped onion
¼ cup chopped toasted almonds

Blend chicken with butter. Add sherry and onion. Sprinkle with almonds.

MRS. WILLIAM E. HENSON

CAVIAR PIE

4 8-ounce packages cream cheese
Chopped onion and salt to taste
Cream to moisten cheese

Lemon juice to taste
4 3½-ounce jars of domestic caviar
12 hard-boiled eggs

Soften cheese with cream until you can easily mold with hand after adding onion. Mold on 8-inch cardboard, covered with aluminum foil. Have cheese about 2 inches high in the middle of cardboard and shaped out to edge of board—like the shape of a pie. Put in refrigerator until firm. When ready to serve, add lemon juice to caviar and ice the cheese mold with it.

Place on 12-inch cardboard, also covered with foil. Grate egg yolks and whites separately (or put through a ricer). Put yolks around cheese mold, and then on the outer edge, the whites. Serve on a large platter with crackers. The 8-inch and 12-inch cardboards can be obtained from a bakery. Serves fifty, can be halved.

MRS. E. B. BRADFORD

CHEESE BALLS

½ pound sharp Cheddar cheese
¼ pound Roquefort cheese
1 medium onion
3 packages cream cheese

1 cup chopped parsley
1 cup chopped pecans
Dash of Worcestershire
Tabasco

Grind Cheddar cheese, Roquefort cheese, and onion in food chopper. Add cream cheese and ½ of the parsley and pecans and seasonings. Form in 1-inch balls. Roll in remaining parsley and pecans.

MRS. WILLIAM O. KINNEBREW

CHEESE THINS

1 cup flour
1 teaspoon salt
¼ teaspoon paprika

2 cups grated cheese
¾ cup pecans, chopped fine
½ cup butter, creamed

Sift flour, and add salt, paprika, cheese and nuts. Add to creamed butter and make into 2 rolls. Put in refrigerator overnight. Slice thin and bake at 350° until light brown (10 to 15 minutes). (If you use margarine use a trifle less.)

MRS. GEORGE NETTLES

CHEESE AND OLIVE LOAF

½ pound bleu cheese
½ pound cream cheese
¼ cup butter
1 tablespoon minced chives

1 tablespoon brandy
½ cup minced ripe olives
1 3½-ounce can toasted almonds,
  chopped
Chopped watercress

Cream together bleu cheese, cream cheese and butter. Stir in chives, brandy and ripe olives. Form mixture into 2 rolls. Chill 2 to 3 hours. Cover with chopped toasted almonds and chopped watercress. Chill. Serve with crackers. Serves 30 to 40 people. This loaf can be made the day before serving. Can be frozen for future use.

MRS. J. BROWN FARRIOR

CHEESE ROLL

1 8-ounce package cream cheese
½ pound sharp Cheddar cheese,
  grated
1 cup finely minced pecans

1 clove garlic, pressed
½ teaspoon salt
1 tablespoon mayonnaise
Paprika

Soften cream cheese; blend with other ingredients. Mixture will be fairly soft. Chill slightly, then form into roll and chill until party time. Sprinkle with paprika. Serve with round crackers or Melba rounds. Serves from 20 to 30.

MRS. WM. C. MCLEAN, JR.

CHEESE SAVORIES

½ pound sharp Cheddar cheese,
  grated
1 stick butter or margarine
1 cup flour

¼ teaspoon salt
Dash paprika (optional)
Dates, pitted

Have cheese and butter at room temperature. Mash cheese until smooth; add butter and mix well. Sift together flour, salt and paprika, and add to cheese mixture. Form into 1-inch balls, and insert a date into each. Bake at 450° for 8 to 10 minutes, or until only delicately brown. Makes 30.

MRS. E. A. UPMEYER

CURRIED CHEESE ROUNDS

¾ cup grated Cheddar cheese
⅓ cup chopped scallions
¾ cup chopped ripe olives

⅓ cup mayonnaise
½ teaspoon curry powder

Mix well, place on toast rounds or fingers and run under the broiler for a few minutes.

MRS. HUGH MITCHELL

COCKTAIL CHEESE BISCUITS

1 stick butter (no substitute)
1 cup sharp yellow New York cheese
1 teaspoon salt

½ teaspoon red Cayenne pepper
1 cup flour
Pecan halves

Cream butter; add cheese, then salt and pepper and flour. Roll into small balls and press half-pecan on each ball to flatten. Place on cookie sheet and bake 15 minutes in 350° oven. Makes 40 to 45 biscuits.

MRS. GARRETT W. JUDY

RICE-CHEESE BALLS

4½-ounce package pre-cooked rice
3 tablespoons butter
3 tablespoons all-purpose flour
1 teaspoon salt
⅛ teaspoon ground white pepper
⅛ teaspoon Cayenne
½ teaspoon dry mustard

1 cup milk
1½ cups finely grated sharp cheese
1 teaspoon Worcestershire
1 teaspoon grated onion
1 egg
2 cups dry bread crumbs

Prepare rice according to label directions. In a saucepan, melt butter. Blend in flour, salt, pepper, Cayenne, and dry mustard. Gradually add milk, stirring constantly over low heat until very thick. Add cheese, Worcestershire, and onion. Add rice; chill. Shape into 1-inch balls. Dip each ball in slightly beaten egg; roll in bread crumbs. Deep fry at 375° about 2 minutes or until golden brown. Drain on paper towels and serve. Makes about 5 dozen.

MRS. CHARLES J. YOUNGER

LIPTAUER

2 3-ounce packages cream cheese
¼ cup butter
1 teaspoon capers
1 teaspoon paprika

2 anchovies, finely chopped
1 shallot or onion, finely chopped
½ teaspoon caraway seed
½ teaspoon salt

Put all ingredients in bowl and allow to soften to room temperature. Mix thoroughly. Line a small mold with thin aluminum foil, leaving edges of foil protruding for easy removal. Press above mixture into mold and allow to stand in refrigerator overnight to mellow. Serve with small rye bread, crackers, etc. Yield: 1½ cups.

MRS. J. BROWN FARRIOR

OLIVE-CHEESE NUGGETS

1 cup shredded sharp Cheddar
   cheese (¼ pound)
¼ cup soft butter
¾ cup sifted flour

⅛ teaspoon salt
½ teaspoon paprika
Stuffed green olives

Blend cheese and butter. Sift in flour, salt and paprika. Mix to form dough. Shape dough around olives, using about 1 teaspoon of dough for each olive. Bake on ungreased cookie sheet at 400° about 12 to 15 minutes, or until golden brown. Serve hot or cold.

MRS. NOVELL HALL

CURRIED SHRIMP IN CHUTNEY

Crab boil
3 pounds shrimp
   (size: 24 to a pound)
½ stick butter

1 teaspoon curry powder
   (or more to taste)
2 cups chutney, finely chopped

Use crab boil according to directions. Allow to boil 5 to 10 minutes before adding shrimp. Boil unpeeled shrimp 1 to 2 minutes. (The shrimp continue cooking in the chafing dish, so do not overboil.) Peel. Melt butter and add curry powder and finely chopped chutney. Stir in part of the slightly cooked shrimp and serve in chafing dish with toothpicks. Add more shrimp to chafing dish as needed. Serves about 30 people.

MRS. J. BROWN FARRIOR

MARINATED SHRIMP

5 pounds shrimp
Celery tops

½ cup mixed pickling spices
2 tablespoons salt

Cover the shrimp with boiling water to which other ingredients have been added. Cook approximately 10 minutes. Drain; cover with ice cubes; then clean and devein.

2 cups chopped green onions
and tops
2½ cups salad oil
1 cup white vinegar

Juice of 2 lemons
5 teaspoons celery seed
3 teaspoons salt
Dash of Tabasco

Alternate layers of shrimp and green onions. Combine other ingredients and pour over the shrimp and onions. Cover. Store in refrigerator for 12 hours. Stir gently. Serve as hors d'ouevres.

MRS. NOVELL HALL

SHRIMP RINGOLD

2¼ pounds boiled shrimp
4 hard boiled eggs
2 envelopes plain gelatin
1 small bottle tomato catsup
½ pint of mayonnaise
Tabasco to taste

Salt to taste
½ tube anchovy paste
Juice of 2 lemons and grated
rind of 1
1 small jar of chopped olives

Grind shrimp and eggs—not too fine. Soften gelatin in cup of cold water, then melt over hot water. Blend into the catsup and mayonnaise. Season to taste with Tabasco and salt. Add other ingredients. Pour into a quart ring or fish mold which has been greased with salad oil. Congeal in refrigerator. Serve sliced on beaten biscuit halves or crackers, or use the mold for salad.

MRS. PAUL LeBLANC

SHRIMP ROUNDELAYS

½ pound sharp Cheddar cheese
¼ pound soft butter
5 tablespoons grated onion
1 teaspoon Worcestershire
½ teaspoon dry mustard

½ teaspoon paprika
¼ cup lemon juice
2 cups ground cooked shrimp
3 dozen tiny whole cooked shrimp

Shred Cheddar cheese and combine with soft butter. Add onion, Worcestershire, dry mustard, paprika and lemon juice. Stir in ground shrimp. Spread on toast rounds. Place a tiny whole cooked shrimp on each canapé. Broil 3 inches from heat until cheese browns and bubbles. Makes about 3 dozen canapés.

MRS. J. BROWN FARRIOR

SHRIMP PASTE

2 pounds cooked, shelled and
  deveined shrimp, ground fine
1 small green pepper,
  chopped very fine
1 small onion, chopped fine
1 tablespoon finely chopped celery

¼ teaspoon dry mustard
Dash of Cayenne
1 teaspoon salt
2 tablespoons butter
1½ tablespoons flour
¾ cup milk

Mix shrimp, vegetables and seasonings. Make a thick cream sauce with the butter, flour and milk. Combine the two mixtures and pack into a quart mold, which has been brushed with salad oil. Chill thoroughly (3 to 4 hours) turn out of mold, and serve with crackers as a spread.

MRS. J. BROWN FARRIOR

SWEET AND SOUR SHRIMP

2 pounds raw shrimp,
  shelled and deveined
3 tablespoons minced onion
4 tablespoons margarine
1½ teaspoons salt

⅛ teaspoon Tabasco
2 tablespoons flour
1 cup beer (this is the secret)
1 bay leaf
2 tablespoons chopped fresh parsley

Wash and dry shrimp. Sauté shrimp and onion in margarine until shrimp turn pink. Add salt, Tabasco and flour; add beer, stirring constantly to boiling point. Add bay leaf; cook over low heat 5 minutes. Discard bay leaf and pour off juice. Sprinkle with parsley. Store in sealed jar in refrigerator until party time. Arrange and serve on cocktail picks. Two pounds will serve 6 or 8.

MRS. J. P. CORCORAN

Dips

BACON-CHEESE DIP

½ cup sour cream
¼ pound Roquefort or bleu cheese
1 3-ounce package cream cheese
¼ teaspoon Tabasco

4 slices crisp bacon
1 small clove diced garlic or
  2 tablespoons diced onion
¼ teaspoon whole celery seed

Put all ingredients into electric blender and blend until smooth. Chill and serve with potato chips or crackers. Yields 1½ to 2 cups.

MRS. CHARLES J. YOUNGER

CHUTNEY DIP

4 hard-boiled eggs
1 3-ounce package cream cheese
1 tablespoon Worcestershire
1 tablespoon curry powder
Dash of Cayenne
2 to 3 dashes Tabasco

¼ teaspoon celery seeds
2 tablespoons mayonnaise
Salt and pepper to taste
3 to 4 tablespoons chutney, chopped fine

Mash eggs with cheese. Add other ingredients, adding chutney last. Chill. Serve as a dip. This keeps well in the refrigerator for several weeks.

MRS. J. BROWN FARRIOR

DESSIE SMITH'S CLAM DIP

1 7½-ounce can minced clams and juice
3 heaping tablespoons mayonnaise

1 tablespoon Worcestershire
1 tablespoon pepper sauce
1 ounce crushed potato chips

Blend together and let stand approximately 1 hour in refrigerator. Serve in bowl as dip for crackers and potato chips.

WITHLACOOCHEE RIVER LODGE
Inglis, Florida

HOT CLAM DIP

1 8-ounce package cream cheese, (cartons of whipped cream cheese save much time and energy)
1 10½-ounce can minced clams
1 tablespoon lemon juice

2 tablespoons clam broth
1 tablespoon prepared mustard
2 teaspoons Worcestershire
⅛ teaspoon garlic powder
Dash Cayenne

Bring cheese to room temperature. Drain clams and reserve liquid. Combine cheese, lemon juice, clam broth, and seasonings. Blend in clams. Heat before serving with Melba toast or onion rounds. This can be made a day ahead and refrigerated. In fact it improves with age. It may seem thick when taken from refrigerator, but heating brings it to proper consistency. Triple the recipe and it will fill chafing dish and serve a party of 25 or 30.

MRS. CHARLES J. YOUNGER

CLAM CHEESE DIP

1 8-ounce package cream
  cheese (softened)
1 tablespoon lemon juice
½ teaspoon salt
1 teaspoon Worcestershire
1 teaspoon horseradish

1 tablespoon sherry wine
4 tablespoons clam liquid
1 7½-ounce can minced
  clams, drained
1 clove garlic, quartered
Corn chips, potato chips, etc.

Mix cream cheese with lemon juice, salt, Worcestershire sauce, horseradish, sherry wine and clam liquid until smooth. Add minced clams and garlic. Let stand for 1 hour. Remove garlic and serve as dip with corn chips, potato chips, etc. Serves 10 generously.

MRS. VICTOR B. YEATS

CRAB DIP

½ cup crabmeat
Juice of 1 lemon
2 to 3 dashes Tabasco
1 teaspoon Worcestershire
8 ounce package cream cheese
½ cup sour cream
⅛ teaspoon salt

½ cup mayonnaise
1 tablespoon minced onion
1 teaspoon chopped chives
1 clove garlic, minced
1 teaspoon cream-style
  horseradish

Marinate crabmeat in lemon juice, Tabasco and Worcestershire. Blend cream cheese and sour cream until smooth. Add salt and beat in mayonnaise. Add onion, chives, and garlic. Fold in crabmeat. Add horseradish. Serve with potato chips or crackers.

MRS. J. BROWN FARRIOR

EDAM CHEESE DIP

1 Edam cheese
¼ cup butter
½ teaspoon dry mustard
Dash of Tabasco

¼ cup chopped stuffed olives
¼ cup minced green onion
Beer

Cut the top from an Edam cheese, and carefully scoop out the inside. Mash the cheese thoroughly or put through the meat grinder. Mix it with butter, dry mustard, Tabasco, olives and green onion. Add enough beer to give the mixture a spreading consistency. Put the mixture back into the cheese shell and serve surrounded by crisp crackers.

LEISURE HOUSE, TAMPA ELECTRIC COMPANY

FONDUE NEUFCHATELOISE

1 pound Swiss cheese, shredded
1½ tablespoons sifted flour
1 clove fresh garlic
1 cup Neufchatel wine (or any
  light dry wine — Chablis
  or Rhine)
Salt, pepper and nutmeg to taste

3 tablespoons Kirsch or
  2 tablespoons cognac or light rum
1 loaf French or white bread with
  hard crust or 4 hard rolls, cut
  into bite-size pieces, each of which
  must have at least one side of crust.

Dredge Swiss cheese in flour. Rub·chafing pan well with garlic. (Do not preheat chafing pan.) Pour wine in chafing pan and set over low flame. When wine is heated to point where air bubbles rise (never boil wine), stir with wooden spoon and add cheese by handfuls; completely dissolve each addition of cheese before adding more. Stir until mixture starts bubbling lightly. Now add, to taste, salt, pepper, and nutmeg. Finally stir in Kirsch or cognac or light rum. Snuff out flame and set fondue in pan of hot (not boiling) water. This is the "traditional way" to eat Swiss fondue; everybody dunks into the chafing pan. Spear a bite-size piece of French bread or hard roll with a fork and dunk the bread in the fondue in a stirring motion. The stirring maintains proper consistency of the fondue. It must be kept bubbling lightly. If water becomes too cool, set it all over low flame. If the fondue becomes too thick at any time, add a little preheated wine.

MRS. ARTHUR D. BROWN

GUACAMOLE

Garlic clove
1 large peeled avocado
¼ teaspoon salt
¼ teaspoon chili powder

1 teaspoon lemon juice
2 teaspoons finely minced onion
Mayonnaise

Rub a wooden bowl with cut garlic clove. Place avocado in bowl and mash with a silver fork. Add salt, chili powder, lemon juice, and minced onion. Mix well and taste for seasoning. Put the Guacamole in a serving bowl and cover with a thin layer of mayonnaise (to prevent the avocado from blackening). Stir well just before serving. This can be used as a canapé spread or a raw vegetable dip, and it is very good as a dressing for head of lettuce salad.

In Spanish "aguacate" means alligator pear and served as spread, dip, hors d'oeuvre is called "Guacamole".

MRS. REGAR HICKMAN

HERB DIP

1 cup sour cream
1 8-ounce package cream cheese
1 tablespoon chives, chopped
1 tablespoon parsley, chopped
1 teaspoon each minced onion,
  tarragon, dill, soy, and
  curry powder

Dash Worcestershire sauce
Dash Tabasco
Salt and pepper to taste
Enough cream to soften dip

Combine all ingredients and blend well.

MRS. GLEN EVINS

RANCHO AUBREY BEAN DIP

4 cups pinto beans
3 cloves garlic
2 onions
Salt to taste
½ pound butter or margarine

½ pound Wisconsin sharp cheese
¼ pound New York sharp cheese
2 cans green chili peppers
Juice of 2 lemons or limes

Clean pinto beans and soak overnight. Add fresh water, enough to cover well, garlic and onions. Boil until well done and liquid has cooked down (not dry). Drain the beans, and while hot cream well in mixer or blender. Add salt to taste. Add butter, cheeses, peppers and lemon juice. Mix again in the mixer or blender until it is a smooth paste. This can be stored in the freezer and used as needed. Serve from chafing dish. Makes about 2½ pints.

MRS. ECKFORD HODGSON

SEAFOOD DIP OR ENTREE

½ pound butter (at least)
2 pounds crabmeat
2 pounds scallops

1½ pounds mushrooms
3 cans crab or shrimp bisque

Sauté crabmeat, scallops, and mushrooms in butter. Add crab bisque and season to taste. Keep over low flame as long as you like. Since the bisque is sometimes hard to find in local stores, a good homemade cream sauce (about 3½ cups, using juice from the sautéed seafood and milk) is even more tasty. Serve as a dip or as an entree. Serves 24. Good with Melba toast or toast points.

MRS. ERNEST L. GREEN

ROQUEFORT DIP FOR SHRIMP

1 small section imported
  Roquefort cheese
1 glass Roquefort cheese spread
¾ teaspoon cream-style horseradish

2 to 3 dashes Tabasco
½ tablespoon scraped onion
Mayonnaise

Crush and blend imported Roquefort with Roquefort cheese spread until smooth and without lumps. Add horseradish, Tabasco and onion. Add mayonnaise until of dip consistency. Serve cold with cold boiled shrimp on picks. Serves 12 people generously.

MRS. J. BROWN FARRIOR

SMOKED OYSTER DIP

1 8-ounce package cream cheese
¼ teaspoon lemon juice
1 teaspoon Worcestershire sauce

½ teaspoon soya bean sauce
1 clove garlic, peeled and halved
1 can smoked oysters

Mix first 4 ingredients. Add garlic and leave in mixture until oysters have been chopped and added. Remove garlic. Serve with crackers.

MRS. CHARLES H. DEVOE

BLACK BEAN DIP

1 can black bean soup
2 8-ounce packages cream cheese
1 small onion, chopped fine

2 teaspoons mayonnaise (or more)
2 teaspoons chopped parsley
¼ teaspoon Worcestershire sauce

Mix all ingredients and blend thoroughly in an electric mixer or blender. Serve with corn chips or potato chips. For a cocktail party, double the recipe for 100 people.

MISS MARY LOUISE LEE

CHAPTER II

Beverages

Florida is a wonderful place for parties. The leisurely mode of living enhances the will to entertain. We all work, and work hard, but Florida people are not inclined to carry the office with them into their free time. After all, it's hard not to relax when practically any day of the year you can have a barbecue, a picnic, a coffee party on a terrace glowing with azaleas, or a peaceful day in the country where wayward breezes make changing patterns on cypress lakes. Indoors or out, there is always a favorite beverage which suits the occasion and makes it more enjoyable. If you're a julep fan, pick a sprig of mint from under the garden faucet. Pluck a few fruits from the citrus trees in the yard for tropical drinks. Prepare a frosted punch with icy sherbets. The land abounds with the ingredients for delicious and hospitable beverages.

CAFÉ BRÛLOT FOR FOUR

4 lumps sugar
4 sticks cinnamon
2 pinches cloves
A few lemon and orange peels

1½ ounces brandy per person
    (must be heated to flame)
2 inches of vanilla bean

Mix these ingredients in hard metal bowl, light flame and dim lights. Ladle 20-30 seconds and then add 4 demitasse cups double strength hot coffee. The second batch is even better than the first.

This recipe was given to me by Louis at Arnaud's in New Orleans where it is served with lights dimmed and great flourish; I use a copper and alloy Brûlot bowl with a strainer ladle and have had considerable success except for the time I was ladling from so great a height the flaming mixture spilled over and took the finish off the table.

Dr. C. Frank Chunn

ARTILLERY PUNCH

1 cup sugar	1 quart sherry
Juice of 6 lemons	1 quart bourbon (rye or Scotch)
2 tablespoons bitters	1 quart brandy
1 quart claret	1 quart soda water

Pour all over ice in a large punchbowl. Makes slightly more than 5 quarts of punch or approximately 20 servings.

This recipe was given me by (then) Major John Eisenhower at Fort Belvoir, Va. in 1957.

DR. WILLIAM MOORE

COFFEE MOCHA

2 quarts strong coffee	1 quart homogenized milk
2 cups simple syrup (one cup water and one cup sugar boiled together)	1 quart vanilla ice cream

Make coffee and simple syrup in advance and have cold. Mix all liquid ingredients in punch bowl. Spoon 1 quart of vanilla ice cream on top. Serve immediately.

MRS. LEFFIE M. CARLTON, JR.

INSTANT COFFEE PUNCH

6 quarts homogenized milk	½ cup sugar (or ½ teaspoon
¾ cup instant coffee (or 1 rounded	for each cup milk)
teaspoon for each cup milk)	2 quarts vanilla ice cream

Scald milk, mix with coffee and sugar. Put in refrigerator and chill. Improves the flavor to stand. To serve: pour mixture in a chilled bowl and add the ice cream. Serves 50. To serve 125 use 15 quarts of milk and 5 quarts ice cream, increasing coffee and sugar proportionately.

MRS. WILLIAM C. GILMORE, JR.

PING'S SPECIAL—PEACH SLUSH

½ overripe peach	2 jiggers whiskey
1 heaping teaspoon sugar	Crushed ice

Mash together peach and sugar, add whiskey and stir well. Fill glass with crushed ice. This recipe makes 1 glassful (large 12 to 14 ounces).

MRS. E. B. BRADFORD

MOCHA PUNCH

1 cup whipping cream
4 cups freshly made coffee
1 quart chocolate ice cream
2 tablespoons rum or
  ½ teaspoon almond extract

⅛ teaspoon salt
Freshly grated nutmeg or
  grated sweet chocolate

Whip cream until stiff. Chill coffee. Pour chilled coffee into a large chilled bowl. Add ½ the ice cream. Beat until cream is partly melted. Add extract and salt. Fold in remainder of ice cream and all but a cupful of whipped cream. Place punch in tall glasses. Garnish tops with reserved cream. Sprinkle with nutmeg or chocolate. Makes 12 servings.

LEISURE HOUSE, TAMPA ELECTRIC COMPANY

IRISH COFFEE

Put ½ teaspoon sugar in an Irish coffee goblet (glass smaller than a water goblet, larger than a cocktail goblet). Fill nearly to brim with hot, strong coffee. Add 1 jigger Irish whiskey. Then put dollop of fresh whipped cream on top.

MRS. JACK ECKERD

RICH EGGNOG

1 pint heavy cream
1¼ cups sugar
6 eggs, separated

¾ cup whiskey (blend or light
  bourbon)
⅓ cup light rum
1 quart milk

Whip cream until stiff, adding ¼ cup sugar. Separate eggs. Whip whites very stiff, adding ½ cup sugar. Whip yolks until creamy, adding ½ cup sugar; continue beating until all sugar is dissolved. Add the liquors to the yolk-sugar mixture, mix well. Stir in the milk. Fold in the egg whites thoroughly, then the whipped cream. This recipe can be doubled, but since the quantities get a bit unwieldy, it is better to make two batches if a larger amount is desired. It makes 2 or 3 quarts.

This is a very thick and light eggnog. The secret of its smooth flavor is thoroughly mixing the liquors with the egg yolks; this kills the raw taste of the yolks and takes the bite out of the alcohol. The eggnog can be made up a day in advance, refrigerated, and folded gently together just before serving. I serve it in large punch cups with a demitasse spoon, adding a sprinkle of nutmeg to each cup.

MRS. DAVID J. KADYK

CLARET LEMONADE

⅓ cup sugar
Juice of 3 lemons

½ cup claret wine
3 cups sparkling water

Combine sugar and lemon juice; stir to dissolve sugar. Slice in some of the rind for more lemon flavor. Add wine. Pour over ice in pitcher; then add sparkling water. Add more sugar if you like it sweet. Garnish with fresh mint. Serves 4.

MRS. LOUIS M. SAXTON

ROMAN PUNCH

Combine:
2 cups sugar boiled in 2 cups
    water for 5 minutes
2 cups strong tea
Juice of 4 oranges
Juice of 6 lemons

2 teaspoons almond extract
2 teaspoons vanilla extract
1 quart bottle of grape juice
Add sufficient water to make
    1 gallon

Excellent served hot at Christmas.

MRS. J. J. SUDDATH

SEMINOLE PUNCH

3 lemons
1 quart water
1 pound sugar
1 teaspoon vanilla

1 teaspoon almond extract
1 cup strong tea
Fruit juices to taste
2 quarts ginger ale

Squeeze lemons and reserve juice. Combine lemon rinds, water and sugar. Boil 5 minutes and strain. Add vanilla, almond extract, lemon juice and strong tea. When cool add 1 pint cold water. This is the base. For punch add assorted fruit juices to taste. Just before serving add chilled ginger ale for snap.

MRS. E. C. DEPURY

Baking Cuban Bread in Ybor City

CHAPTER III

Breads

When a true Florida Cracker speaks of bread he means biscuits, corn bread or muffins. Loaf bread and rolls are "light bread". Perhaps this stems from the necessity (before the days of refrigeration or air conditioning) of baking hot breads for each meal because the dampness and humidity of the weather encouraged mold to form on yeast breads. Whatever the origin, there are still many families of pioneer background in this region who have hot breads at every meal. There is a story told of a large family gathering at which the table was laden with foods prepared by the female members of the clan. At the foot of the table sat the old grandfather·who ignored the array of dishes and concentrated on eating a superb golden pound cake chunk after chunk. Finally, the daughter who had baked the cake with loving care, proffered a plate of biscuits in his direction. "Father," she said, "wouldn't you like to try some of these nice biscuits with your ham and grits?"

"No thanks, Daughter," he replied, "This light bread's good enough for me."

There are Tampa families of northern origin who still know the delights of homemade bread baked every Saturday, with a pan of rolls fashioned for those who can't wait until the loaves cool. French bread, Italian bread, Greek bread, Jewish rye and pumpernickel line the shelves in the grocery stores, while one bread particularly typical of Tampa, the amazing Cuban bread, stands in a bin at the side of the counter because it's too long to lay flat. Cuban bread is one yard long! It's a crusty beige on the outside and 36 inches of delicate white fluff on the inside. There is nothing better in the world than buttered Cuban bread with coffee for breakfast. Long ago, when the 20th Century was still young, Cuban bread was delivered in a horse-drawn bakery wagon, and the deliveryman, swinging the loaf of bread like a bat would impale it on a nail hammered to the side of the customer's house. Community hygiene has banished the nails, but as long as a Tampan remains alive, there will always be a fierce demand for this marvelous bread.

Bread

HOMEMADE BREAD

1 package yeast	2 teaspoons salt
1 cup lukewarm water	3 tablespoons sugar
1 cup milk, scalded and cooled	3 tablespoons shortening (Crisco)
6 cups Pillsbury flour before sifting	

Dissolve yeast in warm water; add cooled milk. Sift flour, salt and sugar into large bowl. Cut in shortening; add the yeast mixture; mix well to make a soft, firm dough. Put the dough into a well-greased bowl. Cover with a cloth. Let rise 2 hours in warm place. Knead the dough on board. Divide into 2 equal parts and shape into loaves. Put into well-greased loaf pans. Let rise one hour. Bake in oven 400° for 10 minutes, then finish baking at 350° for 40 to 45 minutes. Remove from pans; place on cooling rack; brush with butter. The kneading of dough is most important. Do not use extra flour in kneading.

MRS. STEPHEN M. SPARKMAN

ANADAMA BREAD

The story goes, in the vicinity of Rockport, Massachusetts where the recipe originated, a captain on a fishing schooner came home to find his wife had made a new kind of bread. Since it was a dark bread and he had been accustomed to the white variety, he thought she had burned it, and said, "Anna, dammit, what happened to the bread?" Henceforth it has been called Anadama bread.

½ cup corn meal	2 cups boiling water
½ cup molasses	2 cakes yeast
3 teaspoons salt	½ cup lukewarm water
2 tablespoons shortening	6 to 7 cups flour

Mix corn meal, molasses, salt, shortening and boiling water. Cool. Dissolve yeast in lukewarm water and add corn meal mixture. Add flour. Knead and let rise until double in bulk. Shape into loaves and put into greased bread pans. Let rise until double in bulk. Bake about 45 minutes in a slow oven, about 375°

GASPARILLA INN, Boca Grande, Florida

RUSSIAN KOULICH
(Easter Bread)

1½ cups milk
½ cup melted butter
½ cup white sugar
½ teaspoon salt
2 tablespoons brandy
1 teaspoon vanilla
2 envelopes dry yeast

½ cup lukewarm water
2 beaten eggs
4 cups sifted flour
4½-5 cups sifted flour
½ cup slivered almonds
1½ cups mixed glacé fruits
    (pineapple, cherries, white raisins)

Scald milk and cool. Add butter, sugar, salt, brandy, vanilla. Dissolve yeast in lukewarm water; add to the milk mixture. Stir in eggs and 4 cups of flour. Cover and let rise in warm place until doubled in bulk (about 1 hour). Place the rest of the flour in a ring about the size of a dinner plate on board. Pour mixture in center; knead flour in dough. Knead in almonds and fruit that have been dusted with flour. Grease two 3 pound shortening cans. Place half of dough in each can. Cover; let rise in warm place until dough reaches top of cans. Bake 40 minutes at 375°, or until skewer inserted in center comes out clean. May be topped with confectioners sugar icing.

MRS. JAMES H. KENNEDY

OATMEAL BREAD

1 cup old-fashioned oatmeal
¾ stick butter
2 cups boiling water
1 package of yeast dissolved
    in ½ cup tepid water

½ cup sugar
1 teaspoon salt
Approximately 4½ cups flour

Pour water over the oatmeal and butter; let stand until cool. Add yeast mixture, sugar, salt and flour. Knead well (about 4 minutes). Dough will be sticky because of oatmeal. Cover and let rise overnight. Next morning knead down; divide into 2 portions and pack down well in two greased bread pans. Cover with towel and let rise to ¾ the top of pans. Bake in 450° oven for 10 minutes then in 350° oven for 35 minutes. Remove from pan and place on rack (bread should be placed on its sides to cool). Cover with towel to prevent bread from cooling too fast. This keeps bread tender.

NAOMI STOGNER FULLER

HERB BREAD

2 packages yeast	2 beaten eggs
½ cup warm (not hot) water	1 teaspoon nutmeg
1½ cups scalded milk	2 teaspoons sage
4 tablespoons sugar	4 teaspoons caraway seed
4 tablespoons shortening	4 cups sifted flour
3 teaspoons salt	

Dissolve yeast in warm water. Combine milk, sugar, shortening, salt, and let cool. Add softened yeast. Then add eggs, nutmeg, sage, caraway seed, and sifted flour. Beat until smooth. Add more sifted flour to make dough soft—2 to 2½ cups. Sift about ½ cup flour on pastry cloth, and knead dough until smooth and elastic—about 8 to 10 minutes. Rub softened butter over outside of ball of dough, place in large bowl, cover and let rise in warm place until doubled in size (about 1 hour).

Punch dough down, let rest for 10 minutes. Divide into 2 balls, place each in greased 8 or 9 inch pie pan. Cover, let rise 45 minutes. Brush with slightly beaten egg white, sprinkle generously with caraway seed. Bake at 400° 40 to 45 minutes. Makes two loaves.

Very good served warm with "salad meals", and makes wonderful sandwiches.

MRS. J. BROWN FARRIOR

BANANA BREAD

½ cup shortening or 1 stick of margarine	2 cups sifted flour
1 cup sugar	1 teaspoon salt
2 eggs	½ teaspoon soda
1½ cups mashed bananas (3 to 5 bananas)	1 teaspoon vanilla
	⅔ cup chopped nuts

Cream shortening, add sugar slowly; cream well. Add eggs and beat. Add bananas; then flour, salt, and soda which have been sifted together. Add vanilla and nuts. Bake for approximately 1 hour and 15 minutes at 325° in a greased 2-quart loaf pan. Test center for doneness. Cool thoroughly, wrap in foil, and keep in refrigerator. Best for slicing after at least one day.

MRS. OLIVER WALL KUHN

HONEY-WHEAT BREAD

2 packages dry yeast
1 cup lukewarm water
½ cup shortening
1 cup boiling water
2 tablespoons salt

1 cup honey
1 cup powdered milk
2 cups cold water
12 cups whole wheat flour,
   sifted before measuring

Before gathering other ingredients, stir dry yeast into lukewarm water. Combine shortening, boiling water, salt and ½ cup honey. Stir until ingredients are blended, then add powdered milk and cold water. Cool until lukewarm, add yeast mixture, stir well, and add 4 cups sifted whole wheat flour. Beat with rotary beater until smooth, or about 1 minute. Cover and set in a warm place at 85° to 90°. Let rise until double in bulk, or about 1 hour. Blend in ½ cup honey and 8 cups sifted whole wheat flour.

Mix well and knead on lightly floured surface until smooth and satiny. During kneading a ½ cup or more of sifted flour may be absorbed. With a sharp knife cut dough in half. Place each half in a greased bowl. Reverse the dough so that the greased part will be on top. Cover and let rise in a warm place free from draughts until double in bulk, or about 1½ hours. Punch down and shape into 3 large loaves or 4 small ones. Place in greased loaf pans. Sprinkle with sesame seeds and press into place. Cover and let dough rise until double in bulk. Bake at 350° for 30 to 40 minutes. Remove from pans immediately and cool on wire racks.

A trick I have found successful for letting bread rise in cold or damp weather is to turn on the oven for 5 seconds. Using a candy or frying thermometer check oven temperature for 85° to 90°. Place bowls or pans in closed oven for dough to rise.

Mrs. James W. Gray, Jr.

PINEAPPLE-NUT BREAD

2¼ cups sifted all-purpose flour
¾ cup sugar
1½ teaspoons salt
3 teaspoons baking powder
½ teaspoon soda
1 cup all bran

¾ cup chopped walnuts
1½ cups crushed pineapple,
   undrained
1 egg, beaten
3 tablespoons butter or other
   shortening, melted

Sift flour, sugar, salt, baking powder and soda together. Stir in remaining ingredients. Bake in a greased loaf pan, 9 x 4 x 3-inches, in a moderate oven, 350°, for 1¼ hours. This bread keeps moist for a week or 10 days and slices best when a day or more old.

Mrs. Albert Thompson

O A T E N   B R E A D

2 cups sifted flour	1 ¼ cups of buttermilk
½ cup sugar	or sour milk
2 ½ teaspoons baking powder	2 tablespoons melted shortening
½ teaspoon baking soda	1 cup diced, drained, cooked prunes
1 teaspoon salt	½ cup chopped nuts
1 cup of rolled oats	

Sift flour, sugar, baking powder, baking soda, and salt together
and mix in rolled oats. Add milk and shortening to prunes and chopped nuts. Add this mixture to the dry ingredients and mix well. Pour
into well greased loaf pan 9 x 5 x 3-inches. Bake at 350° for 1 hour
or until done. Make muffins if you are short on time. Bake at 425° for
20 to 30 minutes.

TAMPA ELECTRIC COMPANY, LEISURE HOUSE

O R A N G E   B R E A D

Peeling of 4 small oranges	2 ½ cups flour
1 cup sugar	⅔ cup sugar
½ cup water	3 teaspoons baking powder
1 egg	½ teaspoon salt
1 cup milk	1 cup orange peel

Parboil peeling of 4 oranges. Cook in syrup of 1 cup sugar and
water until dry. Add beaten egg to milk; add orange mixture, sifted
dry ingredients, and 1 cup orange peel cut fine. Put into well greased
loaf pan. Let rise 1 hour. Bake 1 hour at 350°. This is very good served
with tea.

MRS. JOHN LONG

N U T   B R E A D

1 egg	½ teaspoon salt
1 cup sugar	1 cup milk
2 ½ cups flour	1 cup chopped nuts
2 ½ teaspoons baking powder	

Beat egg, add sugar gradually. Reserve a little flour to sprinkle
over nuts. Sift together the flour, baking powder and salt. Add to
the sugar mixture alternately with the milk. Add chopped nuts which
have been sprinkled with the reserve flour. Mix well; pour into a
greased loaf pan. Let stand for 20 minutes. Bake at 350° F. for one
hour. Bread will be better and more moist the second day.

MRS. JOHN WHITEHURST

FRUIT NUT BREAD

½ cup dried apricots
Juice and rind of 1 large orange
Boiling water
½ cup raisins
1 teaspoon soda
1 cup sugar
2 tablespoons melted butter

1 teaspoon vanilla
1 beaten egg
2 cups sifted flour
¼ teaspoon salt
2 teaspoons baking powder
½ cup chopped nuts

Soak apricots ½ hour. Drain. Add enough boiling water to orange juice to make 1 cup liquid. Put apricots, raisins, and orange rind through food chopper. Add orange juice and water. Stir in soda, sugar, butter and vanilla. Add beaten egg and dry ingredients. Add nuts and bake 1 hour at 350°. Makes 1 loaf.

MRS. BERT FETZER

GARLIC GREEK BREAD

Long loaves of Greek (or French) bread
½ pound butter

6 cloves of fresh garlic, finely minced

Melt the butter in a skillet and add garlic. Heat but do not cook. Slice bread 1½ inches thick and toast under broiler until golden brown and hot. Immediately brush both sides of bread with the garlic butter, place on a cookie sheet, and return to broiler to brown the bits of garlic, being careful not to burn. May be made in advance, wrapped in foil, and kept in a warm oven until ready to serve.

PAPPAS' RESTAURANT, Tarpon Springs, Florida

Corn Bread

SPOON BREAD

1 pint milk
¾ cup meal
1 tablespoon butter

½ teaspoon salt
3 eggs, separated

Scald milk. Add meal and simmer until thick or about 5 minutes. Add butter and salt and let cool. Add egg yolks. Fold in stiffly beaten egg whites. Put in greased baking dish. Place baking dish in warm water and bake at 325° for 45 minutes. Serves 6.

MRS. JOHN DICKSON

CORN STICKS

½ cup sifted flour
1 cup corn meal
½ teaspoon baking soda
1 teaspoon salt
1 teaspoon sugar

1 egg, beaten
1 cup sour milk
2 tablespoons melted shortening
  (bacon fat is the best)

Sift flour once, measure, add corn meal, baking soda, salt, and sugar, and sift together. Combine egg and milk. Add to flour mixture, stirring only enough to blend. Add melted shortening. Spoon into corn stick pans which have been liberally greased with bacon fat or shortening and heated in the oven. Bake in 425° oven 20 to 25 minutes.

This recipe also makes standard corn bread which is delicious with cooked crumbled bacon added to the batter. Makes 12 corn sticks.

MRS. ROGERS MORGAN

GRATED-CORN BREAD

1 cup grated corn (4 tender ears)
2 well beaten eggs
1 tablespoon sugar
1 teaspoon salt

2 teaspoons baking powder
3 tablespoons bacon drippings
½ cup milk
2 tablespoons flour

Grate corn from about 4 tender ears of corn or enough to make 1 cup. Use back of knife to scrape the ears after grating. Add eggs, sugar, salt, baking powder, bacon drippings and milk. Add 2 tablespoons of flour or enough to make a medium batter. Bake in greased pan (lined with paper) in 425° oven for about ½ hour or until brown on top. Be sure pan is on rack in center of oven. This may also be cooked very slowly on top of stove in an omelet pan. It serves 4.

MRS. VICTOR H. KNIGHT, JR.

BOONE TAVERN HUSHPUPPIES

½ teaspoon salt
½ teaspoon baking powder
1 cup white corn meal
¼ teaspoon baking soda

½ cup buttermilk
1 egg
½ cup onion, finely grated

Sift salt, baking powder and corn meal. Mix soda with buttermilk. Mix above 2 mixtures. Add beaten egg and mix well. Add grated onion. Shape into small balls or drop off end of teaspoon into deep hot fat (400°) and fry until golden brown.

HUSHPUPPIES

2 cups coarse water ground
white corn meal
1 teaspoon salt
2 teaspoons baking powder

1 large sweet onion, chopped
1 bell pepper, chopped
2 cups sweet milk

Sift corn meal, salt and baking powder together into bowl. Stir in onion, pepper and milk. Drop by teaspoons into deep fat (400°) for 5 minutes. For flavor use the fat in which fish, shrimp, scallops or other seafoods have been fried. Serves 6 to 8.

MRS. THOMAS M. EDWARDS

FRANK'S SPOON BREAD

1 cup boiling water
½ cup corn meal
½ cup milk
½ teaspoon salt

1½ teaspoons baking powder
1 tablespoon soft butter
2 well beaten eggs

Pour boiling water over meal. Beat in milk, salt, baking powder, soft butter and eggs. Pour into buttered one-quart baking dish and bake in 400° oven until set or about 20 minutes. Serve hot with butter. Serves 4.

MRS. W. FRANK HOBBS

Biscuits, Muffins and Rolls

LOUISE'S BISCUITS

2 cups flour
3 teaspoons baking powder
2 teaspoons salt

1 tablespoon sugar
½ cup shortening
¾ cup milk

Sift first four ingredients together into a large mixing bowl. Cut shortening into mixture until it is the size of a pea. Add milk slowly, mixing well. Roll out dough on a floured board and cut biscuits to desired size. Place on a greased pan and bake at 400° for 20 minutes. Allow 10 minutes on bottom rack in oven and 10 minutes on top rack to brown.

MRS. H. L. CROWDER, JR.

ORANGE BISCUITS I

2 cups flour	2 tablespoons butter
2 teaspoons baking powder	½ cup orange juice
½ teaspoon salt	½ cup milk
2 teaspoons sugar	Sugar
1 teaspoon grated orange rind	Orange juice

Sift together flour, baking powder, salt and sugar. Add orange rind. Cut in butter. Stir in orange juice and milk, mixing well. Knead lightly and form biscuits. Make an indentation in the top of each biscuit. Put a little sugar in the hole and moisten it with orange juice. Bake at 450° 12 to 15 minutes.

MRS. WALTER BARRET

ORANGE BISCUITS II

Make a biscuit dough by your favorite recipe. Roll ½ inch thick; cut in strips 6 inches wide, then spread with the Orange Paste given below. Roll like a jelly roll and cut with a sharp knife into 1-inch slices. Place these in greased muffin tins or on a baking sheet, and bake in a hot oven (400°).

ORANGE PASTE FILLING:

6 tablespoons butter	Grated rind of 1 orange
2 tablespoons flour	½ cup sugar
⅓ cup orange juice	

In a double boiler, cook all ingredients, except sugar, until thickened. Add sugar and remove from fire. If sugar is added sooner a chemical action takes place which prevents thickening. Let cool before spreading. It may be made in advance and kept in the refrigerator.

TONA W. PERRY and PEARL HALL BOND

GRAPEFRUIT BISCUITS

2 cups sifted flour	¾ cup milk at room temperature
3 teaspoons double-acting baking powder	¼ cup grapefruit juice
¾ teaspoon salt	¼ teaspoon Durkee's powdered lemon rind
¼ cup cooking oil	

Mix ingredients in order listed, stirring well until flour is damp. Then drop by spoonfuls into a warm, well-greased muffin tin. Bake at 375° about 12 to 15 minutes or until tops are brown. Yields 12 medium biscuits.

MRS. WILLIAM E. HENSON, JR.

WHOLE WHEAT BISCUITS

2 cups white all-purpose flour
2 teaspoons baking powder,
   double-acting
1½ teaspoons salt
½ cup whole wheat flour

½ cup Crisco (¾ cup for
   a richer dough)
Enough milk to make dough easy
   to handle

Sift white flour with baking powder and salt into bowl containing whole wheat flour. Do not sift whole wheat flour. Blend in Crisco until well mixed with flour and add milk. Knead lightly for just a few minutes. Roll out and cut biscuits. Bake on ungreased cookie sheet in 425° oven for 20 to 25 minutes. Makes approximately 2 dozen 1½-inch biscuits.

MRS. M. LEO ELLIOTT, JR.

UP AND DOWN BISCUITS

2 cups enriched flour
½ teaspoon salt
4 teaspoons baking powder
½ teaspoon cream of tartar
3 tablespoons sugar

½ cup shortening
⅔ cup milk
¼ cup melted butter or margarine
¼ cup sugar
1 tablespoon cinnamon

Sift dry ingredients into mixing bowl; cut in shortening until mixture resembles coarse crumbs. Add milk all at once and stir until dough follows fork around the bowl. Turn onto floured board and knead gently ½ minute. Roll dough ¼ inch thick. Brush with melted butter and sprinkle with ¼ cup sugar and cinnamon. Cut in 2-inch strips. Stack strips 5 high. Cut off 2-inch pieces and place, cut side down, in greased muffin pans. Bake in hot oven (425°) for 12 minutes. Makes 12 large biscuits. For bite-size party biscuits, bake in doll muffin tins. Makes 3 dozen.

MRS. MYRON GIBBONS

ADDIE'S MUFFINS

⅔ cup white cream meal
⅓ cup flour
3 teaspoons baking powder
½ teaspoon salt
1 egg
½ cup milk

½ cup water
½ medium onion, chopped fine
1 teaspoon sage
¼ teaspoon sugar
1 tablespoon bacon drippings

Mix all ingredients together; fill greased muffin tins 2/3 full. Bake at 400° about 25 minutes.

MRS. J. BROWN FARRIOR

APPLE BREAKFAST MUFFINS

1 cup all-purpose flour
1 tablespoon white sugar
2 tablespoons brown sugar
½ teaspoon salt
¼ teaspoon soda
2 tablespoons baking powder
⅓ cup wheat germ
1 apple, diced fine
2 teaspoons sugar

1 teaspoon cinnamon
⅛ teaspoon powdered cloves
⅛ teaspoon grated nutmeg
1 egg
½ to ⅔ cup sour milk or
   buttermilk
3 tablespoons melted shortening
   (½ melted bacon drippings and
   ½ margarine)

Sift flour, measure, resift with 1 tablespoon white sugar, 2 table-spoons of brown sugar, salt, soda and baking powder. Add wheat germ. Sprinkle diced apple with 2 teaspoons of sugar and spices. (If apple is mealy, sprinkle first with a few drops of lime or lemon juice.) Dredge lightly with a spoonful or two of flour mixture. Beat egg, add milk, then mix with dry ingredients. Add melted shortening, then fold in diced apples. Put into hot, greased muffin pans and bake 20 min-utes in 400° oven. The batter may be thinned and fried as pancakes.

JACK FESSENDEN

MAPLE SYRUP MUFFINS

¼ cup milk
1 egg
1¾ cups flour
2½ teaspoons baking powder

¼ teaspoon salt
1 cup maple syrup
¼ cup melted butter

Whip milk into beaten egg, using egg beater. Sift flour, baking powder and salt together. Add to egg and milk mixture a little at a time, alternating with maple syrup (this is important). Fold in melted butter. Bake 25 minutes in 325° oven in muffin pan. Makes 9 large muffins.

MRS. WHITING PRESTON

MOTHER CARRIE'S ENGLISH TEA MUFFINS

½ cup Snowdrift
2 tablespoons sugar
2 eggs
1½ cups flour

3 teaspoons baking powder
1 teaspoon salt
1 to 2 tablespoons milk if needed

Cream shortening and sugar; add eggs. Mix well; add other in-gredients. Mix quickly. Cook in well greased iron muffin pans at 450°. They are crisper if no milk is used. Makes 2 dozen muffins.

MRS. ROD SHAW, SR.

SALLY LUNN

1 cake yeast
¼ cup luke warm water
   with a little sugar
2 cups milk
4 level tablespoons sugar

2 teaspoons salt
3 pints flour (6 cups sifted
   before measuring)
3 eggs
1 scant cup shortening (melted)

Dissolve yeast in warm water. Warm milk and mix with other ingredients, adding melted shortening last. Leave batter in bowl and set in warm place to rise for 2 hours. Put in angel food pan and let rise to within 1 inch of top. Put Sally Lunn in cold oven, then set at 350°. Bake 1 hour. Serve hot.

MRS. CHARLES C. BEVER, JR.

SHORTBREAD OR MUFFINS

3 cups sifted all-purpose flour
3 teaspoons baking powder
1 teaspoon salt
2 teaspoons sugar

2 tablespoons vegetable shortening
2 eggs
1 cup milk

Sift dry ingredients into bowl; cut in shortening until mixture is coarse in texture; add eggs, beat quickly; add milk and again beat quickly. Pour into greased square pan or muffin pans. Fill well greased muffin pans half full. Bake in 375° oven 20 to 25 minutes for square pan, 15 to 20 minutes for muffins, or until a golden brown. Cut in squares if in square pans. Makes 1 dozen large muffins. Serve hot. This is also a wonderful base for turkey dressing.

MISS CAROLINE HARRIS

FRENCH BREAKFAST PUFFS

⅓ cup soft shortening
½ cup sugar
1 egg
1½ cups sifted flour
1½ teaspoons baking powder
½ teaspoon salt

¼ teaspoon nutmeg
½ cup milk
6 tablespoons butter, melted
½ cup sugar
1 teaspoon cinnamon

Mix shortening, sugar and egg thoroughly. Sift dry ingredients together and stir in alternately with milk. Fill greased muffin tins 2/3 full. Bake until golden brown in 350° oven. Immediately roll in melted butter, then in mixture of sugar and cinnamon. Serve hot. Makes 12 medium sized muffins.

MRS. J. C. COUNCIL

BLENDER POPOVERS

1 cup milk
3 eggs
1 tablespoon melted shortening

1 cup flour
½ teaspoon salt

Put all ingredients in blender jar and beat for 2 minutes. Pour into well greased muffin tins. Bake for 35 minutes at 450° and 20 minutes at 350°. Yields 1 dozen popovers.

TAMPA ELECTRIC COMPANY, LEISURE HOUSE

BUTTERMILK ROLLS

2½ cups flour
1 teaspoon baking powder
1 teaspoon salt
1 cup buttermilk

1 package yeast
¼ teaspoon baking powder
1 teaspoon sugar
3 tablespoons melted butter

Sift together flour, 1 teaspoon baking powder and salt. Heat buttermilk just to lukewarm (it can't be scalded as it goes to clabber). Dissolve yeast in the milk. Stir in ¼ teaspoon baking powder and sugar. Stir in the melted butter, add dry ingredients and mix well. Turn out on floured board and knead lightly until smooth. Make into rolls at once—Parker House, clover leaf, twists or whatever you wish. Place in greased pan, brush with butter. Cover and let rise until light— 1 to 1½ hours. Bake at 400° about 10 minutes. Makes 15 to 18 rolls. These are delicious and never fail!

MRS. LESLIE McGEE

CHARLOTTE'S ONION ROLLS

3 ounces fresh yeast or
  3 packages dry yeast
1 teaspoon sugar
¼ cup lukewarm water
2 teaspoons salt
2 tablespoons sugar

2 tablespoons shortening or oil
2 cups warm milk
6 cups flour
Salt, oregano and finely
  chopped onion for topping

Dissolve yeast, 1 teaspoon sugar and salt in the lukewarm water; add 2 tablespoons sugar, oil, and warm milk. Mix well and slowly add flour. Cover and let rise. Knead and let rise twice more. Break off pieces of dough about the size of a tennis ball and put on floured board. Let rise about 10 minutes. Flatten and place on pan. Brush with melted butter and sprinkle with salt and oregano. Put finely chopped onions on top. Let rise until double in bulk. Bake in 375° oven for 15 to 20 minutes. Yields about 2 dozen rolls.

TONY'S RESTAURANT, TAMPA, FLORIDA

CINNAMON TWISTS

1 package dry yeast	2 beaten eggs
¼ cup lukewarm water	½ cup sour cream
4 cups sifted flour	1 teaspoon vanilla
½ teaspoon salt	1½ cups sugar
1 cup butter	3 teaspoons cinnamon

Soften yeast in water. Sift flour and salt into a bowl. Cut in butter. Blend in eggs, sour cream, vanilla, and softened yeast. Mix. Cover and chill at least 2 hours. Combine sugar and cinnamon.

Roll out half of chilled dough, leaving other half in refrigerator, using board that has been sprinkled with about ½ cup of the sugar-cinnamon mixture. Roll out to about 16 x 8-inch rectangle. Sprinkle with 1 tablespoon of the sugar mixture. Fold one end of dough over center. Fold other end to make 3 layers. Turn ¼ way around and repeat folding and rolling, sprinkling each time with 1 tablespoon sugar, about 4 more times. Roll out to about 16 x 8-inch rectangle about ¼ inch thick. Cut in 4 x 1-inch strips. Twist each 2 or 3 times. Place on ungreased sheets and bake in 375° oven for 15 to 20 minutes. Let cool before removing from sheet.

MRS. T. W. SAMUELS

POPPY SEED ROLLS

1½ cups milk	2 cakes yeast
2 tablespoons sugar	4 cups sifted all-purpose flour
2 tablespoons shortening	2 tablespoons melted butter
(never butter)	1 teaspoon celery or poppy seeds
2 teaspoons salt	

In saucepan, combine first four ingredients. Heat until shortening melts. Pour in bowl and cool to lukewarm. Add yeast. Stir until dissolved. Stir in flour, cover, and let rise until double in bulk (about 30 minutes at 85°). Punch down and turn onto floured board. Divide into two balls and let rest 15 minutes. Roll into circles ¼ inch thick. Brush with butter. Cut into 12 wedge-shaped pieces and roll. Brush with butter, sprinkle with seeds or coarse salt. Let rise 15 minutes and bake at 450° for 12 or 15 minutes. Makes 2 dozen rolls.

MRS. GLEN EVINS

ICEBOX ROLLS

1 package dry yeast
½ cup warm water and a
   pinch of sugar
⅔ cup Crisco
1 cup mashed potatoes

½ cup sugar
1 teaspoon salt
2 eggs
1 cup scalded milk
6 cups flour

Add yeast to warm water and sugar. Let stand. Mix Crisco, mashed potatoes, sugar and salt. Add eggs and beat well. Add the scalded milk. When the dough is warm (not hot), add yeast mixture. Stir in 3 cups of the flour and mix well. Then add remaining flour and mix well. Cover and let rise. Push down, cover well and store in refrigerator to use as needed. Take out about 2 hours before baking; shape as desired and let rise. Bake about 20 minutes at 425°. These rolls are crusty and delicious. They have much the texture of homemade bread.

Mrs. W. Carson McNab

RYE ICEBOX ROLLS

2 yeast cakes
¼ cup lukewarm water
¾ cup sugar
2 teaspoons salt
1 cup butter or other shortening
1 cup hot water

¾ cup cold water
2 eggs
2 or 3 cardamon seeds (optional)
1 cup rye flour sifted with
6½ cups white flour

Mix yeast with 2 tablespoons of the sugar and lukewarm water. Place remaining sugar, salt, and shortening in a bowl. Add hot water and stir until shortening is melted; add cold water. Mixture should be lukewarm now. Add eggs, then yeast mixture. Crush cardamon seeds and add. Gradually add flour, mixing to smooth, soft dough. Knead on lightly floured board until smooth and satiny. Shape into ball, place in greased bowl. Cover and set in refrigerator until needed. Remove from refrigerator; knead lightly to permit gas to escape. Let rise until double in bulk. Knead; shape into rolls, and let rise again until double in bulk. Bake 20 minutes at 400°. Makes 2½ to 3 dozen rolls.

Mrs. Bert Fetzer

LITTLE HOUSE ALMOND CROQUETTES

1 pint milk, scalded
2 egg yolks, beaten
3 tablespoons flour
3 tablespoons cornstarch
½ cup sugar
⅛ teaspoon salt
¼ cup cold milk

½ cup blanched almonds, slivered
10 drops almond extract
For dipping croquettes:
  1 egg, slightly beaten
  Cracker crumbs
Fat for deep frying

Scald milk. Beat egg yolks well. Sift together flour, cornstarch, sugar and salt; add half to egg yolks. Stir in cold milk, add rest of dry ingredients. Then add scalded milk, and cook mixture over boiling water until smooth and thick. Add almonds and almond extract. Pour into 8 inch square pan, cool. Place in refrigerator until thoroughly chilled and firm. Cut into 2½-inch squares (makes 9 squares); dip in slightly beaten egg and then in cracker crumbs. Fry in a basket in deep fat until golden brown. Serve immediately to 8 or 9.

MRS. BLACKBURN LOWRY

Pancakes, French Toast, Waffles

BANANA PANCAKES

1 egg
1 tablespoon sugar
3 tablespoons flour

½ teaspoon baking powder
3 ripe bananas, peeled and mashed
Butter and sugar

Beat egg with sugar. Add flour, baking powder, and bananas. Mix together with a fork. Drop a tablespoonful at a time into a hot buttered frying pan. Turn when bubbles appear. These cook quickly. Be careful not to burn the butter. Add more butter to frying pan as needed. Remove to platter and sprinkle with granulated sugar. These are so delicious that no syrup is needed. Makes 14-16 small pancakes.

This recipe came from a native cook at Round Hill, Montego Bay, Jamaica. It is better to make 2 batches of pancake batter, rather than double this recipe. Recipe can be doubled if blender is used.

MRS. ROBERT A. FOSTER

CORN MEAL PANCAKES

1 cup flour	½ teaspoon soda
1 cup corn meal	2 cups buttermilk
1 teaspoon salt	2 eggs, well beaten
2 teaspoons baking powder	½ cup water

Sift all dry ingredients together. Add to dry ingredients 2 cups buttermilk and 2 well-beaten eggs. Thin batter with ½ cup water. (Pancakes must have thin batter to be good). Pour tablespoon of batter on hot greased gridle and flip once. They should be size of silver dollar. As you are cooking pancakes, stir batter because corn meal settles to bottom of bowl. Serves 4. This is an old southern family recipe.

H. L. (Dusty) Crowder

SOUR MILK PANCAKES

2 cups flour	2 eggs
1 teaspoon soda	2 cups sour milk or buttermilk
1 tablespoon sugar	2 tablespoons melted shortening
1 teaspoon salt	

Sift, then measure flour. Sift again with baking soda, sugar, and salt. (To sour sweet milk artificially place 8 teaspoons vinegar in a 2 cup measure and fill to the 2 cup mark with sweet milk. Mix well). Beat eggs until fluffy. Combine eggs, milk, and melted shortening. Add dry ingredients to liquid, beating until smooth. Bake on a greased griddle turning each cake when it is browned on the underside and before bubbles burst on the top. Turn only once. Serve immediately. Makes 1½ dozen cakes.

Mrs. Rogers Morgan

FRENCH TOAST

2 eggs	⅓ cup milk
1 tablespoon sugar	4 slices day-old bread
¼ teaspoon salt	(should be ½ inch thick)
⅛ teaspoon flour	Butter
½ teaspoon vanilla	

Beat eggs well. Mix in sugar, salt, flour, vanilla, and milk. Dip bread in egg-milk mixture. Sauté in butter. Thick bread, well-soaked in batter makes superb French toast. Serve with maple syrup or cinnamon sugar.

Mrs. Louis M. Saxton

CHOCOLATE BROWNIE WAFFLES

½ cup shortening
1 cup granulated sugar
2 squares unsweetened chocolate, melted
2 eggs, well beaten
½ teaspoon salt
1¼ cups sifted cake flour

½ teaspoon cinnamon
½ cup milk or ¼ cup evaporated milk and ¼ cup water
1 teaspoon vanilla extract
½ cup chopped walnuts (optional)

Work shortening with a spoon until fluffy and creamy. Gradually add sugar, while continuing to work with a spoon until light. Add melted chocolate and eggs and blend well. Sift together the dry ingredients and add alternately with milk, to which the vanilla has been added. Add nuts and mix thoroughly. Bake on a waffle iron. Makes 6 waffles. Serve topped with vanilla or coffee ice cream. These waffles require no baking powder. They are quite rich.

MRS. G. B. HOWELL, JR.

CRISP WAFFLES

2 eggs
1 cup salad oil
½ cup milk
2 cups flour

1 teaspoon salt
1 tablespoon sugar
4 teaspoons baking powder
¾ cup water

Beat eggs. Pour in oil and beat with rotary egg beater until smooth. Add milk. Sift all dry ingredients together and add alternately with water. Beat until smooth. This makes 8 regular round waffles.

MRS. C. E. HOLTSINGER

SOUTHERN WAFFLES

2 cups flour
2 teaspoons baking powder
¼ cup yellow corn meal
¾ teaspoon soda
1 teaspoon sugar

1 teaspoon salt
1 egg, beaten
2 cups clabber or buttermilk
¼ pound melted butter (½ cup)

Mix and sift all dry ingredients together. Add beaten egg, clabber and melted butter. Combine carefully, folding in rather than beating. Best if made day before and allowed to stand in refrigerator overnight. Take out of refrigerator before heating iron. This serves 6 or 8.

MRS. B. C. SKINNER

PAIN PERDU

3 slices bread per person	Nutmeg
1 egg per person	Shortening and butter
Milk	Powdered sugar
Sugar	Cinnamon
Orange Flower Water (or vanilla)	

Pour milk in a soup bowl; add sugar and orange flower water to taste. If unable to get orange flower water, vanilla can be used. Beat the egg yolks and whites separately. Add the yolks to the whites and a dash of nutmeg. Dip the slices of bread into the milk mixture first and press lightly to extract surplus milk. Then cover 1 side with egg mixture and put in frying pan with lard and butter. Paint the other side with egg mixture and turn bread over. When brown on both sides remove and cover each slice with plenty of powdered sugar and cinnamon.

MRS. VIRGINIA ROBINSON

CORN MEAL BATTER CAKES

1 scant cup white corn meal	2 or 3 tablespoons melted shortening
1 cup boiling water	½ cup sweet milk
1 large or 2 small eggs	3 scant teaspoons baking powder
1 teaspoon salt	

Scald meal with boiling water, stirring to prevent lumps. When cool, add well-beaten eggs, salt, shortening and milk. Beat well, then add baking powder. Grease griddle lightly and drop batter by spoonfuls onto hot griddle. When bubbles appear and edges begin to dry turn with a spatula and brown other side. Yields 8 to 10 pancakes.

MRS. NELSON MASON

CHAPTER IV

Salads

October in other areas means a land run riot with the flame colors of turning leaves, stubbled fields patterned precisely with corn shocks and fat orange pumpkins like a new kind of Chinese checkers, air so sharp and clear the most familiar sounds bear a hint of distant sadness. October in other areas is an ending, a turning in of the earth upon itself to rest the long winter through.

On the shores of Tampa Bay, October is a beginning, an opening up of the earth after the long hot summer, a time to plant the waiting seed, a time to tend the new-sprung plant. This is the growing season in the sunny South, the months from October 1st to the end of June. Just north of the beautiful Little Manatee River in the farming community of Ruskin, a gridwork of green fields produces the nation's salads. Each field is protected on four sides by towering black-green Australian Pines, and when the sun is overhead, its rays are funneled as into a well. The tender young plants absorb the warmth, well shielded from strong winds or creeping cold. It's a farmer's paradise. It's paradise for those who delight in crisp green salads.

Ruskin is a favorite spot for picnics and barbecues where the appetizers make the main dishes practically superfluous. On mounds of crushed ice repose luscious vine-ripened tomatoes, halved, thick slices of the incomparable Ruskin onions which are so sweet that they can be eaten like slices of apple, crunchy stalks of pale green celery, crisp slices of unpeeled cucumber, radishes as bright and juicy as raspberries. Nested in the ice are great bowls of homemade mayonnaise and creamy French dressing. Just spread the vegetable of your choice with the dressing of your choice, or try them all at once; it's a treat beyond description. But this is not all. Small delicate ears of pearly white corn are steaming in kettles to be eaten smeared with butter and pepper and salt while the juice dribbles down your chin and your sighs of satisfaction add to the general hum of contentment. If it's not paradise, it's just an inch this side of it.

Salad Dressings

ANCHOVY AND ROQUEFORT DRESSING

⅔ cup olive oil or salad oil
1 can (or 2 ounces) anchovies
  with oil
3 tablespoons vinegar
3 tablespoons lemon juice
1 sliver of garlic
½ teaspoon prepared mustard

½ teaspoon sugar
½ teaspoon onion salt
½ teaspoon celery salt
¼ teaspoon Worcestershire sauce
¼ teaspoon Tabasco
3-ounce wedge Roquefort cheese
¼ teaspoon paprika

Blend all ingredients in blender until smooth. This yields a little less than a pint. It is good with tossed salad, green salad, or vegetable salad.

MRS. JAMES A. WINSLOW

BLEU CHEESE DRESSING

1 4-ounce package bleu cheese
1 ⅓ cups mayonnaise
½ teaspoon salt
¼ teaspoon pepper

1 ½ tablespoons Worcestershire
½ teaspoon Tabasco
4 tablespoons catsup

Grate bleu cheese coarsely and mix with the other ingredients. Chill if desired. Serve over head lettuce, sliced tomatoes, celery, cucumbers or avocado. Yields approximately 1 pint.

MRS. GEORGE E. NETTLES

FRUIT SALAD DRESSING

½ cup sugar
1 ½ teaspoons salt
1 ½ teaspoons dry mustard
1 teaspoon celery seed

¼ cup lemon juice or vinegar
1 ½ teaspoons grated onion or
  onion juice
1 cup salad oil

Mix sugar, salt, mustard and celery seed well. Add lemon juice (or vinegar) and onion. Add oil slowly and beat well with rotary beater until thick. Keeps well in refrigerator.

MRS. PRENTISS HUDDLESTON

FRENCH DRESSING I

1 ¼ cups salad oil
7 tablespoons wine vinegar,
   cider vinegar, or lemon juice
2 ½ teaspoons salt
¼ teaspoon pepper
½ teaspoon paprika

1 teaspoon sugar
3 tablespoons chili sauce
1 teaspoon bottled horseradish
1 teaspoon prepared mustard
Peeled garlic

Combine ingredients. Shake vigorously and store in refrigerator.

Mrs. J. Wallace Gray

FRENCH DRESSING II

1 ½ teaspoons dry mustard
2 teaspoons paprika
5 tablespoons sugar
2 teaspoons onion salt
1 teaspoon salt

6 tablespoons vinegar (for tart
   dressing use 8 tablespoons)
1 cup salad oil
1 clove garlic (optional)

Mix dry ingredients well, add vinegar and mix thoroughly. Add oil and beat until thick (use egg beater). Put clove of garlic in jar with dressing.

Mrs. G. Pierce Wood

GREEN GODDESS DRESSING

1 clove garlic, minced
½ teaspoon salt
½ teaspoon dry mustard
1 teaspoon Worcestershire
2 tablespoons anchovy paste
3 tablespoons tarragon wine
   vinegar

3 tablespoons snipped chives
⅓ cup snipped parsley
1 cup mayonnaise
½ cup sour cream
⅛ teaspoon white pepper

Early in the day or day before, combine all ingredients; refrigerate covered. Use on green salad or as a dip. Makes 1 ¾ cups.

Tampa Electric Company, Leisure House

"HONEY" DRESSING FOR FRUIT SALAD

½ cup sugar
4 tablespoons vinegar
Scant teaspoon onion juice

1 cup olive or salad oil
1 teaspoon celery seeds

Add sugar, vinegar, and onion juice to oil. Soak an hour or so, stirring occasionally, until sugar is dissolved and the mixture is the consistency of honey. Whip with egg beater until thick. Add celery seeds. Keep refrigerated.

MRS. BROWN WALLACE

ITALIAN SALAD DRESSING

¼ cup sugar
1½ teaspoons salt
1 teaspoon mustard
1 teaspoon paprika
1 teaspoon oregano
1 cup catsup

1 cup olive oil (or ½ cup olive oil
    and ½ cup salad oil)
½ cup vinegar
1 clove garlic
1 onion chopped fine

Combine ingredients in a quart jar. Cover tightly and shake until well mixed. Let stand for 2 hours and strain. Makes enough dresssing for 12 salads.

MRS. J. G. SPICOLA, JR.

SOUR LEMON DRESSING

1 cup salad oil
1 teaspoon water
¾ cup freshly squeezed lemon juice
¼ teaspoon salt

⅛ teaspoon fresh ground pepper
¼ teaspoon Tabasco
½ teaspoon Worcestershire sauce
1 teaspoon Lawry's salt

Add oil and water to lemon juice. Then add the salt, pepper, Tabasco, Worcestershire sauce, and Lawry's salt. Stir well and refrigerate. Shake well immediately before serving. This recipe makes about 15 servings.

It is good on any type of green salad, vegetable salad, tomato stuffed with cottage cheese, or half an avocado. It was concocted by Mother and "Honey", our cook of 30 years from Grand Cayman Island.

MRS. WALTER A. BALDWIN, JR.

MAYONNAISE

1 egg and 2 egg yolks
1 quart salad oil
⅓ cup lime juice

1 teaspoon salt
Tabasco and paprika to taste

Beat eggs well in mixer. Begin very slowly adding drops of oil. Continue adding oil, increasing amount as mixture begins to thicken, until the entire quart has been used. Add lime juice and seasonings. Note: Add Tabasco for zip. If mayonnaise is too tart, decrease lime juice by 1 teaspoon.

MRS. H. L. CROWDER, JR.

HOMEMADE MAYONNAISE

2 whole eggs
1 clove garlic (squeezed with
   garlic press or rub bowl with it)
1 heaping teaspoon salt

3 or 4 drops Tabasco
Juice of 1 lemon
2 or 3 dashes paprika
1 pint of salad oil

Beat eggs, garlic, salt, paprika, and lemon juice in electric mixer. Add small amount of oil; then at intervals gradually add oil until all is used and the mayonnaise is right consistency. Store in refrigerator.

MRS. JOHN G. RANKIN

MINUTE EGG DRESSING

1 clove garlic
1 egg
½ cup salad oil
½ cup grated Romano cheese

Several drops of Tabasco
½ teaspoon salt
1 to 2 tablespoons white vinegar

Crush garlic in egg. Beat well with mixer or rotary beater. Add oil very slowly, beating until it thickens. Add cheese, Tabasco and salt. Beat well. Add vinegar and beat. This yields 1 cup or enough for 12 salads.

I serve this over a tossed salad of greens, croutons and artichoke hearts.

MRS. E. P. TALIAFERRO, JR.

"PELICANT-BE-BEET" SALAD DRESSING

"Al", our kitchen genius, got this recipe from the "summer" chef of the late King Alphonso of Spain.

1 pint mayonnaise
1 ⅓ cups best catsup
1 cup finely chopped, drained
   beets
½ cup dill relish

½ cup finely chopped
   green pepper
Onion juice to taste
1 large egg, hard boiled
   and chopped fine

Put all ingredients into a large mixing bowl and blend well with fork. Some homemakers add 1 tablespoon olive oil and 1 teaspoon paprika as a matter of taste. Yields approximately 1 quart.

PELICAN RESTAURANT, Clearwater Beach, Florida

ROQUEFORT DRESSING
(for head lettuce)

3 ounces Roquefort cheese
   (not bleu)
2 teaspoons scraped onion
1 teaspoon vinegar
½ teaspoon Worcestershire

¼ teaspoon Tabasco
½ teaspoon salt
Pepper
¾ cup mayonnaise

Let cheese soften at room temperature before mashing with a fork to a semi-coarse consistency. Add other ingredients and mix well. Let blend at room temperature for 20 minutes before refrigerating. Serves 4 or 6.

MRS. HARLAN LOGAN

SOUR CREAM SALAD DRESSING

1 cup sour cream
¾ cup mayonnaise
¼ cup chopped parsley

¼ cup finely chopped onion
2 tablespoons tarragon vinegar
Garlic salt and cayenne to taste

Combine ingredients. Mix well. Place in jar and cover tightly. This is excellent over grapefruit and avocado slices or head lettuce. Better the second day.

MRS. P. J. SCUDDER

SALAD DRESSING

1 heaping tablespoon Mr. Mustard
3 tablespoons (overflowing) wine
   vinegar

6 tablespoons (overflowing)
   olive oil
½ teaspoon salt
¼ teaspoon cracked pepper

Dissolve mustard in vinegar in salad bowl rubbed with garlic. Add salt, olive oil and pepper to taste. Wash greens. Dry thoroughly. Add to dressing in salad bowl and toss.

PIERRE JACQUET

TOMATO DRESSING

1 cup sugar
1 tablespoon salt
1 teaspoon pepper
¾ cup vinegar

1 cup salad oil
1 cup tomato soup
3 cloves garlic

Shake all together in glass jar. Keeps well in refrigerator and is good on green salads.

MRS. EARL H. McRAE

ZESTY SALAD DRESSING

1 large onion
1 teaspoon Worcestershire sauce
⅓ cup red wine vinegar
1 teaspoon dry mustard
½ teaspoon fresh ground pepper
1 tablespoon salt
¼ tablespoon Cayenne pepper

¼ cup water
1 clove garlic
2 tablespoons sugar
Juice of ½ lemon
1 cup olive oil
½ pint sour cream

Put all ingredients except oil and sour cream into an electric blender. Blend thoroughly. Still blending, add oil and sour cream gradually. Can be stored in the refrigerator almost indefinitely. Yields approximately 3 cups. This is good on green or mixed salad.

MRS. CHARLES J. YOUNGER

THOUSAND ISLAND DRESSING

1 pint Hellman's mayonnaise
½ cup catsup
¼ cup chili sauce
Juice of 1 lime

1 small clove of garlic (use garlic press)
4 tablespoons sweet pickle juice
2 hard boiled eggs, finely chopped (optional)

Combine all ingredients except hard boiled eggs. Chill. Add eggs just before serving.

MRS. M. LEO ELLIOTT, JR.

Vegetable Salads

LOUIS PAPPAS' FAMOUS GREEK SALAD

Make a potato salad from these ingredients:

6 boiling potatoes
2 medium-sized onions or
    4 green onions
¼ cup finely chopped parsley

½ cup thinly sliced green onion
½ cup salad dressing
Salt

Salad ingredients:

1 large head lettuce
3 cups potato salad
12 roka leaves (Greek vegetable) or 12 sprigs watercress
2 tomatoes cut into 6 wedges each
1 peeled cucumber cut lengthwise into 8 fingers
1 avocado pear peeled and cut into wedges
4 portions of Feta (Greek cheese)
1 green bell pepper cut into 8 rings

4 slices canned cooked beets
4 peeled and cooked shrimp
4 anchovy fillets
12 black olives (Greek style preferred)
4 fancy cut radishes
4 whole green onions
½ cup distilled white vinegar
¼ cup each olive and salad oil blended
Oregano

Line a large platter with outside lettuce leaves. Place 3 cups of the potato salad in a mound in the center of the platter. Cover with the remaining lettuce which has been shredded. Arrange the roka or watercress on top of this. Place the tomato wedges around the outer edge of salad with a few on the top, and place the cucumber wedges in between the tomatoes, making a solid base of the salad. Place the avocado slices around the outside. Slices of Feta cheese should be arranged on the top of the salad, with the green pepper slices over all. On the very top, place the sliced beets with a shrimp on each beet slice and an anchovy fillet on the shrimp. The olives, peppers and green onions can be arranged as desired. The entire salad is then sprinkled with the vinegar (more may be used) and then with the blended oil. Sprinkle the oregano over all and serve at once. Garlic toasted Greek bread is served with this salad, and Louis Pappas called this a "Salad for 4 persons".

LOUIS PAPPAS RESTAURANT, Tarpon Springs, Florida

ANNIE LAURIE'S POTATO SALAD
FOR GREEK SALAD

2 pounds medium Idaho potatoes
1 large sweet onion, finely chopped

3 tablespoons wine vinegar
2 teaspoons salt
1 cup mayonnaise

Boil unpeeled potatoes in unsalted water. While potatoes are cooking soak chopped onion in the vinegar. When potatoes are done, cool slightly and peel, then cut in slices and cut the slices in half. Add onion and vinegar mixture to still-warm potatoes. Sprinkle in the salt and mix in the mayonnaise.

I use equal parts of wine vinegar and olive oil to dress the complete salad, and I also put lots of shrimp on each portion instead of just one for garnish as in the Greek restaurants.

MRS. LOUIS M. SAXTON

SALAD A LA DEEDEE

1 head Bibb lettuce
1 head Boston lettuce
1 head leaf lettuce
8 large leaves iceberg lettuce
1 large cucumber
1 bell pepper (use seeds)
3 or 4 ribs of celery and leaves
6 to 8 scallions
4 tablespoons salad oil

8 tablespoons vinegar
4 firm tomatoes
1½ to 2 cups diced baked ham
8 slices Swiss cheese
½ to 1 cup toasted almonds
    or cashew nuts
3 to 4 teaspoons oregano
½ cup grated Parmesan or Romano
    cheese
2 to 3 hard-boiled eggs

Tear lettuce into bite-size pieces. Slice unpeeled cucumber and quarter slices; dice bell pepper; diagonally slice celery and scallions. Combine lettuce, cucumber, pepper, celery and scallions. Add oil and toss *thoroughly* (30 to 40 times). Add vinegar and repeat. Add diced tomatoes, ham, Swiss cheese (torn into bite-size pieces) and nuts. Toss lightly. Rub oregano between palms of hands to sprinkle over salad. Add grated cheese. Toss lightly. Garnish with finely chopped hard-boiled eggs. Serves 8 as main course or 16 as salad course.

MRS. JAMES W. GRAY, JR.

K I N G   G A S P A R I L L A   X L V I I   S A L A D

2 large heads of lettuce
3 stalks of celery
½ cup finely chopped salted
    peanuts

4 strips crisp breakfast bacon
1½ packages dried beef,
    well shredded
1 8-ounce jar processed bleu cheese

Have all ingredients cold before starting. Wash and shred lettuce and chop celery. Mix in large salad bowl. Add the peanuts. Add crumbled bacon, then the dried beef. Toss ingredients well, then stir in bleu cheese dressing.

Other leafy vegetables, carrots, cucumbers, tomatoes, and onions may be added for variety. This serves 6.

JAMES L. FERMAN, KING GASPARILLA XLVII

H O T   P O T A T O   S A L A D   W I T H   C H I V E S

¼ cup white vinegar
2 cups sour cream
6 slices crumbled crisp bacon
1 minced onion
Salt

Freshly ground black pepper
Celery seed
2 pounds cooked, peeled,
    sliced hot potatoes
¼ cup chopped chives

Mix together vinegar and sour cream. Add bacon and minced onion, sautéed in the bacon fat until golden. Add salt, pepper and celery seed to taste. Toss potatoes with this dressing. Sprinkle the salad with chives and serve it hot.

MRS. REGAR HICKMAN

P O T A T O   S A L A D   W I T H   S M O K E D   M U L L E T

Hot boiled potatoes, cubed
Red wine vinegar
Basic French dressing
Salt and pepper (coarse grind)
Capers
Sliced onions, crisped in vinegar

⅛ teaspoon dried dill
Sliced radishes
Smoked fish
Diced hard-boiled eggs
Parsley, finely cut
Mayonnaise

Over the hot potatoes pour vinegar, then a little French dressing. Watch that the potatoes absorb the mixture and that there is no excess. Add salt and pepper, capers, onions, dill, radishes for color, enough flaked fish to flavor but not overpower, eggs, and a lot of parsley. Bind all together with mayonnaise.

MRS. J. BROWN FARRIOR

THE SALAD
(From The Broiler Restaurant in Honolulu)

Mix and keep in jar on the shelf:

2¾ teaspoons salt

1 teaspoon sugar

1 teaspoon dry mustard

1 teaspoon monsodium glutamate

2 teaspoons oregano

½ teaspoon garlic powder

3 teaspoons freshly ground
   black pepper

½ pound (2 cups) freshly grated
   Romano cheese

To make the salad:

Mixed salad greens

Garlic croutons

Crisp bacon, crumbled

1 tablespoon cheese mixture per person

Lemon juice

Olive oil

Raw egg, whipped

Toss lightly in a large salad bowl.

MRS. J. BROWN FARRIOR

UNIQUE COLESLAW

4 cups finely chopped cabbage

1 cup purple chopped cabbage

1 cup finely chopped celery

1 green pepper, finely chopped

1 medium onion, chopped

3 hard-boiled egg whites, chopped

Salt and pepper to taste

Combine ingredients and set aside until dressing is ready.

DRESSING:

3 hard-boiled egg yolks

1 tablespoon butter

2 tablespoons sugar

1 teaspoon mustard

3 tablespoons vinegar

⅓ cup evaporated milk

While egg yolks are hot, add soft butter, sugar, and mustard; mix until creamy and then gradually add vinegar. Mix well and keep in refrigerator until time to serve. When ready to add to slaw, gradually add milk and stir until smooth. Pour over slaw and let soak in. *Do not stir.*

This is delightful served with hamburgers or barbecue of any kind.

MRS. THOMAS W. HARRIS

SOUR CREAM POTATO SALAD

4 cups sliced cooked potatoes	½ pint sour cream
1 cup diced celery	¼ cup vinegar
¼ cup sliced green onions	1 tablespoon bleu cheese
¼ cup sliced radishes	salad dressing

Combine potatoes, celery, onions, and radishes. Blend sour cream, vinegar and dressing; then pour over the potato mixture, tossing lightly. Put this mixture in an 8-inch ring mold and cover wih aluminum foil. Chill for several hours. When unmolding, loosen edges with knife and invert. Garnish with lettuce, parsley, and sliced radishes.

MRS. JOHN CULBREATH

COLESLAW WITH BACON

5 slices bacon	½ cup water
2 eggs	½ cup heavy cream
1 teaspoon salt	1 head cabbage, finely sliced
5 tablespoons sugar	Chopped hard-boiled eggs
½ cup vinegar	

Fry crisp the bacon and set aside 2 slices for topping. Beat the eggs and add salt, sugar, vinegar and water to the crumbled bacon and fat in the saucepan. Heat slowly, beating constantly until it thickens, being careful not to boil mixture. Remove pan from heat and stir in cream. Pour over sliced cabbage, toss lightly, and sprinkle with remaining crumbled bacon and the chopped egg.

MRS. J. BROWN FARRIOR

TOSSED SALAD WITH GREEK CHEESE

Mixed salad greens (Boston, Bibb, iceberg, few spinach leaves for color)	Feta cheese broken in pieces (about 1 tablespoon per person)
Onions thinly sliced and soaked in ice water until translucent	Olive oil
	Lemon juice
	Salt
	Freshly ground black pepper

Toss lightly in a large salad bowl. For variety, smoked oysters, avocado, ripe olives, artichoke hearts, or tomatoes may be added, singly or in various combinations to suit your taste.

MRS. J. BROWN FARRIOR

TONY'S SALAD

Garlic cloves
1 head lettuce, shredded
1 medium Bermuda onion
1 bell pepper, chopped
2 stalks celery, chopped
1 tomato, sliced
1 hard-boiled egg, chopped
¼ pound Swiss cheese, cut
   into thin strips
¼ pound ham, chopped

8 Greek olives
8 green Spanish manzilla olives
½ pound Parmesan cheese,
   coarsely grated
Salt and pepper
2 ounces olive oil
1 ounce wine vinegar
Juice of 1 lemon or lime
2 teaspoons oregano

To prepare garlic soak in lukewarm water and the thin skin slips off easily. Never peel by hand. Crush garlic into semi-purée and pour into jar. Cover with olive oil. Store in refrigerator.

Rub wooden salad bowl with 1 tablespoon oil-garlic mixture. Tear lettuce into small pieces with hands. Pile lettuce lightly in bowl and add very thinly sliced onion on top. This is foundation of layered salad.

Next add slivers of green pepper and celery. Place slices of tomato around edge of bowl. Add chopped egg, tiny Swiss cheese strips and ham (salami or shrimp can be substituted), olives and grated cheese. Place these in small evenly spaced piles over the lettuce base for easier mixing. Salt and pepper thoroughly. Drizzle olive oil over salad, then wine vinegar on top. *Always* add oil before vinegar. Squeeze lime juice over all, which Tony feels is the most important step, then add oregano. Using knife and fork, cut tomatoes into salad as last step, mixing down and up to get the right "shine" on the entire salad. Serve at once. Serves 4 to 6.

TONY'S RESTAURANT, Tampa, Florida

TOSSED SALAD

1 head lettuce (or equivalent
   mixed salad greens)
1 can anchovy fillets
   (or rolled), drained

1 cup broken garlic rounds
   (or croutons)
Olive oil
Lemon juice
Salt and pepper

Combine first 3 ingredients in a large salad bowl and toss lightly with oil, lemon juice, and salt and pepper to taste. Serves 6.

MRS. WILFRED BREGLER

WILTED LETTUCE SALAD

1 head lettuce
1 small bunch Bibb or Limestone
 lettuce
½ pound bacon

½ cup tarragon vinegar
⅛ teaspoon seasoned salt
¼ teaspoon freshly ground pepper

Tear lettuce into bite-size pieces in large salad bowl. Slice the bacon crosswise into ¼-inch pieces and fry. When bacon is crisp remove from pan to salad bowl. Pour vinegar into bacon grease in pan and bring to boil. While very hot pour over lettuce and bacon mixture, tossing as you pour. Add seasoned salt and fresh pepper. Serve in 6 or 8 individual salad bowls. An ideal first course.

ANSLEY WATSON

Meat and Seafood Salads

CHICKEN SALAD DE LUXE

2 tablespoons lemon or lime juice
2 cups cooked chicken, diced
1 cup diced celery
1 cup seedless grapes
¾ cup toasted almonds

1 tablespoon capers
⅓ cup mayonnaise
Dash of nutmeg
Salt, pepper, to taste
Crisp lettuce

Sprinkle 1½ tablespoons lemon juice over chicken and the remaining ½ tablespoon over celery. Allow to stand at least 1 hour. Mix together chicken, celery, grapes, almonds, capers, mayonnaise and seasonings. Serve on crisp lettuce.

MRS. VIRGINIA ROBINSON

KINGFISH SALAD

Steam chunks of kingfish (including skin) in water seasoned with crab-boil, lemon juice, and salt. Drain. Flake the fish, then marinate in basic French dressing with coarsely ground pepper and thinly sliced onions. Chill.

Drain, and mix with:

½ cup mayonnaise that has
 been seasoned with —
1 teaspoon lemon juice
½ teaspoon dry mustard

2 tablespoons horseradish
Onion juice
Chopped chives

Serve in a large bowl or in lettuce cups.

MRS. J. BROWN FARRIOR

TURKEY SALAD

6 cups cooked diced turkey
1 cup minced celery
¼ cup green pepper, chopped fine
¾ to 1 cup broken pecans

¾ cup mayonnaise or enough
    to hold mixture together
Salt and pepper to taste
Parsley for garnish

Toss all ingredients together and chill before serving. If desired cut the amount of mayonnaise to about ½ cup and thin with about ¼ cup of turkey broth. Serves 12 to 14.

MRS. JACKSON LOGAN

FLORIDA LOBSTER SALAD

1 cup cooked Florida lobster meat
2 tablespoons French dressing
1 tablespoon onion, finely chopped
1 cup celery, chopped
¼ cup green pepper, chopped
3 slices pimiento, cut up

1 cup mayonnaise
1 hard-boiled egg, chopped
Lemon juice
½ teaspoon salt
½ teaspoon black pepper
½ teaspoon Tabasco

Bowl should be rubbed with garlic. If lobster shells are used, sprinkle with lemon or lime juice. Cut cooked lobster meat with scissors into ¼-inch cubes. Marinate in old-fashioned (four seasons) French dressing and onion. Add celery, green pepper, and pimiento. Mix together. Add mayonnaise and egg. Salad should have plenty of lemon juice and be seasoned well with salt, pepper and Tabasco.

MRS. JAMES E. WALL

PICKLED SHRIMP

5 pounds cooked shrimp

10 white mild onions sliced
    in thin rings

Into a deep, flat pan place layers of shrimp and onion alternately until ingredients are consumed.

DRESSING:

1 pint olive oil
¾ pint cider vinegar
1 large bottle of capers
    with juice

1 tablespoon sugar
1 teaspoon Worcestershire
3 or 4 drops Tabasco
Salt to taste

Mix ingredients thoroughly and pour over shrimp and onion. Cover and place in refrigerator for 12 hours before serving, stirring at intervals. To serve, drain shrimp, place on large platter and garnish with crisp lettuce leaves or parsley.

MRS. J. HARDIN KIRBY

S H R I M P   S A L A D   S P E C I A L

6 cups water
1 stalk celery with leaves, chopped
2 tablespoons salt
2 tablespoons vinegar
2 tablespoons mixed pickling
    spices or shrimp spice
1 sprig parsley
1 bay leaf

1½ pounds uncooked fresh or
    frozen shrimp, peeled and
    deveined
¼ cup tarragon vinegar
1 cup celery
3 hard-boiled eggs, cut in eighths
¼ cup mayonnaise
1 tablespoon chopped onion
1 tablespoon drained capers
Salt to taste

Combine first 7 ingredients and bring to boil. Add shrimp; cover and bring to boil. Lower heat and simmer gently until shrimp turn pink (about 5 minutes). Drain. Add tarragon vinegar and let stand about ½ hour. Drain thoroughly. Add remaining ingredients and toss lightly. Chill well. Serve in lettuce cups and top with mayonnaise. Serves 6 to 8.

MRS. CLIFF McELVEY, JR.

Combination Salads -- Congealed

A V O C A D O - B U T T E R M I L K   R I N G

1½ tablespoons plain gelatin
½ cup cold water
1½ cups sieved avocado
2 cups buttermilk
½ cup mayonnaise
1½ teaspoons salt

Sprinkle of celery salt
½ teaspoon grated onion
1 tablespoon lemon juice
Dash Tabasco sauce
2 or 3 drops green food coloring
Watercress & grapefruit sections
    for garnishing

Soften gelatin for 5 minutes in cold water and dissolve over hot water. Add to avocado and combine with next 8 ingredients. Pour into an 8-inch ring mold that has been lightly oiled, and chill until firm. To serve, unmold, pile grapefruit sections in the center and garnish with watercress. Serves 8.

MRS. WILLIAM E. HENSON, JR.

COLD BROCCOLI SALAD MOLD

1 package frozen broccoli spears
3 hard-boiled eggs, chopped
2 teaspoons lemon juice
1½ teaspoons salt

4 teaspoons Worcestershire
Dash of Tabasco
2 envelopes plain gelatin
1 can beef consommé (undiluted)
¾ cup mayonnaise

Thaw broccoli in small amount of water in skillet and cook slightly until able to mash with fork. Mix with the eggs, lemon juice, salt, Worcestershire sauce and Tabasco. Soften gelatin in small amount of consommé. Add remaining consommé and heat until thoroughly dissolved. Cool. Combine consommé and broccoli mixtures and then add the mayonnaise. Pour into a greased mold and chill. Serve with lettuce that has been tossed in French dressing.

MRS. B. J. SKINNER, JR.

CHICKEN SALAD LOAF

2 envelopes unflavored gelatin
½ cup cold water
3 cups chicken broth
4 sliced, hard-boiled eggs
2 cups tiny green peas (cooked)

4 cups diced cooked chicken
2 cups chopped celery
½ cup chopped almonds
2 cups mayonnaise

Soak gelatin in cold water for 5 minutes. Stir into 3 cups of hot chicken broth until dissolved. Cool. Place sliced eggs in the bottom of a pyrex loaf pan. Drain the green peas and put a layer over the eggs. Cover with chicken broth-gelatin mixture to depth of 1 inch. Place in refrigerator to harden. Into the remaining chicken broth-gelatin mixture, put the chicken, celery, almonds, and mayonnaise. Stir thoroughly.

When the 1 inch gelatin layer is firm, add the rest of the mixture, being careful not to disturb this layer. Pat down with a spoon and place in the refrigerator to harden. This takes about 2 hours. Remove congealed loaf from pan, slice and place on lettuce leaves. Serve with mayonnaise if desired.

MRS. MORRIS E. WHITE,
MRS. R. E. NOBLE

CHICKEN SALAD, MOLDED IN LAYERS

2½ tablespoons gelatin
4 cups chicken broth
2 cups white meat, diced
2 cups dark meat, diced
12 hard-boiled eggs
⅓ cup sliced stuffed olives

¾ cup finely diced celery
3 tablespoons finely diced
  green pepper
2 tablespoons vinegar (optional)
1 teaspoon grated onion
  (optional)

Boil one 5 to 5½ pound hen until nearly tender. Season to taste with salt and 3 leafy stalks of celery. Cook until meat is very tender. Remove celery. Chill and remove fat. Remove bones and skin from chicken and dice the meat, keeping the light and dark meat separated.

Strain 4 cups of broth. You will not use quite this much. Soak gelatin 5 minutes in 1 cup of the cold broth. Dissolve in 1 cup of boiling broth. Add remaining 2 cups broth (scant) and season with vinegar and onion. Decorate the bottom of a 5½ x 9½ inch loaf pan with sliced stuffed olives and thin strips of pimento in artistic pattern. Next add a layer of finely chopped white meat and celery mixed together. Pat down evenly. Carefully add enough broth to saturate. Add egg yolks which have been sieved. Smooth layer with additional broth. Next add the dark meat and olives, and more broth. Then add the diced egg whites and green pepper with more broth. It is necessary to pat each layer gently and to add the broth with caution in order to keep a definite line between layers. Place in refrigerator to congeal.

Several hours before serving, unmold and return to refrigerator. Serve on platter of lettuce, garnished with stuffed and ripe olives, and top with mayonnaise. Serves 12.

MRS. WILLIAM C. BLAKE, JR.

CHICKEN-ALMOND MOLD

1 tablespoon (1 envelope)
  unflavored gelatin
¼ cup cold water
1 cup mayonnaise
1 cup heavy cream, whipped

½ teaspoon salt
1½ cups diced chicken
¾ cup almond meats, toasted
  and chopped
¾ cup sliced stuffed olives

Soften gelatin in cold water and dissolve over hot water. Cool slightly and combine with mayonnaise, whipped cream, and salt. Fold in remaining ingredients. Chill in individual molds until firm. Unmold on crisp greens. Serves 6 to 8.

MRS. EDWIN DUNN, JR.

CHRISTMAS SALAD

2 tablespoons gelatin
½ cup cold water
2 cups boiling water
Juice of one lemon
½ cup sugar
½ cup vinegar

½ teaspoon salt
Red pepper to taste
1 cup nut meats (pecans)
2 cups celery, cut fine
1 cup apple, cut fine
1 small can pimientos

Soften gelatin in cold water; dissolve in boiling water and add lemon juice, sugar, vinegar, salt and red pepper. When nearly congealed, add remaining ingredients and chill. Serve on lettuce with mayonnaise.

MRS. WILLIAM J. BULLARD

SALMON MOUSSE

1 large can red salmon
1 teaspoon dry mustard
1 cup milk
1 stick butter
2 eggs, separated
2 tablespoons Worcestershire
1 medium onion, grated
Tabasco, celery salt, and salt to taste

4 envelopes of plain gelatin —
    dissolved in ½ cup strained
    salmon liquor and ½ cup hot water
¾ cup finely chopped celery
¼ cup grated green pepper
2 tablespoons lemon juice —
    or more to taste

Clean and flake salmon. First dissolve mustard in 3 tablespoons milk, then melt butter, add remaining milk, well beaten egg yolks, Worcestershire, onion, the dissolved mustard, Tabasco, salt and celery salt. Mix in gelatin. Toss celery and green pepper with salmon. Add lemon juice, then fold into the milk and gelatin mixture. Beat egg whites until stiff and fold in. Pour into an oiled 2 or 3 quart melon mold. Chill until firm. Turn out on lettuce platter, slice and serve with mayonnaise.

MRS. E. P. TALIAFERRO

SHRIMP SALAD

2 tablespoons unflavored gelatin
½ cup cold water
1 cup mayonnaise
1 pound cooked shrimp
3 tablespoons stuffed olives, sliced
¼ cup lemon juice

1½ teaspoons horseradish
2 teaspoons onion juice
¼ teaspoon salt
¼ teaspoon paprika
1 cup sour cream

Soften gelatin in water over boiling water. Stir in mayonnaise. Add other ingredients. Put in fish mold and let congeal in refrigerator.

MRS. WILLIAM O. KINNEBREW

BLENDER TOMATO ASPIC

1 quart tomato juice	1 teaspoon Worcestershire
3 packages plain gelatin	1 teaspoon salt
Juice 1 lemon (or lime)	4 green spring onions and tops
1 teaspoon sugar	¾ cup parsley
½ teaspoon Tabasco sauce	4 or 5 stalks celery and leaves
(less if desired)	Small jar stuffed olives (about
	¾ cup) optional

Heat 1 cup tomato juice and gelatin in sauce pan until gelatin is dissolved. Put aside. Put 1½ cups tomato juice in blender and add other ingredients except olives. Cut or chop the bulky ingredients just enough to make the work of the blender easier. Blend on high speed for about 30 seconds. Combine blender mixture with gelatin mixture and remaining tomato juice. Slice olives and add.

Pour into 2 oiled 9-inch ring molds. Chill until firm. To serve, place mold in hot water for a few seconds. Unmold on bed of lettuce. Aspic may be served in individual ring molds. Heap the center with boiled shrimp and serve with Thousand Island Dressing. Serves 12.

Mrs. M. Leo Elliott, Jr.

TUNA OR LOBSTER MOUSSE

2 envelopes unflavored gelatin	2 tablespoons lemon juice
½ cup cold water	1½ teaspoons horseradish
1 cup mayonnaise	¼ teaspoon paprika
2 cups tuna or lobster, flaked	1 package chopped almonds
½ cup diced celery	(optional)
¼ cup chopped stuffed olives	1 pint heavy cream
1 tablespoon finely cut onion	

Soften gelatin in cold water. Dissolve over boiling water; stir into mayonnaise. Add remaining ingredients except cream. Mix well. Whip cream and fold into mixture. Pour into 10 x 6 x 1½-inch pan. Chill until firm. Cut in squares to serve. Makes 8 to 10 servings.

Mrs. Cliff McElvey, Jr.

ROSY TOMATO ASPIC

2 cups tomato juice
1 tablespoon grated onion
1 tablespoon horseradish

3 tablespoons vinegar
Pinch of salt
1 package raspberry gelatin

Combine tomato juice and seasonings and bring to boil. Pour over gelatin powder. Stir well, cool and chill. This aspic combines two un-related flavors but is delicious and a beautiful rose-red color. If you would like, try molding it in layers with the Snow-White part.

SNOW-WHITE LAYER

1 3-ounce package cream cheese
½ cup mayonnaise
½ teaspoon salt

½ teaspoon onion juice
½ envelope plain gelatin
2 tablespoons water

Mix softened cream cheese with mayonnaise, salt and onion juice. Soften the gelatin in the water, and then dissolve over boiling water. Add to cheese mixture, mixing well. To mold, pour half the tomato aspic into loaf pan that has been rinsed with cold water; chill. When it is set, add cheese mixture; chill. Then add remaining aspic; chill. Serve on greens with mayonnaise; garnish with stuffed olives.

MRS. LOUIS M. SAXTON

CUCUMBER ASPIC

2 tablespoons plain gelatin
½ cup cold water
1 cup boiling water
2 large cucumbers, grated
1 small onion, grated

3 tablespoons vinegar
2 tablespoons lemon juice
Salt to taste
Several dashes of Tabasco
Few drops green food coloring

Soften gelatin in cold water. Dissolve over hot water. Pour boil-ing water over the cucumbers and onions. Let steep 10 minutes. Add warm gelatin and remaining ingredients. Strain and turn into ring mold. This makes a clear jelly, but a few chopped cucumbers may be added if desired. Pretty with the center of mold filled with cottage cheese.

MRS. WALTER BARRET

Frozen Salads

FROZEN CREAM CHEESE SALAD

1 3-ounce package cream cheese, softened
1 No. 2 can diced pineapple chunks

½ cup drained, chopped, maraschino cherries
30 to 40 tiny marshmallows
½ cup chopped nuts

Cream the cream cheese and mix in the remaining ingredients. Freeze in a refrigerator tray or mold. Serves 6.

Mrs. John R. Culbreath

EASY FROZEN FRUIT SALAD

½ cup heavy cream
¼ cup sugar
¼ cup mayonnaise
2 teaspoons cherry juice
1 teaspoon lemon juice

½ cup seedless grapes
½ cup canned apricots
½ cup canned pineapple
½ cup maraschino cherries

Whip cream. Add sugar, mayonnaise, and juices, then fruits. Place in wax paper-lined ice trays and freeze for 8 hours. This serves 6.

Mrs. S. Denny Herndon, Jr.

RED AND WHITE FREEZE

1 1-pound can jellied cranberry sauce
2 or 3 tablespoons lemon juice
1 3-ounce package cream cheese, whipped

¼ cup mayonnaise
¼ cup sifted confectioners sugar
1 cup chopped pecans or walnuts
1 cup heavy cream, whipped

Crush cranberry sauce with fork and add lemon juice. Pour into 1-quart refrigerator tray. Combine cream cheese, mayonnaise, and sugar. Blend well. Add nuts. Fold in whipped cream and spread over cranberry mixture. Freeze firm. Cut in wedges and serve on lettuce. Makes 6 to 8 servings.

Mrs. John R. Culbreath

Fruit Salads -- Congealed

HOLIDAY SALAD

DRESSING:

1 tablespoon sifted flour

1 tablespoon granulated sugar

1 teaspoon of salt

1 teaspoon Coleman's dry mustard

5 tablespoons cider vinegar

6 beaten egg yolks

1 teaspoon of butter

In an enameled pot, blend the flour, sugar, salt and mustard, then add the vinegar slowly, mixing thoroughly. Add the beaten egg yolks and butter and cook in double boiler until smooth, stirring constantly. The heat must be as low as possible and you must stir and beat constantly. When dressing begins to get hot and thickens at the bottom, remove from heat and beat until smooth. Repeat several times until dressing is as thick as honey, then remove and let cool. Your patience will be rewarded when all is blended. Use a silver fork and spoon to avoid a brackish taste.

MIXTURE:

1 No. 2½ can sliced pineapple

1 quart of whipping cream

2 cups broken pecans

1 pound of "extra soft" marshmallows

Drain the pineapple and dice coarsely. Whip cream and add the dressing. Combine pineapple, nuts and marshmallows and add to the whipped cream mixture. Chill in refrigerator, but do not freeze, for 12 hours. Serve on lettuce and top with a maraschino cherry. Serves 12.

MISS CAROLINE HARRIS

BING CHERRY SALAD

2 packages cherry gelatin

2 cups hot water

2 Coca-Colas

1 9-ounce can drained crushed pineapple

1 16-ounce can black pitted cherries (drained)

1 cup chopped pecans

Dissolve gelatin in hot water, then add Coca-Colas. Let partially congeal. Add fruit and nuts. Chill in refrigerator several hours.

MRS. J. H. WILLIAMS, JR.

FIVE - CUP FRUIT SALAD

1 cup Mandarin oranges,
   drained overnight
1 cup pineapple chunks,
   drained overnight

1 cup miniature marshmallows
1 cup shredded cocoanut
1 cup sour cream

Mix altogether and put in refrigerator overnight or for a few hours.

Variation: Add 1 envelope of plain gelatin dissolved in ⅓ cup warm water.

MRS. PAUL JACOBS,
MRS. ETHEL WILLIS

DELICIOUS FRUIT SALAD

2 tablespoons gelatin
½ cup cold water
2 cups homemade mayonnaise
1 cup heavy cream, whipped
3 egg whites, beaten stiff

1 No. 2 can pineapple chunks,
   drained
1 No. 2 can Queene Anne cherries,
   seeded and drained
½ pound blanched almonds

Soften gelatin in cold water. Dissolve over hot water. Stir into mayonnaise. Fold in whipped cream and egg whites. Chill until slightly thickened, then stir in fruits and nuts. Chill until firm.

MRS. WALTER BARRET

GRAPEFRUIT MOLDS

2 envelopes of gelatin
½ cup cold water
2 cups grapefruit sections,
   cut in pieces, with juice
3 tablespoons maraschino
   cherry juice

1 teaspoon almond extract
SAUCE:
½ cup mayonnaise
3 tablespoons cream
¼ teaspoon curry powder

Soften gelatin in cold water. Place over hot water to melt. Add grapefruit sections, cherry juice, and almond extract and pour into individual molds. Combine mayonnaise, cream and curry powder. Blend well and spoon over molds when ready to serve. Serves 6.

CHALET SUZANNE, Lake Wales, Florida

ROQUEFORT CHEESE RING WITH FRUIT SALAD

1 package lemon gelatin
1 cup boiling water
1 tablespoon vinegar
1 small package cream cheese
1 small package Roquefort cheese
1 cup crushed pineapple
½ cup whipped cream

1 grapefruit, sectioned
2 oranges, sectioned
1 pineapple, cut in cubes
Mayonnaise
Whipped cream
Lemon juice

Dissolve gelatin in boiling water. Add vinegar. Mash cheeses together, and add to partially cooled gelatin, mixing to a smooth paste. Add drained crushed pineapple and when almost cold, fold in whipped cream. Turn into ring mold and chill. To serve, unmold on platter of shredded lettuce. Fill center with fruit sections mixed with mayonnaise blended with whipped cream and lemon juice. Serves 8 to 12.

MRS. LEM BELL, JR.

FRESH STRAWBERRY SALAD

2 packages strawberry-
  flavored gelatin
2 cups hot water
1½ cups cold water

1 8-ounce package cream cheese
½ cup finely chopped nuts
1 pint fresh strawberries
  (slightly sugared)

Pour the hot water over gelatin and stir well to completely dissolve. Add 1½ cups cold water. Shape cream cheese into balls (using 1 teaspoon for each). Roll in the chopped nuts. Place cheese balls evenly spaced in 9-inch ring mold. Cover with the lightly sugared strawberries. Pour cooled strawberry gelatin over cheese balls and berries. Chill until the gelatin is set. Unmold on large serving plate. Serves 8.

MRS. SAM GIBBONS

SWEET 'N SOUR SALAD

1½ cups sugar
1 cup water
1 cup vinegar
12 whole cloves
1 tablespoon gelatin
2 tablespoons cold water

1 9-ounce can crushed pineapple
  with juice
1 dozen small sweet pickles,
  sliced
1 cup chopped pecans

Cook sugar, water, vinegar, and cloves until syrup forms. Pour over gelatin which has been softened in cold water. Remove cloves. When gelatin has dissolved add pineapple, pickles, and pecans. Chill until firm. Serves 8.

MRS. H. L. CULBREATH

TROPICAL FRUIT TRAY

1 No. 2½ can pineapple slices
Whole strawberries
1 small honeydew melon
1 cantaloupe or papaya
1 pint cottage cheese
1 3-ounce package cream cheese
4 tablespoons bleu cheese

4 tablespoons sour cream
¼ cup chopped walnuts
2 large ripe bananas
Lime juice or mayonnaise
Flaked coconut
French dressing

Chill pineapple, berries, melon and papaya. Mix cheeses with sour cream and chill. Put in bowl in center of large serving tray. Top with walnuts, surround with strawberries, and line up pineapple slices on either side. Cut bananas in bite-size chunks; roll in lime juice or thinned mayonnaise, then in coconut. Place next to pineapple. Fill in rest of plate with alternate slices of cantaloupe (or papaya) and honeydew melon. Tuck in fresh mint sprigs and plenty of lime wedges. Serve separately a tart French dressing. Serves 6 to 8.

MRS. LEM BELL, JR.

MELON RINGS WITH CHICKEN SALAD

2 ripe honey dew melons or
3 or 4 ripe cantaloupes (depends on size)
1 envelope unflavored gelatin
¼ cup cold water

1 No. 2 can crushed pineapple, undrained
1 package lemon gelatin
1 6-ounce bottle Vernor's ginger ale

Cut tops from melons, scoop out seeds and drain well. Soften unflavored gelatin in cold water for few minutes. Heat crushed pineapple and juice until hot; then add unflavored gelatin and lemon gelatin. Stir until dissolved. Cool and add ginger ale. Fill melons with mixture. Chill overnight. Before serving, pare skins from melons and cut in slices. Serve on lettuce leaves and top with chicken salad. Usually some gelatin mixture will be left over which can be molded for family use. This recipe makes 12 to 16 generous servings.

Variation: Add 4 or 5 slices finely cut crystallized ginger to mixture.

MRS. JAMES V. BUDD

CRANBERRY SALAD

2 cups raw cranberries
1 orange, seeded
1 cup sugar
2 envelopes gelatin
½ cup cold water

½ cup boiling water
1½ cups canned apple sauce
½ cup chopped nuts
1 cup diced celery

Using a medium blade, grind cranberries and orange (rind and pulp). Add sugar and mix well. Soften gelatin in cold water; let stand 5 minutes; add boiling water to gelatin and dissolve. Combine cranberry mixture, applesauce, nuts, and celery. Gradually add gelatin; mix well. Pour into lightly oiled 1½-quart mold.

MRS. RICHARD PITTMAN, JR.

GRAPEFRUIT ASPIC SALAD

1 package lemon gelatin
¾ cup boiling water
1 cup grapefruit juice
¼ teaspoon salt

1 tablespoon sugar
2 cups grapefruit sections
½ tablespoon grated onion
½ cup blanched almonds

Sprinkle gelatin into boiling water and stir until dissolved; add juice, salt and sugar. Chill. When aspic begins to thicken fold in the grapefruit sections, onion, and almonds. Mold and serve.

TONA W. PERRY AND PEARL HALL BOND

SUNDAY SALAD

2 tablespoons gelatin
½ cup cold water
1 cup boiling water
1 tablespoon sugar
1 teaspoon salt

¼ cup lemon juice
1 cup crushed pineapple, drained
1½ cups cranberry sauce or jelly
1 cup finely chopped celery
½ cup chopped pecans

Soak the gelatin in cold water for 10 minutes. Dissolve in boiling water, then add sugar, salt, lemon juice, and pineapple. Allow to cool but not congeal. Add cranberry sauce, stirring thoroughly. Add celery and pecans last. Put into individual molds which have been rinsed in cold water and not dried. Chill until set. Serve with mayonnaise. Serves 8.

MRS. MORRIS WHITE

Replica of a Spanish Courtyard at Las Novedades Restaurant

CHAPTER V

Soups and Chowders

If you ever visit a Spanish Restaurant in Tampa for the purpose of sampling a variety of Spanish foods, be forewarned. The soup is so delicious and so filling you may never get past the first course. These soups not only have flavor, they have substance, so much so, in fact, that a favorite lunch here is a bowl of soup with Cuban bread and butter, or soup and a Cuban sandwich. Those who do not have large appetites have learned to order only a cup of soup before a full-course dinner.

During Gasparilla Week one of the main attractions for tourists is the serving of free Spanish bean soup from the sidewalks of Ybor City. Visitors line up for blocks to wait their turn at the gleaming cauldrons where white-aproned chefs ladle out steaming cups of bright yellow Garbanzo soup rich with beans, potatoes, and Chorizo sausage. It's almost unbelieveable to see the curbings lined with tourists of every age and description sitting happily savoring their soup and Cuban bread. As the Mock Turtle sang,

> "Soo--oop of the e-e-evening,
> Beautiful, beautiful Soup!"

ASPARAGUS SOUP

½ pound fresh asparagus	3 cups chicken broth
¼ pound fresh mushrooms	3 cups skimmed milk
1 small onion, chopped	Black pepper to taste
5 or 6 tablespoons butter	Parsley

Cook asparagus on stems, in water to cover, until tender. Save tips, blend stems in blender. Sauté mushrooms with onion, in 3 tablespoons butter until tender. Add 2 or 3 tablespoons butter in small pieces. Blend well in blender. Add chicken broth, heated skim milk, and blended asparagus stems. Add whole tips, sprinkle lightly with fresh ground black pepper. Garnish with chopped fresh parsley. Serves 6.

MRS. J. BROWN FARRIOR

COLLARD GREENS SOUP
(Verzada)

½ cup northern beans
2 quarts water
1 small ham bone
1 small ham hock
½ pound beef short ribs
1 bay leaf
1 teaspoon salt
2 potatoes, diced

1 bunch fresh collard greens
   (or 2 packages frozen),
   chopped fine
½ onion, chopped
½ green pepper, chopped
1 blood sausage (Morzilla)
3 tablespoons bacon drippings

Soak beans overnight. In a large pot put water, ham bone, ham hock, short ribs, bay leaf and salt. Bring to a boil, removing foam with a skimmer. Lower heat and simmer approximately 30 minutes. Add beans and cook until tender. Add potatoes and collard greens. Sauté onion, green pepper and sausage (cut in 3 pieces) in the bacon drippings. When onion is soft, add to collard greens. Bring to a boil and cook uncovered for 10 minutes. (This eliminates bitterness from greens.) Cover the pot and simmer until potatoes and greens are done.

LAS NOVEDADES RESTAURANT, Tampa, Florida

FLORIDA FISH CHOWDER

1 cup diced potatoes
1 cup sliced carrots
½ cup diced celery
½ teaspoon salt
2 tablespoons butter (or more)
1 medium onion (thinly sliced)
1 to 2 pounds snapper, grouper,
   snook or other firm-meat
   fish, skinned, boned, and cut
   into 1-inch pieces

1 teaspoon Worcestershire sauce
1 teaspoon salt
¼ teaspoon pepper
2 to 3 cups milk
Paprika

Cook potatoes, carrots, celery and salt in water to cover until vegetables are almost tender. Melt butter in large saucepan. Add onion and cook over low heat until limp but not brown. Add fish and Worcestershire sauce and cook 1 minute, stirring gently. Add vegetables and water and cook this mixture 10 minutes. Add salt, pepper and milk; heat slowly to boiling. Sprinkle paprika on each bowlful of chowder. Serves 6 to 8.

MRS. DAVID J. KADYK

BORTSCH

1 medium onion, chopped
3 tablespoons bacon drippings
⅛ pound butter
2 beef bouillon cubes

1 cup hot water
2 tablespoons sugar
1 pint sliced beets

Sauté the onion until transparent in the bacon drippings and butter. Do not brown. Add bouillon cubes to hot water. Combine all in blender and blend for at least 2 minutes.

W. F. LENFESTEY

FRANK COOPER'S GROUPER CHOWDER

1 large grouper
2 pounds Irish potatoes, diced
1 large onion

¾ pounds white bacon
1 No. 2 can tomatoes
½ teaspoon pepper
¼ teaspoon Tabasco

Boil potatoes and onion in enough water to cover for 15 minutes. Dice and fry white bacon. Add bacon and drippings to potatoes. Add tomatoes and boil 15 minutes. Skin grouper, cut from bone, and then cut in 1½ inch fingers. Add fish and boil 45 minutes longer. Garnish with thin slices of lemon.

MRS. JAMES E. WALL, JR.

SEAFOOD GUMBO

1 large soup bone
½ pound beef stew meat
1 6-ounce can tomato paste
2 bay leaves
Salt and pepper to taste
3 packages frozen chopped okra

3 or 4 chopped onions
1 cup flour
½ to 1 cup bacon drippings or
    cooking oil
2 pounds shelled raw shrimp
1 pound crabmeat
1 tablespoon gumbo file

Put the soup bone, stew meat, tomato paste, bay leaves, salt and pepper in a pot with about a gallon of water. Cook for several hours over a low fire. Fry okra, onions, and flour in ½ cup bacon drippings until quite brown, adding additional fat as necessary. This will take 30 minutes at least since frozen okra is used. Add this mixture to the soup and cook at least 2 hours more. Shrimp and crabmeat should be added about an hour before serving; the gumbo file about ½ hour before. Serve in soup bowls, topping the gumbo with a large tablespoon of cooked rice.

MRS. CHARLES FORD, JR.

GREEK LEMON SOUP

3 cups chicken broth
3 cups water
½ cup rice

2 eggs
½ cup lemon juice

Bring chicken broth and water to a boil. Add rice and boil for 14 minutes. Meanwhile beat eggs well. Add ½ cup of the boiling broth to the lemon juice. Now the only hard part: add the lemon-broth mixture to the eggs very slowly, and beating constantly. It must not curdle! Now add the lemon-egg mixture to the chicken rice broth. Marvelous hot or cold.

ONION SOUP LOUISA

½ pound of butter
1 medium onion per serving
1 small potato per serving

1½ cups water per serving
Salt to taste
Grated Swiss cheese

Melt butter in frying pan; cook onion rings in it until soft but not brown. Meanwhile in another pot, cook the potatoes in water. Sieve potatoes, return to water, and add butter and onions. Season to taste—it requires plenty of salt—and cook for about ½ hour until all flavors blend. To serve, pour over small squares of toast sprinkled with grated Swiss cheese. This is quite different from the usual French Onion Soup.

MRS. LOUIS M. SAXTON

OYSTER STEW

½ cup celery, diced
1 small onion, chopped
2 tablespoons butter

1 quart milk
½ teaspoon salt
1 pint oysters

Cook celery and onion in butter until tender, add milk and salt. Let milk get hot but do not boil. Add oysters and their juice; cook gently until edges of oysters begin to curl. Serve at once.

MRS. W. F. McLANE

GAZPACHO

½ cup olive oil	¼ teaspoon Tabasco
4 tablespoons lemon juice	2 teaspoons salt
6 cups tomato juice	½ teaspoon freshly ground
2 cups beef broth	black pepper
½ cup finely minced onion	2 green peppers, finely chopped
2 tomatoes, peeled and cubed	2 cucumbers, diced
2 cups finely minced celery	Croutons

Beat together the oil and lemon juice. Stir in the tomato juice, broth, onions, tomatoes, celery, Tabasco, salt and pepper. Taste for seasoning. The mixture should be well seasoned. (It may require more salt or Tabasco depending on individual taste.) Chill the soup at least 3 hours. Pour into a tureen. Serve the green peppers, cucumbers and croutons separately, to be passed and added to each serving. The soup will keep several days in the refrigerator. This serves 8 to 10.

This Spanish vegetable soup usually creates quite a sensation, and of course it is best on a hot summer day.

MRS. HARRY A. MCEWEN

DESSIE SMITH'S SHRIMP CHOWDER

Wash shrimp well. To boil 5 pounds of shrimp use 2½ quarts of water. Add 1 chopped onion, 6 bay leaves, 2 tablespoons vinegar, salt and pepper to taste. When water boils, add shrimp and cook 5 minutes for small shrimp, 10 minutes for large shrimp. Drain water off carefully as a little silt may be in bottom of kettle. Set liquid aside.

Dice and fry crisp ⅓ pound white bacon, and then add:

2 bell peppers, chopped fine	3 spears celery, chopped fine
3 medium onions, chopped fine	4 medium potatoes, diced fine

Cook over medium heat until half done, add shrimp juice and 2 (No. 2) cans of tomatoes. Cook gently for 20 minutes. Add 4 to 5 shrimp per person. Before serving place 1 soupspoon of dry sherry in bottom of soup bowl.

The chowder was discovered accidentally. After I had been throwing away the cooking water for years, one day I realized that most of the flavor was there, and decided to experiment with it.

WITHLACOOCHEE RIVER LODGE, Inglis, Florida

PEANUT BUTTER SOUP

½ cup peanut butter
1 cup boiling water
2 cups milk

1 teaspoon salt
Dash of pepper
Dash of paprika
½ teaspoon onion juice

Heat peanut butter in top of double boiler and gradually stir in boiling water, mixing well. Add milk and seasoning. For a thicker soup add paste made of 1 tablespoon flour and 2 tablespoons cold water. Cook 10 minutes more.

MRS. WILLIAM E. HENSON

TOMATO BOUILLON

1 quart canned tomatoes
12 peppercorns
4 cloves
1 tablespoon salt
1 slice of onion

1 pint water
1 bay leaf
2 teaspoons sugar
2 tablespoons butter

Mix all ingredients together and cook for 20 minutes. Strain and serve with thin slice of lemon. Serves 8.

MRS. BRIGHTMAN J. SKINNER, JR.

SPANISH BEAN SOUP

½ pound garbanzo beans
1 tablespoon salt
1 beef bone
1 ham bone
2 quarts water
4 ounces white bacon
Pinch of paprika

1 onion
2 ounces lard
1 pound potatoes
1 pinch saffron
Salt to taste
1 Chorizo (Spanish sausage)

Soak garbanzos overnight with a tablespoon of salt in sufficient water to cover beans. When ready to cook, drain the salted water from the beans, and place them with the beef bone and ham bone in the 2 quarts of water. Cook for 45 minutes over slow fire. Fry the white bacon, with paprika and onion in the lard. Add to the beans. Also at this time add the quartered potatoes, saffron and salt to taste. When potatoes are done remove from fire and add Chorizos cut in thin slices. Serves 4.

COLUMBIA RESTAURANT, Tampa, Florida

VICHYSSOISE

4 large Spanish onions	Salt and pepper to taste
1 tablespoon butter	2 cups milk
2½ cups diced potatoes	1 cup heavy cream
2 cups fresh chicken stock	Chopped chives
¼ teaspoon paprika	

Sauté sliced onions in heavy skillet with butter until soft but not brown. Add the potatoes, chicken stock, and seasonings. Simmer covered for 45 minutes. Put mixture into electric blender or run through a sieve. Chill; then add milk and cream. Serve topped with the chives.

MRS. BRIGHTMAN J. SKINNER, JR.

WATER CRESS SOUP

2 bunches water cress	1 teaspoon salt
2 thick slices onion	3 cups chicken bouillon
1 3-inch piece celery, cut up	1 large can evaporated milk
1 tablespoon cornstarch	2 tablespoons butter
1 tablespoon sugar	

Remove leaves from stems of cress. Place leaves, onion, celery, cornstarch, sugar, salt and 2 cups of bouillon in blender and blend until smooth. Place in saucepan and add remaining 1 cup of bouillon. Bring mixture to a boil, reduce heat and cook for 10 minutes, stirring constantly. Add evaporated milk and butter and simmer for 5 minutes. Serves 6.

MRS. CLARE M. PHILLIPS, JR.

TROPICAL JELLIED CONSOMMÉ

1½ cups water	½ cup cold water
2 chicken bouillon cubes	1 10½-ounce can condensed
¼ teaspoon seasoned salt	consommé
2 teaspoons unflavored gelatin	¾ cup orange juice

Heat water to boiling, add bouillon cubes and salt, stir until dissolved. Sprinkle gelatin over cold water, let stand 5 minutes to soften. Remove bouillon from heat, stir in gelatin until completely dissolved. Stir in consommé and orange juice. Chill in refrigerator until set. Then beat lightly with a fork, serve in chilled bouillon cups, topped with thin orange slices and mint leaves.

MRS. J. BROWN FARRIOR

CHAPTER VI

Eggs and Cheese

Every Spanish menu has a section on "Huevos", which means eggs. Omelets are a specialty, and the Spanish omelet is a masterpiece. Chopped onions, green peppers, and garlic are sautéed in olive oil, then combined with tomatoes, pepper and salt, and simmered until the sauce is a rich tawny red. Tiny green peas are added just before the sauce is spooned gently into the center of a fluffy golden omelet. Omelets with ham, omelets with mushrooms, omelets with the mellow tang of Swiss cheese—all these are disguised under the prosaic word, "Huevos".

At Gasparilla time eggs are an important stand-by for those who celebrate until the small hours. After the Coronation Ball the restaurants are crowded with those in search of a midnight breakfast, and much of the social calendar is filled with sumptuous breakfasts after the festivities, or light-hearted champagne breakfasts in the mornings. These are perhaps the most sought-after invitations, for these are the hours when the hectic pace slows a little, affording time for quiet conversation and unhurried enjoyment.

Eggs

EGGS A LA SAXTON

1 small onion, chopped
2 tablespoons butter
½ pound chicken livers
2 cups medium cream sauce
1 Jalapeno pepper, seeded and
    minced
1 sweet chili pepper, sliced
1 tablespoon chopped pimiento
2 or 3 dashes Tabasco
½ teaspoon Worcestershire sauce
¼ teaspoon black pepper
4 hard-boiled eggs, cut
    in quarters
¼ pound sharp cheese, cubed

Sauté onion in butter until soft; add chicken livers and sauté until done. Add cream sauce and other ingredients, except cheese. Test for salt. (If you have made your cream sauce with salt, you probably won't need any.) Cook gently 5 minutes. Add cheese; when cheese starts to melt, serve on toast points. This dish can be prepared with quite a flair in a chafing dish. Mushrooms or sweetbreads may be substituted for the livers. Serves 4. Jalapenos and chilies are available in cans in most food stores, or wherever Mexican foods are sold.

COLONEL LAMONT SAXTON

BAKED EGGS

1 slice bacon
6 chicken livers
2 tablespoons butter
Cayenne pepper
Dry mustard

6 tablespoons heavy cream
6 eggs
Salt
Freshly ground black pepper

Cut bacon into 6 pieces and sauté until crisp. Drain and save bacon; discard fat. Sauté chicken livers in butter for 5 minutes or until lightly browned. Put 1 liver in each of 6 buttered individual baking dishes. Add a few grains of Cayenne and a pinch of mustard to cream and stir well. Put 1 tablespoon cream into each dish and break 1 egg on top of the cream. Sprinkle with salt and pepper. Put a piece of bacon on top of each egg. Cover the baking dishes and bake eggs in a moderate oven (375°) for 10 minutes, or until eggs are set. Custard cups covered with foil may be used instead of individual baking dishes.

MRS. CLARE M. PHILLIPS, JR.

CRAZY EGGS

1 large sweet onion, minced
1 bell pepper, minced
⅓ cup bacon drippings
1 tomato, chopped
12 eggs, beaten until frothy
6 ounces Swiss or American
    cheese, cubed

2 teaspoons oregano
½ teaspoon salt
    (or more to taste)
⅛ teaspoon pepper
½ teaspoon monosodium glutamate
2 tablespoons fresh parsley,
    chopped

Using a large skillet with a close fitting lid, sauté onion and bell pepper in bacon drippings until onion is golden. Add tomato, cover and simmer 5 minutes. Combine beaten eggs with last 6 ingredients. Pour egg mixture into skillet, stir well, cover closely, turn heat very low and let stand 5 minutes. Stir again, cover, let stand 5 minutes. Repeat, if necessary, until eggs are fluffy but not dried out. Constant stirring is not necessary because the sautéed vegetables and cheese steam the eggs. Bacon crumbled over the top lends a final crowning touch. Serves 6.

MRS. ALONZO REGAR

BAKED EGGS PIQUANTE

⅔ cup mayonnaise	½ teaspoon grated onion
¼ teaspoon salt	¼ cup milk
⅛ teaspoon pepper	1 cup grated sharp cheese
1 teaspoon Worcestershire	6 eggs

In a saucepan combine the mayonnaise, salt, pepper, Worcestershire, and onion. Add milk gradually, blending until smooth. Add cheese. Cook over low heat, stirring constantly till cheese has melted and mixture is thick and smooth, about 5 minutes. Put 2 tablespoons of mixture in bottom of each of 6 buttered custard cups. Break an egg into each cup, then add another 2 tablespoons of mixture to each.

Place cups in shallow pan of water (about 1 inch deep). Bake in 350° oven until eggs are of desired consistency—15 to 30 minutes.

MRS. LOUIS SAXTON

CREOLE EGGS

2 tablespoons butter	2 tablespoons butter
2 tablespoons flour	1 No. 2 can tomatoes
1 cup milk	½ teaspoon chili powder
Salt and pepper to taste	6 hard-boiled eggs, sliced
½ cup chopped onion	½ cup buttered cracker crumbs
1 clove garlic	½ cup grated American cheese
½ cup chopped green pepper	2 cups cooked rice

Make white sauce of butter, flour and milk. Add salt and pepper. Sauté onion, garlic and green pepper in 2 tablespoons butter until soft but not brown. Add tomatoes and chili powder and cook until thick. Add to white sauce. Place alternate layers of sauce and sliced eggs in casserole, top with bread crumbs and cheese and bake in moderate oven 350° for 15 minutes. Serve over rice. This makes 6-8 servings. We have this every year after Easter to use up the Easter eggs.

MRS. LEM BELL, JR.

Cheese

CHEESE CROQUETTES

3 tablespoons margarine
¼ cup flour
⅔ cup milk
2 egg yolks
½ cup sharp cheese, grated

1 cup mild cheese, cut in cubes
Salt, pepper and Cayenne
Bread crumbs
2 egg whites

Make a thick white sauce using margarine, flour and milk. Add yolks of eggs without beating and stir until well mixed. Add grated cheese. As soon as cheese melts remove from fire and add cheese cubes and seasonings. Spread in shallow pan and chill. Then cut in small squares and roll into croquettes. Dip in fine bread crumbs, whites of eggs, then crumbs again. It is a good idea to put croquettes back into refrigerator for a short while before frying. Fry in deep fat and drain on paper.

MRS. C. S. ROBINSON

TYROPITTA
(Cheese Pie)

1 pound Feta (white Greek
  cheese)
1 12-ounce package cottage
  cheese
1 8-ounce package cream cheese
10 eggs, slightly beaten

Pepper to taste
⅛ pound butter (½ stick)
¼ cup flour
2 cups milk
1 pound pastry sheets (Phyllo) *
¼ pound butter, melted

Crumble the Feta and add to cottage cheese, cream cheese, eggs and pepper. Mix well. Melt ⅛ pound butter in heavy sauce pan and add flour gradually, stirring constantly until it has absorbed all the butter. Add the milk gradually and stir until sauce becomes smooth. Cool. Add sauce to cheese mixture and mix well.

Line buttered 10 x 14-inch baking pan with one sheet of pastry. Brush with butter and add another sheet. Repeat pastry and butter until half the pastry sheets are used. Now pour cheese batter and spread evenly. Cover with remaining pastry sheets, brushing each sheet with melted butter. Trim pastry around the pan before adding the last sheet. Baste with melted butter. With sharp knife score the top sheets into 3-inch squares. Bake in 325° oven for 30 to 45 minutes or until golden brown and pastry is crisp. Cool slightly before cutting the squares. Serve warm. If Tyropitta is refrigerated, then reheat in a 400° oven to make pastry crisp again. Serves 16. This Greek pastry is not sweet and could take the place of potatoes or maccaroni.

*Phyllo may be bought from Greek bakery or delicatessen.

MRS. JOHN T. KARAPHILLIS

CHEESE SOUFFLÉ

4 tablespoons butter
4 tablespoons flour
1 cup milk
¼ teaspoon mustard
Dash of Cayenne pepper
½ to 1 teaspoon salt

¼ teaspoon pepper
1 cup shredded sharp cheese
   (¼ pound)
3 eggs, separated
¼ teaspoon cream of tarter

Melt butter over low heat; stir in flour and cook until bubbly. Add milk, mustard, Cayenne pepper, salt, and black pepper, stirring constantly. When sauce thickens add cheese. Remove from heat; stir in well-beaten egg yolks. Add cream of tartar to egg whites and beat until stiff; fold into cheese mixture. Pour into greased 1½-quart casserole. Bake at 350° until puffed and golden brown (50 to 60 minutes). The soufflé is particularly delicious when ½ cup ground ham is added with the cheese.

MRS. HUGH MITCHELL

BREAD-CHEESE SOUFFLÉ

8 slices stale bread
1½ pounds sharp cheese, grated
6 eggs beaten
2½ cups milk
1 round tablespoon brown sugar
Paprika

1 finely minced green onion
½ teaspoon dry mustard
Pepper
½ teaspoon salt
½ teaspoon Worcestershire sauce
Few grains red pepper

Remove bread crusts and cut in small cubes· Mix all ingredients except bread together. Make layers of bread cubes and cheese mixture in buttered baking dish. Place in refrigerator for 24 hours before baking. Bake at 300° for 1 hour. This is guaranteed not to fall. Serves 8.

MRS. DONALD M. LINS

CHAPTER VII

Rice, Cereals, and Macaroni

Some of the earliest Florida settlers envisioned the land as a vast
sweep of rice fields. This dream was not to be, and the soil was turned
to other, more productive ventures, but rice still remains a favorite item
in the diet of Floridians. Northerners who came to this region think-
ing rice was something to be eaten with cream and sugar or in puddings,
have learned to their delight that rice and gravy, gumbo, pilau, hoppin'
John, and the flavorsome Spanish combinations of yellow rice with
tomato sauces or meats are dishes fit for the gods. There are as many
different ways to cook fluffy white rice as there are cooks. Most of
them couldn't begin to tell you their secret (you have to sneak in the
kitchen and watch), but we did hear of a bride who was told by her
mother how to cook rice in a double boiler. The recipe was simple
enough; it called for one cup of water to one cup of rice, then cook
until done. Carefully, the bride measured one cup of rice into the top
of the double boiler and one cup of water into the bottom of the
double boiler. Two hours later in tears, she called her mother on the
phone to report that the rice was hard as stone. A gentle lecture on the
advisability of putting one cup of water in the top of the double boiler
with the rice set matters straight, but still it is true, the way of the novice rice-maker is fraught with peril.

Tampa, with its large Latin population, is a happy haven for
those who love spaghetti and pasta of all kinds. In Italian homes, the
first course is always a large dish of spaghetti served as the soup course
is served in other homes. This spaghetti is no weak and watery concoc-
tion; it has authority. A whole pod of garlic, unpeeled, is cooked with
the sauce in many an Italian kitchen. Italian specialty stores will sell
you blocks of pungent Romano or Parmesan cheese to be grated at
home just before the spaghetti is served.

And let us not forget grits. Many a transplanted Northerner who
has taken to rice in all its forms will never, ever see the good of grits,
but those who like them, sigh and call them "Georgia Ice Cream". Grits
with ham, grits with fish, grits with bacon and eggs! For a true be-
liever, these are dishes to dream on.

Rice

BAKED BROWN RICE

¼ cup butter or margarine
2 cups uncooked rice
2 10½-ounce cans consommé
   diluted with 2 cans water
1 8-ounce can mushrooms
   (optional)

1 tablespoon chopped parsley
2 teaspoons salt
Dash of thyme or marjoram
   (optional)

Melt butter in iron skillet or Dutch oven; add rice and sauté until golden brown, stirring constantly. Stir in remaining ingredients; pour in a buttered casserole. Bake 45 minutes at 350°, covered. (Can be prepared early and put in oven 45 minutes before serving time.) Serves 6 to 8.

DR. H. J. BLACKMON

SYRIAN RICE

Ingredients for first step:

1 cup boiling water
½ cup uncooked rice

1 teaspoon salt

Pour boiling water over washed rice plus salt. Cover and soak overnight.

Ingredients for second step:

1 tablespoon chopped onion
½ cup butter
¼ teaspoon black pepper
2 teaspoons salt
½ pound ground beef

¼ teaspoon powdered cinnamon
¼ teaspoon grated nutmeg
½ cup blanched almonds
1 cup water

Sauté chopped onion in butter, seasoning with pepper and 1 teaspoon salt. When onion is soft add ground beef seasoned with cinnamon and nutmeg. After cooking mixture slowly for 5 minutes remove from skillet, leaving fat. In the fat sauté almonds until golden brown. Then strain fat into saucepan. Add to the fat 1 cup water, 1 teaspoon salt and the drained rice. Bring this mixture to a fast boil then cover and simmer for 20 minutes or until tender. At this point add the meat and nuts and mix with fork.

MRS. BOB GRASS

GREEN RICE

1 cup uncooked rice
2 teaspoons salt
2½ cups boiling water
4 eggs, separated
1 green pepper, finely chopped
1 small onion, finely chopped

½ cup minced parsley
5 tablespoons grated Parmesan
   cheese
1 teaspoon paprika
1 cup heavy cream, whipped

Add rice and 1 teaspoon salt to boiling water. (½ teaspoon garlic salt and ½ teaspoon salt may be used.) Cover and cook over low heat until rice is tender and water is absorbed (20 to 25 minutes). Beat egg yolks and combine with green pepper, onion, parsley, cheese, paprika and the remaining 1 teaspoon salt. Blend mixture with the cooked rice. Fold in whipped cream. Beat egg whites until foamy and fold into the mixture. Turn into greased 2-quart casserole or ring mold. Place in pan of hot water and bake at 350° until set (50 to 60 minutes). Serves 6 to 8.

MRS. CHARLES J. YOUNGER

CALYPSO RICE

2¼ cups water
½ teaspoon salt

1 cup uncooked rice
1 Chorizo sausage

Add salt to water and bring to boil. Add rice and sausage, cover and simmer until rice is dry. Serve immediately. Serves 3 to 4.

EUGENE KNIGHT

ORANGE RICE

½ cup margarine or butter
2 cups hot water
1 cup uncooked rice
1 tablespoon chopped onion

⅔ cup diced celery
2 tablespoons grated orange rind
¾ cup orange juice
1½ teaspoons salt

Melt butter in hot water; then add the combined other ingredients. Place in a covered 3 quart casserole and bake 1 hour at 350°.

MRS. WILLIAM E. HENSON, JR.

PINEAPPLE RICE

1½ cups uncooked rice	1 cup light brown sugar
2 No. 2 cans crushed pineapple	½ stick of butter
1½ cups white sugar	

Cook rice until dry and fluffy. Place half of rice in a well buttered casserole. Cover with half of pineapple which has been well drained. Mix the sugars and use half over the pineapple. Dot well with half of butter. Repeat. Then pour about ⅔ cup of the pineapple juice over all. Dot with the rest of the butter. As the rice cooks add the juice in small amounts so as not to boil over. Bake uncovered in 325° oven for 3½ hours or a slow oven for 4 hours. Do not stir or mix at any time. Serves 10.

MRS. W. PAUL VANCE

RICE AND SOUR CREAM CASSEROLE

¾ pound sharp Cheddar cheese	3 cups cooked rice
3 cups sour cream, salted	Salt and pepper
2 cans peeled green chile peppers, chopped	½ cup grated Cheddar cheese

Cut cheese in strips. Thoroughly mix sour cream and chile peppers. Butter a 1½ quart casserole well. Season rice with salt and pepper. Layer rice, sour cream mixture and cheese strips in order. Finish with rice as top layer. Sprinkle with grated cheese and bake in a 350° oven for about ½ hour. Serves 6 or 8.

MRS. GEORGE H. KEEN, JR.

SPANISH RICE

2 tablespoons olive oil	1 teaspoon salt
1 onion	¼ teaspoon black pepper
1 bell pepper	1 packet saffron
1½ cups water	1 cup uncooked rice
2 fresh tomatoes, quartered	

In olive oil sauté onion and bell pepper. When tender but not brown, add water, tomatoes, salt, pepper, and saffron, and bring to a boil. Add rice and bring to boil again. Lower heat, cover, and let cook 25 to 30 minutes. Half way through cooking period stir gently with a fork.

MRS. LOUIS SAXTON

WILD RICE AND MUSHROOMS

¼ pound butter
1 cup wild rice (washed and
   drained)
½ cup toasted slivered almonds
3 tablespoons finely chopped
   chives, green onions or green
   pepper

1 4-ounce can of sliced
   mushrooms, drained
3 cups chicken stock
1 teaspoon salt

Melt butter in skillet. Add wild rice, almonds, chives or onions or green pepper, and mushrooms. Sauté, stirring constantly, until rice turns yellow, about 5 minutes. Put mixture in casserole with chicken broth and salt, cover tightly and place in oven at 325° for about 1 hour, or until all liquid is absorbed. Serves 4.

MRS. JAMES W. GRAY, JR.

POPPED WILD RICE

2 cups wild rice

Salt to taste

Wash wild rice well, 2 or 3 times. Dry on a cloth towel. Heat deep fat to 375°. Using strainer with fine mesh wire (4-5 inches across and not over 3 inches deep) lower 2 to 3 tablespoons rice at a time into hot fat. Let cook until it pops, which is almost immediately. Drain on paper towel, salt lightly. Place in covered container (ovenware) and heat before serving.

MRS. R. T. FARRIOR

Cereals

HOMINY PUFF WITH CHEESE

1 cup cold cooked hominy grits
2 eggs
½ cup milk
½ cup grated cheese

Butter size of egg
   (about ¼ cup)
Salt and pepper

Put hominy through potato ricer. Beat eggs well; add other ingredients and mix lightly. Bake in moderate oven (350°) approximately 30 to 40 minutes or until puffed up and golden brown. This dish is just as good reheated. Serves 4.

MRS. EDWARD O. SAVITZ

GRITS SOUFFLÉ

1 cup grits	½ stick butter
2 cups water	½ pound grated cheese
1 cup milk	Salt to taste

Cook grits 10 minutes in water. Add milk, butter, cheese and salt. Bake in casserole 30 minutes at 350°. Double recipe for more than four.

MRS. JOHN B. SUTTON, JR.

Macaroni, Noodles and Spaghetti

LASAGNA

1 large onion	1 small onion
1 clove garlic	4 tablespoons butter
¼ cup olive oil	3 tablespoons flour
1 No. 2½ can tomatoes	¾ cup Parmesan cheese
1 large can tomato paste	Dash of salt
2 bay leaves	2 cups milk
1 teaspoon salt	2 egg yolks
¼ teaspoon pepper	1 package Mozzarella cheese
½ cup water	1 pound package Lasagna noodles
1 pound ground beef	

Chop large onion and garlic and fry slightly in hot olive oil. Add tomatoes, tomato paste, bay leaves, salt, pepper and water. Stir well. Toss in ground beef in small pieces. Cover and cook over low heat for 1 hour stirring occasionally. Chop small onion fine and cook in melted butter 2 minutes. Mix in flour until smooth, add Parmesan cheese and salt. Gradually stir in milk and continue cooking over low heat, stirring constantly until sauce is consistency of heavy cream. Beat egg yolks slightly, mix in a little hot cheese mixture slowly (to prevent egg from curdling) then mix all yolks into cheese mixture and cook over low heat for 10 minutes longer. Remove from heat.

Cook Lasagna noodles as directed, then drain. Grease a large baking dish and put layer of noodles on bottom of dish, pour over enough tomato sauce to cover and add a little cheese sauce to this. Continue with these layers until ingredients are all used. Top with slices of Mozzarella cheese. Bake 20 minutes at 325°, then broil a few minutes until cheese surface is bubbly gold. Serves 6.

MRS. JOHN R. CULBREATH

MOCK LASAGNA

SAUCE:

1½ pounds ground beef
2 onions, chopped
2 cloves garlic, chopped
2 8-ounce cans tomato sauce
Chili powder and red pepper
   to taste

1 bay leaf
A little water
Salt to taste
2 tablespoons chopped olives
1 4-ounce can mushrooms
2 tablespoons raisins

Lightly brown meat, onions and garlic. Then add tomato sauce, chili powder, red pepper, bay leaf, water, salt, and cook over low fire for at least 2 hours. Add olives, mushrooms, and raisins.

FOR LASAGNA:

1 small package of regular
   dried noodles
¼ pound Swiss cheese

¼ pound American cheese
¼ pound Velveeta cheese

Cook noodles until tender. Into a greased casserole place a layer of the noodles, cover with the spaghetti sauce, top with layer of sliced cheeses, alternating kinds. Repeat with one more layer of each and place in a moderate oven (350°) to bake until cheese is melted and whole dish is heated through. (The amounts of cheese are approximate.) Serves 4 generously.

MRS. CHARLES E. FORD, JR.

MACARONI AND CHEESE I

2 quarts water
1¾ teaspoons salt
2½ cups elbow macaroni
1 tablespoon butter or
   margarine

1 egg
1 pint milk
Salt and pepper
2½ cups mild Cheddar cheese

Bring salt and water to a rolling boil. Add macaroni (10 ounces) and cook for about 10 minutes or until firm but not soft. Remove from heat and drain in a colander. Place the macaroni in a casserole. Stir butter into hot macaroni. Break egg into bowl and beat with a wire whip or fork. Blend in milk, salt and pepper to taste. Pour this mixture over the macaroni and blend in 1¼ cups grated cheese. Allow mixture to stand approximately 15 minutes. Top with 1¼ cups grated cheese. Bake in moderate oven about 350° for 10 to 15 minutes. Yield—12 generous servings.

MORRISON'S IMPERIAL HOUSE

PASTITSO

GROUND MEAT SAUCE:

2 pounds ground chuck (include
  a little ground beef fat)
2 medium onions, chopped
2 tablespoons parsley, chopped
½ teaspoon ground cinnamon
Salt, pepper to taste
1 1-pound can tomato purée

WHITE SAUCE:

¼ pound butter
1¼ cups flour
1¼ quarts milk
6 egg yolks, slightly beaten
⅓ cup grated Parmesan or
  Romano cheese
¼ teaspoon grated nutmeg
Salt, pepper to taste

1 pound macaroni

Sauté meat in heavy skillet. Add onions, parsley, cinnamon, salt, and pepper and sauté lightly. Add tomato purée and simmer for 1 hour. Meanwhile cook macaroni according to package directions and drain.

For the white sauce, melt butter in a heavy sauce pan; stir in the flour until thoroughly blended and smooth. Add the milk gradually, while stirring, and cook until smooth and thickened. Now add egg yolks, grated cheese, nutmeg, salt and pepper.

Toss macaroni and meat sauce together and place in an 11 x 16-inch baking tray. Sprinkle with grated cheese and add white sauce. Sprinkle with a little nutmeg. Bake in 325° oven for 45 minutes or until topping is a golden even brown.

If you prefer pastitso in layers, then start by placing macaroni in tray first; then add layer of meat sauce. Repeat this until macaroni and sauce are used, ending with macaroni. Pour white sauce over this, sprinkle with nutmeg and bake. When cool cut in squares. Serves 20.

Pastitso is served in Greece as a first course. It makes a good main dish or it may be served for a buffet.

MRS. JOHN T. KARAPHILLIS

GREEN SPINACH NOODLE CASSEROLE

1 8-ounce package spinach
  noodles (or spinach macaroni)
1 pint sour cream

2 6-ounce packages sliced
  natural Swiss cheese
Garlic salt

Cook noodles in boiling, salted water, uncovered, for about 30 minutes, or until tender. Drain and rinse with hot, hot water. Drain thoroughly. In greased casserole alternate layers of noodles, sour cream and Swiss cheese. Sprinkle cheese with garlic salt. Have bottom layer noodles and top layer of cheese. Repeat. Sprinkle again with garlic salt. Heat in 300° oven until cheese is melted and casserole is heated through. Serves 8.

Spinach noodles or spinach macaroni are green in color and are generally available in specialty food stores. It is a non-starch vegetable since it is made from Jerusalem artichoke flour.

MRS. PAUL D. COCHRAN, JR.

CHICKEN TETRAZZINI

1 3½-pound stewing chicken
2 teaspoons salt
⅛ teaspoon pepper
½ pound fine noodles
7 tablespoons butter
½ pound sliced mushrooms
¼ cup all-purpose flour

½ teaspoon salt
1 cup light cream
¼ cup sherry or cooking sherry
1½ cups grated natural cheese
   or ⅓ cup Parmesan cheese
Paprika

1 stalk of celery
1 small onion
½ cup parsley

Simmer chicken with 2 quarts water, celery, onion, parsley, 2 teaspoons salt, and pepper, covered, 3 to 4 hours. Remove chicken from broth; add noodles, cook 8 minutes. Drain, reserving broth; boil down to 2 cups; strain. Cut meat into pieces; pre-heat oven to 450°. In 3 tablespoons hot butter sauté mushrooms, set aside. Into 4 tablespoons melted butter, stir flour, ½ teaspoon salt, broth, cream. Cook until thickened. Add chicken, mushrooms, sherry; heat. Place noodles in greased casserole and pour sauce over them. Top with cheese and paprika. Bake 10 minutes in 450° oven. Serves 8. This may be prepared and frozen ahead of time.

Mrs. Fred R. Martin

Mrs. Perry M. Shoemaker

OYSTERS TETRAZZINI

2 pints oysters
4 cups noodles (½ pound)
SAUCE:
½ stick butter
½ cup flour
2 teaspoons salt
1 teaspoon white pepper
1 teaspoon paprika
2 teaspoons Worcestershire sauce

2½ cups milk
½ cup sherry
½ cup Romano cheese
TOPPING:
½ stick butter
1 cup bread crumbs
1 cup grated Romano cheese

Drain oysters and reserve ½ cup liquor. Cook noodles and place in buttered baking dish. Make sauce using ingredients in order. Add the cheese and oyster liquor to sauce. Put oysters on top of noodles. Sprinkle with salt and pepper. Pour on sauce and add topping. Bake 15 minutes at 400°. Serves 8.

Mrs. Walter W. A. Boden

CRAB SAUCE LORENZO

⅓ cup olive oil
2 large onions, minced
2 cloves garlic, minced
1 green pepper, minced
1 bay leaf
1 6-ounce can tomato paste
1 1-pound, 12-ounce can
    tomato purée

1 1-pound, 12-ounce can water
2 tablespoons sugar
1 tablespoon salt
¼ teaspoon black pepper
⅛ teaspoon oregano
⅛ teaspoon Tabasco (optional)
1 pound cooked crabmeat

Heat olive oil in large saucepan. Add onions, garlic, green pepper. Sauté slowly until soft (5 to 10 minutes). Add remaining ingredients, except crabmeat, and simmer uncovered 2 to 2½ hours, stirring occasionally. Leaving saucepan uncovered during cooking makes sauce much thicker. Add cooked crabmeat and simmer 20 minutes. Allow to stand 30 minutes before serving. Serve over cooked spaghetti; top with grated Parmesan cheese. Serves 6.

Mrs. W. J. Williamson

TOMATO SAUCE

½ cup olive oil
1 bell pepper, finely chopped
2 medium onions, finely chopped
2 stalks celery, finely chopped
1 clove garlic, finely chopped
3 sprigs parsley, finely chopped
2 pounds coarsely ground lean beef
½ teaspoon sugar
1 teaspoon salt
¼ teaspoon freshly ground pepper
½ teaspoon oregano

½ teaspoon bitters
1 teaspoon Worcestershire sauce
2 bay leaves
1 teaspoon monosodium glutamate
3 6-ounce cans tomato paste
1 No. 10 can tomato purée
    (Italian type tomatoes are best)
2 cups very dry red wine
1 8-ounce can whole mushrooms
    (optional)

Heat olive oil in large skillet; add and cook until lightly browned all the chopped vegetables. Add beef, and stir until brown. Add remaining ingredients (except mushrooms), and simmer very slowly for 2 hours. If sauce is too thick, thin with tomato juice. Remove bay leaves; add mushrooms. Makes 6 quarts. A delicious sauce for spaghetti, lasagna, manicotta, pizza, omelette, or as a base for chili. The sauce will freeze well.

Mrs. Thomas M. Edwards

ITALIAN-STYLE PIZZA PIE

½ cup olive oil	2 tablespoons tomato paste
3 cloves garlic, chopped	1 tablespoon salt
1 small onion	1 teaspoon sugar
1 small green pepper	15 dashes hot sauce
1 cup whole tomatoes	1 dash oregano

Heat olive oil, chopped garlic, onion, and green pepper. When onion is half done, add whole tomatoes and cook for 5 to 10 minutes, then add tomato paste, salt, sugar, and hot sauce. Let it simmer for 5 minutes, cover pizza dough with mixture, and sprinkle oregano on top. Bake at 425° for 30 minutes.

PIZZA PIE DOUGH:

2 cups all-purpose flour	2 tablespoons olive oil
1 teaspoon salt	1 package dry yeast
	1 cup lukewarm water

Sift flour; add salt and olive oil. Dissolve yeast in a cup of lukewarm water and add to flour mixture. Work dough until it is well mixed; let rise at room temperature for 45 minutes. Turn dough onto lightly floured surface; knead lightly. Mold into flat loaf. Place loaf in greased 8-inch layer pan and work just as a pie.

Serve pizza hot, cut into wedges. Makes 8 servings. To this pizza you can add anchovies, meat sauce or shrimp. Sprinkle with grated Parmesan or Mozzarella cheese.

COLUMBIA RESTAURANT, Tampa, Florida

CHICKEN AND SPAGHETTI

3 pound hen	1 clove garlic, chopped
Salt and pepper	2 stalks of celery, chopped
2 onions, chopped	1 8-ounce package spaghetti
1 green pepper, chopped	Grated cheese

Barely cover hen with water. Simmer with salt and pepper to taste until tender. Reserve broth. Remove meat from bones and cut in small pieces. Line a large greased baking dish with the chicken.

Cook spaghetti according to package directions. Drain, rinse, and drain again thoroughly. Place spaghetti in casserole on top of chicken. Sauté onion, green pepper, garlic, and celery in a small amount of bacon drippings until tender. Drain, then mix with spaghetti. (Mushrooms may be added if desired.) Pour chicken broth over spaghetti. The broth will be absorbed in cooking but use sparingly or dish will be soggy. Top with grated cheese. Bake for 1 hour at 350°.

MRS. GUY BURNETT

SPAGHETTI A LA MARADEL

¼ pound white bacon
1 large or 2 medium onions,
  finely chopped
1 pound ground beef
5 small cans tomato sauce
1 can mushrooms, medium
1 large clove garlic, crushed

½ cup chopped parsley
⅛ teaspoon pepper
¼ teaspoon salt
1 cup water
2 tablespoons dry basil
1 ½ pounds thin spaghetti
¼ pound grated Romano cheese

Cut bacon into small strips and fry in a large pot. When bacon is browned, add onions and sauté. Add ground meat and stir until cooked through. Add tomato sauce, mushrooms, garlic, parsley, pepper, salt, and water. Bring to a boil, then simmer for about 30 minutes. Add basil and simmer for about 15 minutes more. Stir occasionally.

Cook spaghetti according to package directions. Sprinkle grated cheese in soup plate; fill with spaghetti; sprinkle more cheese over spaghetti; add ¾ cupful of sauce; top with cheese. Serves 6 to 8.

MRS. R. S. CLARKE

MACARONI AND CHEESE II

1 ¼ cups scalded milk
¾ cup soft bread crumbs
3 tablespoons butter
1 ½ cups cooked macaroni

½ tablespoon chopped onion
½ teaspoon salt
3 cups grated cheese
2 well beaten eggs

Pour scalded milk over bread crumbs and add remaining ingredients. Mix well. Place buttered casserole in a pan of water and bake in 375° oven for 45 minutes. Serves 6.

MRS. A. PICKENS COLES

CHAPTER VIII

Sauces for Meat, Fish, and Vegetables

Every cook, at some time or another, must have wished someone would invent an entirely new meat or a deliciously different vegetable. When this happens, we know instinctively, we must get out the cook-books because we have been lazy in our cooking. The amount of food products available to the American housewife is staggering in its variety, and if we are bored with our meals, ergo we have been serving the same thing in the same way for too long. We have not troubled to concoct that which makes of a usual food an exciting experience. We have not prepared the sauce! To the kitchen then! Prepare to create!

WHITE SAUCE

2 tablespoons butter	¼ teaspoon salt
2 tablespoons flour	Few grains pepper
1 cup milk	

Melt butter in small saucepan. Add flour, salt and pepper and stir until well blended. Pour in milk gradually, while stirring constantly. Bring to boiling point. Boil 2 minutes, being careful not to burn. For a thin white sauce use 1 tablespoon butter and 1 tablespoon flour. For thick white sauce use 4 tablespoons butter and 4 tablespoons flour.

ALLEMANDE SAUCE

2 tablespoons butter	¼ teaspoon salt
2 tablespoons flour	⅛ teaspoon pepper
1 cup chicken or veal stock	1 egg yolk, beaten
(bouillon cubes may be	1 teaspoon lemon juice
used but omit salt)	

Make cream sauce with butter, flour, and stock. Add salt and pepper. Reduce heat and add egg yolk. When the mixture has thickened slightly add lemon juice. Yields 1 cup.

MRS. ROBERT FRANK

SPECIAL "LITTLE HOUSE" CREAM SAUCE

5 tablespoons butter
5 tablespoons flour
1 can clear chicken broth
1 cup milk
2 egg yolks

½ cup grated sharp American
   cheese
2 teaspoons salt
1 teaspoon Worcestershire sauce
Tabasco to taste

To the melted butter add flour. Slowly add chicken broth and milk, stirring constantly, and simmer for a few minutes. Add beaten egg yolks, then the grated cheese and seasonings. To this sauce can be added diced chicken, cooked shrimp, crab meat, or chipped beef to be served over toast. A few tablespoons of sherry can be added if desired. Serves 6.

MRS. HENRY HOLMES

CHEESE SAUCE

3 tablespoons butter
3 tablespoons flour
1 cup milk

½ small onion, finely chopped
½ cup Parmesan cheese

Melt butter over low heat; add flour, stirring until blended and smooth. Add milk slowly, stirring constantly. Add onion and cheese. Cook until thickened. Makes about 1¼ cups.

MRS. JOHN B. SUTTON, JR.

DRAWN BUTTER SAUCE

4 tablespoons butter
2 tablespoons flour

1 teaspoon lemon juice
Freshly ground black pepper
1 cup hot water

Melt 2 tablespoons of the butter; add flour, lemon juice, and pepper. Stir until smooth, then add hot water. Bring to a boil, stirring constantly. Reduce heat and cook for 5 minutes. Add remaining butter and stir until melted.

MRS. CLARE M. PHILLIPS, JR.

EASY HOLLANDAISE SAUCE

⅓ cup butter
Yolks of 3 eggs

Juice of ½ lemon
1 tablespoon hot water

Put butter, eggs, and lemon juice in top of double boiler and let stand, without heating, at room temperature several hours. When ready to serve, set over hot, not boiling, water. Add hot water and beat with electric beater until thick and smooth. Will not separate. Keeps in refrigerator and can be reheated by adding another tablespoon of hot water.

MRS. PERRY R. WILSON

CHINESE MUSTARD SAUCE

2 drops oil
1 tablespoon dry mustard

1 teaspoon vinegar

Stir the oil into the mustard (the Chinese prefer sesame oil). Stir in the vinegar. Add enough additional vinegar to make a smooth paste. This condiment is well known in Chinese restaurants.

MRS. BLAINE HOWELL

BARBECUE SAUCE

1 cup minced onion
1 cup butter
½ cup white vinegar
½ cup brown sugar
1 teaspoon grated garlic
1 tablespoon horseradish
2 tablespoons Worcestershire

1 tablespoon dry mustard
1 tablespoon salt
1 teaspoon pepper
1 cup chili sauce
1 cup tomato purée
1 tablespoon liquid smoke

Simmer onion in butter 5 minutes. Add remaining ingredients and simmer 10 minutes longer. This sauce is best served warm with spareribs, beef, hot dogs, or hamburgers. Yield: 1 quart or 20 servings. If refrigerated this sauce will keep for a very long time.

BUCCANEER INN, LONGBOAT KEY, SARASOTA, FLORIDA

BARBECUE SAUCE
(Sweet and Sour)

⅓ cup chili sauce
⅓ cup catsup (or all catsup can be used)
⅓ cup vinegar (or wine vinegar)
1 cup dark brown sugar
1 teaspoon Worcestershire sauce
1 teaspoon garlic juice

1 teaspoon prepared mustard (or ½ teaspoon dry mustard)
2 teaspoons red pepper hot sauce
1 tablespoon lemon juice
⅛ teaspoon salt
⅓ of a stick of butter, or 2 ⅔ tablespoons melted butter

Mix all ingredients in a 1 quart sauce pan. Heat mixture on stove until sugar is dissolved and then simmer slowly for 5 minutes. This recipe keeps approximately 2 weeks in the refrigerator. Makes 1 pint.

MRS. HARRY PORTON

BLENDER—MADE SAUCE VERTE

1 egg
1 teaspoon salt
1 teaspoon sugar
1 teaspoon mustard
Dash of Tabasco

3 tablespoons vinegar or lemon juice
1 ½ cups salad oil
½ bunch parsley
1 clove garlic

Put into blender the egg, salt, sugar, mustard, vinegar or lemon juice and Tabasco. Cover, blend a few seconds, uncover, add oil slowly, keeping motor running. Blend until thick and smooth. Add parsley and garlic and blend until you get a smooth green sauce. Makes 1 pint. Wonderful on fish or as a salad dressing.

MRS. ALONZO REGAR

CRAB SAUCE

½ pint sour cream
1 tablespoon chives
½ teaspoon seasoned salt

Dash of pepper
½ cup crab meat, flaked
¼ teaspoon paprika

Combine all ingredients and blend in blender or beat with rotary beater. This serves 4. Serve over green vegetables or baked potatoes.

MRS. WILLIAM E. HENSON, JR.

HORSERADISH SAUCE

½ cup sour cream
½ teaspoon salt

1 teaspoon sugar
3 or 4 tablespoons horseradish

Mix cream, salt and sugar. Gradually add horseradish. This is delicious with ham.

MRS. H. PHILLIP HAMPTON

SAUCE FOR LEG OF LAMB

1 teaspoon salt
1½ tablespoons vinegar
½ teaspoon sugar

1 teaspoon dry mustard
6 tablespoons salad oil
Garlic salt to taste

Combine all ingredients. Brush well over meat before roasting.

MRS. G. B. HOWELL, JR.

LEMON BUTTER SAUCE

4 eggs, well beaten
Juice of 4 lemons (or ¾ cup
    lemon juice)
½ cup sugar

½ cup water
½ teaspoon salt
2 tablespoons butter

Combine all ingredients except butter. Cook in double boiler, beating constantly until mixture thickens. Stir in butter.

MRS. MARSHALL BIZE

MUSTARD SAUCE

½ cup sugar
1 heaping tablespoon flour
2 tablespoons dry mustard

¼ teaspoon salt
½ pint light cream
½ cup vinegar

Mix dry ingredients thoroughly, add cream, and mix again. Cook mixture in a double boiler until it thickens (it will still be a thin mixture). Remove from heat, add vinegar. Return to heat and "cook up" once. Pour into pint jar, allow to cool, then refrigerate. It will thicken to the consistency of mayonnaise by the next day. Makes 1 pint. Good with ham, fish, and cold meats.

MRS. BLACKBURN LOWRY

WONDERFUL REMOULADE SAUCE

2 cups mayonnaise
Juice of 2 lemons
4 rounded teaspoons whole
    black peppercorns
2 teaspoons prepared mustard

1 teaspoon salt
¼ teaspoon Tabasco
¼ cup chopped dill pickles
⅓ cup coarsley chopped parsley

Place first 6 ingredients in an electric blender and blend thoroughly. Add pickles and parsley and blend only a few seconds. More salt, Tabasco or pepper may be added to taste. Refrigerate. This serves 10. Can be used as a cold shrimp dip or hot sauce for broccoli or asparagus.

MRS. W. F. EDWARDS

NEW ORLEANS COCKTAIL SAUCE

2 tablespoons anchovy sauce
1 tablespoon olive oil
4 tablespoons tomato catsup

1 cup stiff unsalted mayonnaise
2 tablespoons chili sauce
2 tablespoons tarragon vinegar

Mix anchovy sauce in olive oil, add other ingredients, stir until creamy. Juice of ½ lemon and dash of Tabasco may be added.

MRS. EUGENE MURPHY

SHRIMP COCKTAIL SAUCE

2 tablespoons chopped capers
⅛ teaspoon grated onion
½ cup heavy mayonnaise
1 teaspoon dry dill, steeped in
    scalding water and drained dry

2 chopped hard-boiled eggs
¾ cup grapefruit sections,
    cut into pieces
1 teaspoon orange rind

Combine all ingredients and pour over chilled shrimp. Serves 6.

CHALET SUZANNE, LAKE WALES, FLORIDA

BARBECUED CHICKEN SAUCE

1 tablespoon prepared mustard
Juice of 3 lemons
⅛ teaspoon Tabasco

1 stick melted butter
¼ cup Worcestershire sauce

Mix well, pour over pieces of chicken, and bake at 350° for 1 hour. Enough sauce for 1 chicken.

MRS. DONALD M. LINS

CHAPTER IX

Meats

The surest way we know to cook a roast of any kind is to invest in a meat thermometer. Insert the thermometer 2 inches into the lean part of the meat, not touching any bone, and roast at 325° until the indicator points to the name of the meat on the dial. Remove the roast, carve, and know perfect eating. The one exception is a standing rib roast which should be cooked in a 350° oven.

As for stews and pot roast, the secret of succulence is to brown the meat most thoroughly before adding the liquid. This insures a rich brown color and that the meat as well as the gravy will be juicy. Patience is the key word.

On the following pages you will find recipes of varied origins. We, in this region, have incorporated them all in our menus and take pleasure in mixing and matching recipes from different sections to suit our moods. Almost any meal here is rather international in its flavor. We find this makes cooking far more interesting and think you will too.

Beef
BEEF PIQUANT

2 to 3 pounds chuck, round or
   other inexpensive steak
1 lemon
2 tablespoons prepared mustard
Salt and pepper
2 tablespoons Worcestershire sauce

2 teaspoons brown sugar
3 generous dashes Tabasco sauce
2 medium onions, sliced
2 tablespoons butter or margarine
1 tablespoon capers

Select a steak that is about 2 inches thick and place in center of large piece of heavy-duty aluminum foil (18 inches wide) in shallow pan. Rub steak with cut surface of lemon so meat will get rind flavor. Spread both sides of meat with mustard. Fold aluminum foil around meat pan fashion. Place under broiler and brown both sides. Remove steak from oven, sprinkle with salt and pepper, and pour over it the juice squeezed from the lemon. Sprinkle with Worcestershire sauce, sugar and Tabasco. Add onions, which have been sautéed in butter, and capers. Bring the foil up over the meat and seal all edges with a double fold to make airtight package. Bake in slow oven (300°) for 3 hours. When done, remove to a hot platter and garnish with onions and capers. I often seal sliced raw onons, peeled whole raw potatoes and carrots in with the meat.

MRS. W. J. HOULIHAN, JR.

BEEF STEW

¼ pound salt pork
1 clove garlic, peeled and minced
1 large onion, sliced thin
1½ pounds lean stew beef
2 to 3 tablespoons flour
1 cup bouillon
1 8-ounce can tomato sauce
1 tablespoon mixed pickling spice

6 peppercorns
3 large potatoes, peeled and diced
1 No. 1 can small boiled onions
   (save juice)
1 5-ounce can water chestnuts,
   sliced thin
½ teaspoon salt

Remove rind from salt pork. Cut pork into ¼-inch cubes. Fry slowly in ungreased heavy skillet. Add garlic and sliced onion and cook gently. Transfer to casserole. Cut beef into serving pieces and dust with flour. Brown in drippings. Put in casserole, add bouillon and tomato sauce. Put spices and peppercorns in cheese cloth square and tie. Put in casserole. Cover and bake in 350° oven for 1½ hours. Remove from oven. Add potatoes, onions and ½ juice from can, and water chestnuts. Add salt. Bake covered another 45 minutes. Skim fat before serving. Remove spice bag. Serves 6.

MRS. ROBERT T. COZART

BURGUNDY BEEF

2 tablespoons oil
1½ pounds stew beef
12 small onions (or 3 large
   onions quartered)
2 tablespoons flour
1 clove garlic, minced
Red wine (boil for 5 minutes
   before using)
Water
Kitchen Bouquet

2 teaspoons tomato paste
2 teaspoons salt
¼ teaspoon black pepper
Tie together:
   6 sprigs parsley
   1 sprig thyme
   ½ bay leaf
¼ pound fresh pork fat
½ pound mushrooms
Chopped parsley

Heat oil in heavy sauce pan. Brown beef and onions. Sprinkle with flour and brown before adding the garlic and enough wine and water (half and half) to almost cover meat. Add enough Kitchen Bouquet to give an appetizing color. Add tomato paste, salt, pepper, and herbs tied in a "bouquet garni".

While mixture is coming to boil, dice the pork fat and brown over high heat. Add to the meat. Cover and simmer very slowly for 2½ hours. Skim off the fat and add mushroom stems and buttons. Cook 15 minutes longer. Serve and garnish with chopped parsley. Serve over plain or wild rice.

MRS. LAMAR SPARKMAN

CHATEAUBRIAND

1 whole beef tenderloin, 4 to
   5 pounds defatted
1 clove of garlic
4 tablespoons Lea & Perrins sauce

1 lime
Salt and pepper
¼ teaspoon monosodium glutamate

Rub beef tenderloin with garlic and place in pan. Mix Lea & Perrins sauce with juice of 1 lime, salt and pepper, and monosodium glutamate and rub into meat. Let stand 1 hour. Broil to your taste on charcoal broiler. You may wrap tenderloin in foil until ready to serve, then serve in slices. Serves 8.

SPANISH PARK RESTAURANT, TAMPA, FLORIDA

BOLICHI I
(Stuffed Eye of the Round of Beef)

3 to 4 pounds eye of the round
   plus piece of suet
1 Chorizo sausage, chopped
1 medium slice of cured ham,
   chopped
1 clove garlic, minced
1 medium Spanish onion,
   chopped

½ green pepper, chopped
Salt and pepper
Paprika
3 tablespoons bacon drippings
¾ cup hot water
1 bay leaf
4 whole cloves

Ask butcher to cut lengthwise pocket in center of beef, leaving opposite end closed. Mix sausage, ham, garlic, onion and pepper and stuff roast, packing well but not too tightly. Secure open end with skewers or wire. Salt and pepper all over and sprinkle generously with paprika. Brown well in bacon drippings over medium heat. Turn often to get an even browning because the better the browning, the more delicious the sauce. When browned add hot water, scraping the pan well. Lay suet on top of meat, add bay leaf and cloves to liquid. Cover and place in 325° oven. Baste occasionally and cook about 3 hours or until the meat is fork tender.

During the last 30 minutes potato balls may be added. Serve Bolichi cut in round slices and pass gravy separately. Serves 8 to 10.

MRS. LINUS W. HEWIT

BOLICHI II

Have your butcher make a pocket in center of one eye of the round roast (or do it yourself with a very sharp knife).

½ pound ground beef
1 Chorizo sausage, chopped
1 onion, chopped
¼ of a green pepper
¼ cup olives, halved
¼ teaspoon garlic salt

1 teaspoon Worcestershire
Tomato sauce (approximately half can or to consistency for stuffing)
1 can consommé

Mix all ingredients except consommé. Stuff roast with mixture forcing it to end. Flour stuffed roast, and roast at 475° for 20 minutes. Remove from oven, season with garlic salt and pepper. Add consommé to pan. Roast, uncovered, at 325° for 2 hours, basting frequently.

MRS. MANUEL CORRAL, JR.

SPANISH BEEF ANDALUCIA

3 pounds round steak cut in pieces
4 tablespoons butter
1 tablespoon olive oil
1 teaspoon salt
¼ teaspoon pepper
½ teaspoon thyme
1 bay leaf
1 onion stuck with 2 cloves

2 leeks (large scallions)
2 slices salt pork, cut in strips
½ cup meat broth
12 to 18 mushroom caps
2 tablespoons melted butter
1 tablespoon lemon juice
1 cup of small, pitted ripe olives
1 cup sherry (optional)

Flour beef cubes. Add 4 tablespoons melted butter to olive oil in heavy skillet and brown beef. Add salt, pepper, thyme, bay leaf, onion, leeks, salt pork and meat broth. Cover tightly and simmer 2½ hours or until meat is tender. Sauté mushrooms in 2 tablespoons butter and add lemon juice when tender. Add to stew. If liquid cooks down too much add more broth. About 20 minutes before beef is tender add ripe olives and sherry. An additional cup of broth may be used in place of sherry if preferred. Serves 4 to 6.

MRS. GEOFFREY W. STEPHENS

ENTRECOTE BÉARNAISE
(Rib Steak Béarnaise)

3 pounds rib steak, 2 inches thick	2 carrots, cut up
1 cup white wine	1 large onion, cut up
2 tablespoons tarragon vinegar	1 stalk celery
1 tablespoon tarragon leaves	6 egg yolks
1 tablespoon chopped shallots	½ pound butter, melted
1 sprig parsley	⅛ teaspoon Cayenne pepper

Combine in pan the wine, vinegar, tarragon leaves, shallots, parsley, carrots, onion and celery. Cook until mixture is half of original amount. Put aside to cool. In another saucepan put egg yolks, and stir in a little at a time some of the above mixture. Alternately stir in melted butter. When all is added, stir vigorously to the consistency of heavy cream. Blend well over low heat. Strain through a fine sieve and add Cayenne.

Brush steak with melted butter, salt and pepper. Broil on both sides, either rare, medium rare, but not overdone, as the sauce will add some cooking to the meat. Pour the Béarnaise sauce over the steak, or serve on the side. Serves 6. This sauce is also good with non-oily fish.

ROLLANDE AND PIERRE RESTAURANT,
ST. PETERSBURG, FLORIDA

FILETE CACEROLA

3 or 4 pounds of beef	2 bay leaves
1 pound of ham hocks	Salt and pepper to taste
4 or 5 celery stalks	1 tablespoon of flour
2 ripe tomatoes	1 cup of Burgundy
1 clove garlic	4 8-ounce fillets of beef

The base of Cacerola sauce is beef stock. For the sauce, place the above ingredients except flour and wine, in deep pan, cover with water and cook until meat is tender (about 3 hours). Dissolve flour in the cup of wine and add to the cooked meat stock. Let cook 15 more minutes. Strain sauce into another pan. Should be thick and a golden brown in color. Add four 8-ounce fillet steaks, trimmed. Cook for 6 minutes. Serves 4.

LAS NOVEDADES RESTAURANT
TAMPA, FLORIDA

FILETE STEAK SALTEADO

1 pound tenderloin fillet	2 Spanish sausages (Chorizos)
½ cup pure olive oil	15 mushroom buttons
2 garlic cloves, chopped	1 tablespoon salt
1 Spanish onion, chopped	Pinch of white pepper
1 green pepper, chopped	½ cup red wine
2 potatoes, diced	

Braise the diced tenderloin in hot olive oil. When meat is brown, add garlic, onion and green pepper. Fry potatoes in deep fat for 10 minutes at 350°, or until brown. Add Spanish sausages, mushrooms, salt, pepper and potatoes to the meat. When done, add wine. Garnish with peas and parsley. Serves 2.

COLUMBIA RESTAURANT, TAMPA, FLORIDA

GREEN PEPPER STEAK

3 bell peppers	1 tablespoon monosodium glutamate
2 tablespoons shortening	1 tablespoon salt
2 cups beef stock (or water)	1 tablespoon sugar
1½ pounds steak	1 tablespoon cooking sherry
2 tablespoons soya sauce	2 tablespoons cornstarch

Cut bell peppers in 1-inch squares and boil 3 to 4 minutes. Heat shortening in 12-inch frying pan and sauté boiled peppers ½ minute. Remove shortening from pan. Add 2 cups of beef stock and bring to boil. Add steak cut in ½ to 1 inch cubes, soya sauce, monosodium glutamate, salt and sugar. Mix well. Add sherry and diluted cornstarch (dilute cornstarch with about 1 tablespoon water). Stir until gravy thickens. Steak will be medium rare. Serve with rice. Serves 6 to 8.

LAMAS SUPPER CLUB, TAMPA, FLORIDA

MEAT LOAF

Have butcher grind together:	2 cups milk
1½ pounds ground beef	8 saltines, crumbled
¼ pound salt pork	1 small grated onion
1 egg, unbeaten	¼ bottle catsup

Mix all ingredients except catsup and put in ungreased dish (such as a Pyrex bread pan or a casserole dish). Pour ¼ bottle of catsup over top and bake for 2 hours in 350° oven. Wait 30 minutes before slicing. Serves 10.

MRS. JAMES V. BUDD

GRILLADES

4 pounds beef round cut in pieces
Salt and pepper to taste
1½ cups flour
3 tablespoons shortening
2 medium onions, chopped fine
    chopped fine

1 bunch shallots, chopped fine
2 small cans tomatoes
1 sprig thyme
1 small bay leaf
1 small clove garlic, chopped fine
2 tablespoons finely chopped parsley

Season meat with salt and pepper, dip in flour and fry in shortening on both sides until brown. Remove from fat. Add the chopped onion with the white part of the shallots and sauté until onions are limp. Drain tomatoes (save liquid) and put through a sieve or chop fine. Add tomatoes and cook about 20 minutes, then add tomato liquid, thyme, bay leaf, garlic, parsley and shallot tops. Add a little water if necessary for more gravy. Cook in covered heavy aluminum or iron pot until tender. Serves 8.

MRS. JAMES P. VAN PELT

CHILI CON CARNE PIE

1 pound ground beef
½ cup chopped onion
⅓ cup chopped green pepper
1 tablespoon shortening
2 cups canned tomatoes

1 teaspoon salt
3 teaspoons chili powder
¼ teaspoon poultry seasoning
¼ teaspoon ground black pepper
2½ cups canned red kidney beans

Brown meat, onion and green pepper in shortening. Add tomatoes and seasonings. Cook until thickened (10 to 15 minutes). Add kidney beans and heat thoroughly. Turn into a 1½-quart casserole, cover with corn meal pastry, and bake 20 minutes at 425°. Serves 8.

CORN MEAL PASTRY:

1 cup sifted flour
½ cup corn meal
¾ teaspoon salt

½ cup shortening
4 tablespoons cold water

Sift flour, corn meal and salt. Cut in shortening. Add water and toss with fork until barely dampened. Roll out to ⅛-inch thickness on flour-covered board. Put on top of casserole, trim, turn under and flute edge. Cut gash in top to let steam escape.

MRS. LEM BELL, JR.

PICADILLO I

¾ cup olive oil
2 large Spanish onions
2 green peppers
2 cloves garlic
3 pounds ground steak

1 2-pound can tomatoes
  (about 3 large cans)
2 tablespoons capers
1 can pitted black olives
Tabasco (optional)

In the olive oil, sauté the onions, peppers and garlic. When golden add the ground steak and stir until pink of meat disappears. Add the tomatoes and after cooking for about 1 hour add the capers and olives. Tabasco sauce may be added to taste.

MRS. SAM F. DAVIS

PICADILLO II

1 pound ground beef
1 pound ground pork
2 medium onions
1 large green pepper, (optional)
Olive oil
6 small tomatoes (or 2 small cans)
2 teaspoons salt
1 teaspoon garlic powder

Pepper to taste
1 tablespoon brown sugar
¼ cup vinegar
¼ cup stuffed green olives,
  chopped
½ cup raisins
1 tablespoon capers
½ cup red wine or ½ cup
  tomato juice or bouillon

Chop onions and green pepper very fine and brown in the olive oil. Add chopped tomatoes, salt, garlic, pepper, and meat, stirring constantly to break in small bits. Add remaining ingredients slowly until meat is tender, about 1 hour. Serve over rice, mashed potatoes, or split buttered and toasted hamburger buns. Serves 10.

MRS. WILLIAM E. HENSON

STUFFED GRAPE LEAVES

1 pound ground beef
½ to ¾ cup uncooked rice
1 medium onion, chopped fine
Salt and pepper to taste

Dash garlic salt
Basil leaves
1 15-ounce jar grapevine leaves
1 can tomatoes

Combine all ingredients except tomatoes. Mix well. Place heaping spoonful of mixture in center of each grape leaf and fold over. Place in cooking utensil and pour tomatoes over all. Cover and cook slowly for 30 minutes or longer. Serves 4.

MRS. LEFFIE M. CARLTON, JR.

ENGLISH ROAST BEEF AND YORKSHIRE PUDDING

Standing rib or sirloin tip roast

Preheat oven to 450°. Cook roast in open pan for 15 minutes. Reduce heat to 350° and cook 15 minutes to the pound (total time).

YORKSHIRE PUDDING:

1 cup flour	1 cup milk
⅛ teaspoon salt	2 eggs
⅛ teaspoon baking powder	4 tablespoons melted drippings from roast

Sift flour, salt, and baking powder together. Add milk gradually, stirring to make smooth paste; add eggs and beat with egg beater for 2 minutes. Pour in melted drippings, stir again. Pour in flat greased tin. Bake 25 minutes in 375° oven until done. Serve with juices from roast.

Miss Nell Trice

SWEDISH MEAT BALLS

2 cups soft bread crumbs, firmly packed	½ teaspoon salt
¾ cup milk	¼ teaspoon paprika
2 tablespoons minced onion	1 egg, slightly beaten
¼ cup butter	2 tablespoons flour
1 pound ground beef	Fat or salad oil
¼ teaspoon nutmeg	½ cup light cream

Combine bread crumbs and milk; let stand 10 minutes. Sauté onion in butter over low heat until soft but not brown. Combine beef, nutmeg, salt, paprika and egg. Add to bread crumb and onion mixture. Shape in small balls, about 1-inch in diameter. Chill at least 1 hour. Roll meat balls in flour; cook in a little hot fat or salad oil, turning to brown on all sides. Add cream, cover and cook 5 minutes. Serve at once with Almond Noodles. Makes 6 servings.

ALMOND NOODLES:

¼ cup butter	1 tablespoon poppy seeds
½ cup slivered blanched almonds	1 8-ounce package egg noodles, cooked
1 tablespoon paprika	

Melt half the butter; add almonds and cook until golden brown. Add remaining butter, paprika and poppy seeds. To hot cooked noodles, add this mixture, tossing with a fork until thoroughly mixed. Makes 6 servings.

Mrs. D. A. Kafka

HARVEST POT ROAST

5 to 6 pound pot roast (boned and rolled rump or chuck)	2 tablespoons catsup
2 tablespoons shortening	1 tablespoon sugar
1 clove chopped garlic	½ cup claret wine
2 teaspoons salt	4 tablespoons flour
¼ teaspoon pepper	2 cups liquid
3 tablespoons wine vinegar	Salt and pepper to taste
	1 teaspoon Kitchen Bouquet

Brown roast slowly on all sides in hot shortening with the garlic, about 15 minutes. Season with salt and pepper. Add vinegar and steam 30 minutes in tightly covered Dutch oven or skillet. Combine catsup, sugar, and claret. Pour over meat. Turn meat and continue cooking over low heat until fork tender, about 3 hours. When roast is done, remove and keep warm while making gravy. Remove meat drippings and fat from pan. Skim off all fat and return 4 tablespoons of fat to pan. Slowly stir in flour and continue stirring slowly over low heat until the mixture starts to thicken. Gradually add 2 cups of liquid (using the drippings plus enough water or canned bouillon to make 2 cups). Cook slowly and season to taste. For a deeper color add 1 teaspoon Kitchen Bouquet.

MRS. R. A. FOSTER

SWISS STEAK

3 pounds choice round steak	2 cloves garlic, chopped fine mashed with 1 teaspoon salt
Mix 3 tablespoons flour with pepper, salt, monosodium glutamate, and 1 teaspoon oregano	1 pint fresh mushrooms
	3 tablespoons cooking oil
3 medium onions, chopped	1 No. 3 can tomatoes, strained
	2 cups beef stock or bouillon

Dredge steak with seasoned flour and brown in skillet. Place in flat baking pan. Sauté onions, garlic and mushrooms in cooking oil for 3 minutes. Add tomatoes and beef stock. Cook a minute longer. Pour sauce over steak and cover pan but not completely. Bake at 350° for 2 hours.

MRS. JOHN P. CORCORAN, JR.

SAUERBRATEN

Part I

4 to 6 pounds beef (bottom round, shoulder clod or sirloin tip cut to fit a Dutch oven). Wipe meat and trim off rough edges. Put in a deep dish. Make several cuts through meat by plunging a paring knife into it on either side so the spiced liquid will go in deep. Boil together for 5 minutes:

1 cup vinegar
3 teaspoons salt

½ teaspoon each, dry mustard, pepper, cloves, allspice
1 medium onion, chopped fine

Pour hot liquid over meat and let stand in solution several hours. Then take the meat out, heat the vinegar again, and pour it back over the roast. This makes it penetrate better and seasons it quicker. It's best to let meat marinate overnight in the refrigerator, but it can be started early in the morning if you're in a hurry.

Part II:

Take the meat out of the liquid, sift flour over it on all sides, and sear thoroughly in just enough cooking oil to cover the bottom of the Dutch oven. Then remove. Fry in the same drippings:

2 onions, diced
1 turnip, diced

1 carrot, diced

Replace the meat on top with some sprays of parsley. Pour the spiced liquid over all, adding hot water to half cover. Cover closely and simmer about 4 hours, turning the meat once. At the end of the cooking time, remove the meat to a platter, skim fat from the gravy, and thicken gravy with at least ½ cup flour mixed to a thin paste with water, ¼ teaspoon salt and about 1 teaspoon of Kitchen Bouquet. The gravy is characteristically very dark in color, and the pieces of diced vegetables give it added body. Serve Sauerbraten with gravy ladled generously over both mashed potatoes and the sliced meat. Serves 6 to 8.

This is a French version of Sauerbraten.

MRS. E. C. DePURY

ROAST BEEF TENDERLOIN
WITH BORDELAISE SAUCE

BORDELAISE SAUCE:

2 tablespoons butter	½ bay leaf
1 shallot, minced	2 tablespoons flour
1 onion slice	1 can condensed bouillon,
2 carrot slices	undiluted
Sprig of parsley	¼ teaspoon salt
6 whole black peppercorns	⅛ teaspoon pepper
1 whole clove	¼ cup red wine
	1 tablespoon snipped parsley

Day before: Melt butter in skillet; sauté shallot, onion, carrot, parsley sprig, peppercorns, clove and bay leaf until golden and tender. Add flour and cook over low heat, stirring until flour is lightly browned. Stir in bouillon. Simmer, stirring, until thickened and smooth, about 10 minutes. Strain. Add salt, pepper, red wine and snipped parsley. Refrigerate. About 15 minutes before serving, reheat sauce, covered, in double boiler. If sauce is too thick, thin with 1 or 2 tablespoons wine.

Roast Beef Tenderloin (6 pounds whole beef)

About 1¼ hours before serving start heating oven to 450°. Meanwhile from 6 pound whole beef tenderloin (buy lower quality grade as it will have less fat) remove any surface fat and connective tissue. If desired, rub well with garlic. Place on wire rack in shallow pan, tucking narrow end under to make roast more uniformly thick. Insert meat thermometer into center of thickest part. Roast about 60 minutes or to 140° on meat thermometer. Meat is crusty brown outside, pink to red inside. Cut tenderloin into 1-inch thick slices and arrange on heated platter. Serve with Bordelaise Sauce. Serves 8 to 10.

MRS. PAUL D. COCHRAN, JR.

O P E N   P I T   B A R B E C U E
(S l o w   P r o c e s s)

Select pieces of beef and pork of similar size so that they will all be done at the same time. Five to ten pound cuts will cook in about 8 to 10 hours. Dig a pit about 18 inches deep. Use only dying coals under the meat. Coals should be fed from a fire outside the pit, or with charcoal briquets, only a few at a time. Damp hickory sawdust can be used for hickory flavor if desired. Place wire rack over the pit and place the meat on the rack. Turn meat every 15 minutes, basting each time with the following sauce: (Use a new long-handled dish mop.)

1 quart vinegar	2 teaspoons Cayenne
6 tablespoons butter	3 teaspoons salt
3 teaspoons black pepper	1½ pints sieved tomatoes

Bring to boil before using. This will have to be multiplied to suit the amount of meat processed.

Use a thermometer to determine when meat is cooked through. The slower the cooking process, the more thorough the barbecue process. To keep meat from drying out turn and baste frequently.

When meat is ready to be served, use the following sauce:

1 stick butter	1 teaspoon onion juice
1 cup catsup	1 garlic clove
1 cup white vinegar	⅛ teaspoon red pepper
2 teaspoons Tabasco	¼ teaspoon black pepper
2½ ounces Worcestershire	1 tablespoon salt
1 teaspoon brown sugar	1 teaspoon paprika

Mix all ingredients in a pot, boil, and remove from fire. Add ½ cup minced white onion and allow to cool. May be stored without refrigeration.

TOM LENFESTEY

MOCK BEEF STROGANOFF

1½ pounds of round steak or rump	1 teaspoon salt
4 tablespoons butter	¼ teaspoon pepper
½ pound sliced mushrooms,	2 cups stock
or one 8-ounce can	⅛ of a green pepper
1 large onion, sliced	3-inch piece of celery
6 tablespoons meat drippings	Clove of garlic
or shortening	½ cup dairy sour cream
6 tablespoons flour	

Have butcher cut the round steak or rump (I find rump more flavorful) in strips, bias to the grain, approximately 1 x 2½ x ½-inch thick. Melt butter, add mushrooms and onion and cook until onion is soft and yellow, but not brown. Remove from pan. Add drippings to pan. When hot, drop in meat and stir to brown evenly. When meat is a good rich brown, sprinkle with flour, salt and pepper. Stir well and add stock. The liquid from canned mushrooms can be used as part of the stock. Return mushrooms and onion to pan. Add green pepper, celery and garlic, but remove before serving. Cover and cook in 325° oven until meat is tender and gravy is thickened—1½ to 2 hours. More liquid may be added if necessary. However the gravy should be fairly thick as the sour cream thins it. Just before serving, stir in sour cream. Serve on fluffy rice, topped with chopped toasted almonds. This may be prepared 1 or 2 days in advance, except for sour cream.

MRS. LOUIS M. SAXTON

Ham

HAM AU GRATIN

3 tablespoons butter	1 teaspoon dry mustard
3 tablespoons flour	1½ cups of diced cooked ham
1 cup milk	1½ cups of peeled, seeded,
½ teaspoon salt	firm tomatoes
½ teaspoon Tabasco	¼ cup chopped green pepper
	1 cup cubed Cheddar cheese

Melt butter and stir in flour. Gradually add milk and stir until thickened; add seasonings. Toss, lightly, with all other ingredients. Bake in 350° oven for 1 hour. Serves 6 to 8.

MRS. E. P. TALIAFERRO, JR.

HAM JAMBALAYA

2 slices bacon
½ clove garlic
2 onions, finely chopped
2 cups canned tomatoes
1 tablespoon chopped fresh parsley

1 teaspoon salt
¼ teaspoon pepper
2 teaspoons Worcestershire sauce
1 cup cooked rice
1 cup chopped or ground ham, ground preferred

Fry bacon until crisp· Remove from skillet and drain. Sauté garlic and onions in bacon drippings. Add tomatoes and parsley. Season with salt, pepper, and Worcestershire sauce. Simmer 15 minutes. Add rice and ham and mix well. Bake in casserole in 350° oven for 30 to 40 minutes. Serves 4 to 6.

Mrs. Frank P. McMichael

VICKSBURG STUFFED HAM

To cook old ham ("Country Cured"—Smithfield or Talmadge): Soak in cold water overnight, skin side down. Change water next morning. Put on in cold water to cover, skin side up. Add:

1 cup vinegar
1 cup sugar
1 onion, sliced

3 cloves
1 pod red pepper
½ cup whole black peppercorns

Cover and boil 20 minutes per pound.

HAM STUFFING:

2 eggs, beaten
1 cup bread crumbs
1 tablespoon dry mustard
1 tablespoon celery seeds
1 tablespoon black pepper

2 tablespoons brown sugar
1 teaspoon red pepper
1 onion, chopped fine
2 tablespoons vinegar

Mix all ingredients. Remove bone and skin from cooked ham. Put stuffing in place of bone and sprinkle top of ham with sugar. Pour ½ cup vinegar in bottom of pan and bake 1 hour at 325°. Serves 15 to 30 depending on size of ham.

Mrs. C. Frank Chunn

HAM LOAF

1 pound ground cooked ham
1 pound ground fresh pork
1 cup bread crumbs

¼ teaspoon pepper
2 eggs, beaten
1 cup milk

Mix well and pat gently into greased loaf pan. Pour over the loaf the following mixture:

⅓ cup brown sugar
1 tablespoon dry mustard

¼ cup vinegar

Bake at 350° for 1 hour. This is good served with baked beans and brown bread. Serves 8.

MRS. LINUS W. HEWIT

SAVORY HAM-VEAL RING

1½ pounds ground ham
1½ pounds ground veal
3 eggs
2 cups applesauce
3 cups soft bread crumbs

¾ cup catsup
1 teaspoon Worcestershire
½ cup minced onions
Pepper

Mix well all ingredients except 1 cup of the applesauce. Bake in greased ring or pan at 325° for 1½ hours. Unmold if in ring and spread with applesauce. Bake additional 30 minutes.

MRS. LEWIS FRAZEE

HAM OR CHICKEN SALAD, BAKED

2 cups chopped ham or chicken
2 cups chopped celery
½ cup chopped almonds
Salt to taste
1 teaspoon grated onion

¼ cup sweet pickle, chopped
1 cup mayonnaise
½ cup grated cheese
1 cup potato chips, crushed

Mix together ham or chicken, celery, almonds, salt, onion, pickle, and mayonnaise. Put in loaf baking dish and sprinkle with cheese and potato chips. Bake 20 minutes at 400°. Serve hot. Serves 4 to 6.

MRS. JOHN B. SUTTON

Lamb

BARBECUED LAMB SHANKS WITH NOODLES

4 lamb shanks
1 tablespoon salad oil or drippings
1 cup tomato sauce
1 envelope French dressing mix

2 tablespoons brown sugar
1 tablespoon vinegar
½ cup water
8 ounces wide egg noodles

Wipe lamb shanks with a damp cloth. Rub well with salt, pepper, monosodium glutamate, and flour to coat. Brown on all sides in salad oil in Dutch oven or heavy kettle. While meat browns, combine other ingredients, except noodles. Pour over meat in kettle. Cover and heat to boiling. Simmer about 2 hours or until lamb is tender when pierced with a fork. Remove shanks and skim off fat. Return meat to kettle and heat to boiling. Arrange hot cooked noodles and shanks on heated platter; spoon sauce over all. Serves 4.

MRS. ALONZO REGAR

LAMB SHANKS

4 lamb shanks
4 tablespoons flour
½ teaspoon shortening
1 cup water
¼ teaspoon pepper

2 tablespoons Worcestershire
2 tablespoons horseradish
⅛ teaspoon marjoram
2 teaspoons vinegar
½ teaspoon salt

Dredge shanks in 3 tablespoons flour. Brown in skillet with shortening. Put shanks in casserole. Add remaining flour to drippings in skillet, add water and cook, stirring constantly until thick. Add other ingredients and cook 5 minutes. Pour gravy over shanks and cover. Bake in 350° oven 1½ hours.

MRS. J. T. COWART

B A R B E C U E D   L E G   O F   L A M B

1 leg of lamb, about 6 pounds, trim excess fat	¼ cup flour
	¼ cup vinegar
½ cup margarine	1 tablespoon salt
1 teaspoon sugar	⅛ teaspoon red pepper
1 teaspoon Worcestershire sauce	2 garlic cloves, chopped fine

Soften margarine. Add all other ingredients and make a thick paste. Cover entire upper surface of roast which has been placed in roasting pan. Start cooking in 500° oven for 15 minutes; cook at 450° for 15 minutes. Turn oven then to 300° and cook until done, approximately 3½ hours, basting frequently. Sauce makes delicious rich brown gravy when thickened. Serves 6 to 8.

Mrs. Leslie Blank

S H A S H L I K

6 or 7 pound leg of lamb	¼ teaspoon coriander seeds, crushed
¾ cup red wine (the finer the wine, the better the flavor)	6 whole black peppercorns, crushed
5 cloves garlic, halved	1 tablespoon salt
2 sweet onions, diced	3 green peppers
3 bay leaves	6 sweet onions
1 teaspoon basil	6 ripe firm tomatoes
½ teaspoon oregano	1 pound mushrooms
¼ teaspoon dill seeds, crushed	

Have butcher bone leg of lamb and dice meat into 1-inch cubes. Place wine, garlic, onions, and seasonings in a large glass or china bowl. Stir lightly and add lamb. Cover tightly and refrigerate 24 to 60 hours. Stir at intervals to marinate evenly. On skewers alternate lamb with ½-inch green pepper rings, onion quarters, tomato quarters and fresh mushroom buttons. Broil over charcoal fire until lamb is done. Serve with tossed green salad and melon dessert. Serves 6 to 8.

Mrs. James W. Gray, Jr.

CURRY IN A HURRY

½ stick butter or margarine
3 stalks celery, diced
2 small onions, diced
1 large apple, peeled,
 cored and diced
2 tablespoons flour (use 3 if
 leftover gravy not available)
2 cups cold roast lamb, diced
Hot water

Leftover lamb gravy (or 1 teaspoon
 Kitchen Bouquet for color if
 gravy not available)
½ teaspoon salt
⅛ teaspoon pepper
2 teaspoons curry powder
 (less if preferred)
½ cup seedless raisins
⅛ teaspoon ground cloves (optional)

Melt butter in a large skillet, add celery, onion, and apple and sauté until golden. Add flour, stirring well, then add lamb. Add hot water and gravy to cover, stirring well, then add remaining ingredients. Bring to a boil, cover and reduce heat to simmer. Cook ½ hour or until liquid assumes consistency of gravy. Serve with steamed rice. Pass chutney, chopped toasted almonds, etc. Serves 6.

Mrs. Rogers Morgan

Pork

CURRY OF PORK (OR CHICKEN)

1 onion, chopped
1 tablespoon butter
 (may need more)
2 teaspoons curry powder

3 to 4 pounds pork tenderloin, cubed
½ cup fresh cream
2 tablespoons tomato paste
2 tablespoons consommé

Sauté onion in butter in heavy skillet or kettle until golden; add curry powder and mix well. Sauté pork in this mixture until browned. Add cream, tomato paste, and consommé. Move and turn meat frequently. Simmer 30 to 40 minutes or until tender. If sauce needs more liquid, add cream or a little lemon juice. Serve with cooked rice. Serves 6 to 8. (If chicken is used, allow 2 pieces per serving.)

Mrs. John S. Allen

PORK CHOP CASSEROLE

4 large or 8 small pork chops	4 tablespoons chopped onion
4 cups soft bread crumbs	4 tablespoons chopped green pepper
½ cup melted fat	2 tablespoons chopped parsley
½ teaspoon salt	1 apple
¼ teaspoon pepper	

Brown pork chops in frying pan over low heat. Place bread crumbs in casserole bowl; stir in melted fat with fork; stir in salt and pepper, then vegetables. Put browned pork chops on top of dressing. Quarter apple and lay on top. Sprinkle with salt and bake uncovered for 1 hour at 350°. Serves 4.

MRS. WILLIAM C. McLEAN, JR.

LOIN OF PORK WITH PRUNES
(Swedish Style)

4 to 5 pounds loin of pork	½ teaspoon white pepper
20 prunes, halved and pitted	¼ teaspoon ginger
3 teaspoons salt	1 cup prune juice

Trim meat and wipe with cloth. Make deep cut into fleshy part of meat. Soak prunes in warm water ½ hour, then insert deep in meat. Save this water. Rub meat with seasonings and tie with string. Brown on all sides in Dutch oven. Add 1 cup of the water in which prunes were soaked. Cover and simmer over low heat about 1½ hours, or until tender. Baste occasionally; add commercial prune juice after first 45 minutes of cooking. When ready, place meat on hot platter, remove string, cut away back bone, then slice. Strain and skim pan juice. Serve separately.

If thick gravy is preferred, heat 3 tablespoons of the fat, add 2 to 3 tablespoons flour, and stir until browned. Add 2 cups pan juice and 1 cup prune juice. Simmer 10 minutes, stir occasionally, and season with salt and white pepper. Serves 8.

MRS. BENGT TJERNSTROM

PORK CHOPS A LA MARGARET

8 pork chops	½ teaspoon nutmeg
SAUCE:	⅓ cup cider vinegar
½ cup catsup	1 cup water
1 teaspoon salt	1 bay leaf
1 teaspoon celery seed	

Brown chops on both sides. Place in casserole dish or oven-proof platter. Assemble sauce and pour over pork chops. Cook in 325° oven for 1½ hours. Serve over hot noodles. Serves 8.

MRS. GEORGE A. HOCHSCHWENDER

PORK CHOPS A LA NOILLY

4 large lean pork chops, thick sliced	4 large slices Spanish onion
1 teaspoon sage	4 thick tomato slices
1 teaspoon salt	Worcestershire sauce
1 teaspoon pepper	Dry mustard
4 tablespoons catsup	Paprika
	5 ounces dry vermouth

Place chops in buttered oven-proof casserole. Sprinkle each liberally with sage, salt, pepper. Spoon a generous tablespoon of catsup over each chop. Top with a slice of onion and then a slice of tomato. Sprinkle each chop with Worcestershire sauce, dry mustard, and paprika. Pour vermouth into dish at the side to avoid washing off seasonings. Cover and place in 350° oven for 1 hour. Remove lid and bake additional ½ hour to brown tops of tomato slices. Serves 4.

MRS. TOM DALEY

SAUSAGE, BEAN AND APPLE CASSEROLE

½ pound sausage	1 clove garlic
1 No. 2 can red kidney beans	½ cup tomato juice
1 cup sliced apples	2 teaspoons salt
¼ cup brown sugar	¼ teaspoon pepper
1 large onion sliced	½ teaspoon chili powder

Cook sausage slightly in skillet. Pour off fat. Then combine sausage with other ingredients and bake 1½ hours in a very slow oven.

MRS. C. S. ROBINSON

S E G E T I N G E R

3 ½ pounds boned loin of pork	½ teaspoon pepper
3 tablespoons butter	2 bouillon cubes
4 large onions, chopped	2 cups tomato juice
1 tablespoon paprika	1 large can sauerkraut
2 cloves garlic, crushed	1 large potato, grated
1 teaspoon salt	

Cut pork into 1-inch cubes, trimming excess fat, sear in butter 10 minutes in large heavy skillet. Add onions and cook 5 minutes, then add paprika, garlic, salt and pepper. Dissolve bouillon cubes in heated tomato juice and add to pork and onion mixture. Cover and simmer for 1½ to 2 hours. Skim off excess fat from sauce. Cover pork mixture with sauerkraut and simmer ½ hour. Stir in grated potato and cook until slightly thickened, approximately 10 minutes. Serves 6.

MRS. PERRY COLE

S W E E T   A N D   S O U R   P O R K

3 eggs	2 cups cold water
6 tablespoons flour	2 cups sugar
9 tablespoons cornstarch	½ cup cornstarch
¾ teaspoon salt	½ cup water
3 pounds lean pork	4 tablespoons catsup
2 cups vinegar	

Blend eggs, flour, cornstarch, and salt, slowly adding enough water to thin to a medium batter. Cut pork into ½-inch cubes and dip in batter. Deep fry in cooking oil 350° to 400° for five minutes. Remove pork and drain for a few minutes. Over medium heat mix vinegar with water, add sugar, and bring to boil. Add cornstarch diluted with ½ cup cold water. (Pour water slowly into cornstarch; stir as you pour until blended.) Add catsup and stir slowly until sauce thickens (approximately 5 minutes). Add pork to sauce and stir thoroughly. Serve with rice. Serves 6.

P O R K   A   L A   W A M

5 pounds pork tenderloin	1 clove garlic, crushed
1 small jar honey	½ cup sugar
1 bottle soy sauce	1 can chicken stock

Combine last 4 ingredients and marinate the tenderloin in the sauce overnight. Bake in sauce for 1 hour at 350°. Serve hot or cold.

DR. WILLIAM MOORE

Veal

VEAL BIRDS

2 slices veal cut from the round,
about ⅓ inch thick
2 slices fat salt pork
Fine cracker crumbs
Salt and pepper
Cayenne, poultry seasoning,
lemon juice, onion juice

1 beaten egg
Stock
Flour for dredging
Butter for frying
Cream
Chopped parsley and toasted
chopped almonds for garnish

Wipe veal; remove bone, skin and fat, and discard. Pound slices until only ¼-inch thick. Cut in pieces 4 inches long by 2 inches wide, saving trimmings. Chop trimmings and salt pork. Measure and add ½ the measure of cracker crumbs. Season highly with next 6 ingredients. Moisten lightly with egg and stock (or hot water). Spread each piece of veal with thin layer of pork mixture being careful not to get too close to edges. Roll up and fasten with skewers. Sprinkle with salt and pepper; dredge with flour. Fry in butter until golden brown. Add cream to half cover meat. Cook slowly 20 minutes or until tender.

Serve on hot crisp toast, pouring cream from skillet over each. Garnish with parsley and almonds.

MRS. FRANK C. CALDWELL

BAKED SESAME VEAL CUTLETS

6 veal cutlets
1 egg, beaten
½ pint sour cream
1 cup flour
1 teaspoon baking powder
2 teaspoons salt

¼ teaspoon pepper
2 teaspoons paprika
¼ cup chopped pecans
2 tablespoons sesame seeds
½ cup butter

Dip veal into egg and sour cream mixture; then into mixture of flour, baking powder, salt, pepper, parika, pecans, and sesame seeds. Melt butter in shallow pan in hot oven (400°). Remove from oven. As coated pieces of veal are placed in pan, turn to coat with butter. Bake in single layer for 30 minutes. Turn and bake 30 minutes more. If meat cannot be served immediately, reduce heat and baste with melted butter. Serves 6.

MRS. OTTO M. STALLINGS, JR.

CHOP SUEY

1 pound lean veal (1-inch cubes)	1 level teaspoon salt
1 pound lean pork (1-inch cubes)	2 teaspoons Worcestershire sauce
2 tablespoons shortening	1 7-ounce cup of mushrooms
2 cups slivered onions	1 No. 2 can chop suey vegetables
2 cups celery, diced	2 tablespoons flour
1 tablespoon dark molasses	½ cup water
3 or 4 tablespoons soy sauce	1 can chop suey noodles

Brown veal and pork cubes in shortening. Remove meat and sauté onion. Put onion, meat and celery in large pan or kettle; add hot water to cover, then add molasses, soy sauce, salt, Worcestershire sauce. Cover, and cook on low heat for 2 hours. Twenty minutes before done add mushrooms and chop suey vegetables. Thicken by combining flour with water and adding to chop suey. Serve over rice, using a teacup to mold rice in center of plate. Spoon chop suey around mold of rice. Sprinkle crisp chop suey noodles over the top and serve. This recipe makes 6 large servings. If sauce is made the day before, add mushrooms and chop suey vegetables ½ hour before serving.

MRS. ERNEST BROWN

THIN VEAL FORESTIER

1½ pounds veal cutlets (very thin slices)	½ pound mushrooms
Clove of garlic, or ½ teaspoon garlic salt	Salt and pepper
	⅓ cup dry vermouth
Flour	1 teaspoon lemon juice
¼ cup butter	Snipped parsley

Pound veal thinner with wooden mallet. Rub all over with cut garlic clove or sprinkle with garlic salt. Dip slices in flour, coating well. Heat butter until hot in skillet. Add veal and sauté until golden brown on both sides. Heap thinly sliced mushrooms on veal, sprinkle with salt and pepper and vermouth. Cover skillet and cook over low heat about 20 minutes. Add water if necessary to keep veal moist. Just before serving sprinkle lemon juice and parsley over the veal. Serves 4 to 6.

MRS. GEORGE H. KEEN, JR.

VEAL IN PAPRIKA CREAM

3 to 4 pounds veal for stew
½ cup butter
1 clove garlic, thinly sliced
6 tablespoons flour
2 cups consommé
1 bay leaf

1 tablespoon lemon juice
1 tablespoon paprika
1 pound small white onions,
  parboiled
1 cup white wine
½ cup sour cream

Brown veal in butter with garlic. Sprinkle veal with flour, add consommé, bay leaf, lemon juice and paprika. Cook over low heat (or in moderate oven) for 1 hour. Add onions and wine. Cook until onions are tender, then stir in sour cream. Be careful not to boil or cream will curdle. Serve with noodles or rice ring. This dish is even better if prepared a day ahead. Serves 8.

MRS. GEORGE A. HOCHSCHWENDER

BRAZIL NUT-RAISIN STUFFING
FOR BREAST OF VEAL

Breast of veal (2 to 2½ pounds)
¼ cup butter
2 tablespoons finely chopped onion
3 cups soft bread crumbs
½ cup finely chopped Brazil nuts
½ cup finely chopped celery

½ cup raisins
2 tablespoons chopped parsley
1 teaspoon salt
⅛ teaspoon pepper
¼ cup water

Have large pocket cut in the breast of veal. Sprinkle inside and out with salt and pepper. Melt butter, add onion and cook over low heat until onion is tender, but not brown. Add crumbs, nuts, celery, raisins, parsley, and seasonings. Cook about 5 minutes over medium heat, stirring constantly. Add water. Fill cavity of veal with stuffing and skewer edges together. Place the roast, fat side up, on a rack in an uncovered pan. Allow 40 minutes per pound at 325°. Serves 6.

MRS. G. B. WILSON

V E A L   C U T L E T   P A R M I G I A N A

1 pound of veal cutlets

Salt and pepper

2 ounces grated Parmesan cheese

2 eggs

Bread crumbs

6 tablespoons olive oil
  or vegetable oil

2 cans seasoned tomato sauce

¾ pound sliced Mozzarella cheese

Add salt, pepper, and cheese to eggs and beat. Dip cutlets in egg mixture and roll in bread crumbs. Sauté cutlets in hot oil until brown on both sides. Place cutlets in baking dish and cover with tomato sauce. Place slices of Mozzarella on each cutlet and bake for 15 minutes in 350° oven. Serves 4.

MRS. A. V. BELOTT

Liver

L I V E R   A U   V I N G T - C I N Q   P I A S T R E S

1½ pounds beef or calf liver

1 tablespoon onion

1 clove minced garlic

1 tablespoon minced green pepper

1 tablespoon lard

1 tablespoon flour

1 can tomatoes

1½ cups water

Thyme, bay leaf, salt and pepper

Plunge liver into boiling water and remove instantly. Brown onion, garlic, and green pepper in lard. Add flour and stir until it browns. Add tomatoes, water, and other seasonings. Place liver in this tomato mixture and let simmer until tender.

MRS. C. S. ROBINSON

C H I C K E N   L I V E R   S T E A K

8 slices of bacon

1 pound chicken livers

Pinch of salt

¾ cup brown gravy

¾ cup red wine

Wrap chopped chicken livers with bacon, forming a steak much like a fillet. Add a pinch of salt and grill on both sides for 30 minutes. When done, heat brown gravy with red wine, add to chicken livers and serve at once with hot peas and parsley. Serves 2.

COLUMBIA RESTAURANT, TAMPA, FLORIDA

SMOTHERED BEEF LIVER AND ONIONS

1 pound beef liver   Bacon drippings
Salt and pepper to taste   2 medium onions
Flour

Skin liver slices, salt and pepper them and dredge in flour. Heat
enough bacon drippings to brown liver. When grease is hot, brown
thinly sliced onions until almost done. Remove onions, add liver, and
brown on both sides. Arrange onion slices on top of liver, add sufficient water to cover meat and onions. Cover tightly and simmer 30
to 40 minutes. Gravy may be thickened if necessary.

MRS. JOHN RANKIN

LIVER LOAF

1½ pounds beef liver   Milk, enough to moisten crumbs
1 onion   2 beaten eggs
Juice of half lemon   Salt and pepper to taste
1½ cups bread crumbs   Bacon strips
                                       Tomato sauce

Pour boiling water over liver and let stand for few minutes. Drain
and cool. Put liver and onion through medium blade of food chopper.
Combine with remaining ingredients. Line a mold with thinly sliced
bacon. Pour mixture over bacon and bake or steam in medium oven 1
hour or more. Turn out on platter and pour over it tomato sauce.
Serve with French or German fried potatoes.

MRS. BERT FETZER

CHICKEN LIVERS ON TOAST

9 chicken livers, cut in half   6 or 8 fresh mushrooms, chopped
2 tablespoons butter   Salt, pepper, paprika
2 tablespoons dry white wine

Sauté chicken livers in butter in the blazer of a chafing dish over
direct heat until they are brown on all sides (about 3 or 4 minutes).
Add wine, mushrooms, salt and pepper to taste and a dash of paprika.
Cook 3 minutes longer and serve on rounds of freshly made, buttered
toast.

MRS. REGAR HICKMAN

The Duck Hunters

CHAPTER X

Poultry and Game

We offer the same advice on roasting chicken or turkey as given for roasting meats. If you don't have a meat thermometer, get one! Insert the point of the thermometer two inches deep in the fleshy part of the breast next to the thigh, and roast at 325° until the indicator points to "Chicken" or "Turkey" on the dial. The meat will be juicy and tender, and your ears will ring with praise of your cooking skill.

Here in Tampa we women look forward to the Fall of the year when our men go forth in the morning as hunters, and return in the dusk as providers. There are deer in the Ocala Forest and Gulf Hammock, ducks in the rivers and bays, squirrels in the rolling wooded lands near Brooksville, doves and quail in the fields and pastures. Though the region has built-up rapidly, there is still plenty of game for those who enjoy the sport and those who enjoy the tantalizing flavor of wild game. There is nothing to equal plump-breasted doves or quail, floured, fried slowly in butter, then steamed until served browned and juicy with wild rice and gravy. There is nothing better than camp stew made over an open fire by a backwoods guide, or a native colored man, who also knows how to mash potatoes with a bottle and toss a fresh green salad. There is something primitively satisfying in receiving from your man food for the family table.

Chicken

ALMOND GAI DING

1 small stalk Chinese cabbage
  (use bottom 6 inches) diced
1 stalk celery (bottom part)
  diced in ¼-inch pieces
1 8-ounce can mushrooms
½ cup water chestnuts, diced
½ cup bamboo shoots
1 6-ounce package frozen green
  peas
3 tablespoons cornstarch
½ cup water

½ cup salad or cooking oil
3 pounds boneless chicken breast,
  diced in large pieces
1 tablespoon salt
2 tablespoons cooking sherry
1 can beef broth diluted with
  1 can water
1 tablespoon monosodium glutamate
1 teaspoon sugar
3 shakes from pepper shaker
4 ounces whole almonds or
  cashew nuts

In a large bowl mix Chinese cabbage, celery, mushrooms, water chestnuts, bamboo shoots and peas. Dissolve cornstarch in ½ cup water. Put salad oil in a large (at least 2 quarts) pot. Sauté the chicken, adding salt and sherry, for 2 minutes. Add vegetable mixture and sauté for 2 minutes more. Add diluted beef broth and bring to a boil. Cover and simmer for 8 minutes.

To prepare gravy, blend monosodium glutamate, sugar, and pepper and add to cornstarch. Cook over low heat, stirring constantly, until smooth. As soon as gravy thickens stir 30 seconds longer and remove from heat. Pour over chicken mixture and top with almonds. Serve with rice. Serves 4.

LAMAS CLUB, TAMPA, FLORIDA

BAKED TURKISH CHICKEN

1½ pound broiler chicken
Salt and pepper
1 clove garlic (optional)

½ cup olive oil
1 tablespoon oregano

Halve chicken. Rub salt and pepper and garlic generously all over chicken. Place in pan, cavity up, and baste generously with olive oil to which oregano has been added. Place in 250° oven. Baste with olive oil every 5 minutes for the first 15 minutes. After 15 minutes increase oven temperature to 350°, turn chicken, and baste as needed for the next 45 minutes. If you feel the cavity side needs to be turned up again, do so. Before removing from oven, turn cavity down. Serves 2.

JACK LESTER

BAKED CHICKEN GARIBALDI

2½ pounds chicken
½ cup Spanish olive oil
2 cloves garlic
1 onion (cut in half-rings)
1 green pepper (cut in half-rings)
2 cups chicken gravy

1 tablespoon salt
¼ cup red wine
20 buttons or slices of mushrooms
¼ cup grated Parmesan cheese
¼ cup grated toasted almonds
Parsley leaves

Roast chicken until half done. Heat olive oil and simmer garlic, onion and green pepper in the oil. When half done add chicken gravy and salt. Bring to a boil and add red wine and mushrooms. Remove chicken from bones and place in casserole dish. Cover chicken with sauce and sprinkle with Parmesan cheese. Bake at 350° for 30 minutes or until cheese is au gratin style. Garnish with parsley leaves and chopped toasted almonds. Serves 2.

COLUMBIA RESTAURANT, TAMPA, FLORIDA

BRUNSWICK STEW I

1 4-pound stewing chicken,
    cut into pieces
2 quarts water
2 teaspoons salt
½ cup catsup
2 teaspoons Worcestershire sauce
½ teaspoon hot pepper sauce
3 tablespoons butter or margarine
Grated rind and juice of ½ lemon
2 1-pound cans tomatoes,
    or 8 fresh

4 medium potatoes, diced
4 cups fresh baby lima beans
4 cups whole-kernel corn
2 cups fresh okra, cut in ½ inch
    slices
4 stalks celery, cut into ½ inch
    slices
4 cloves garlic, minced
2 medium onions, minced
Salt and pepper to taste

Combine chicken, water and the 2 teaspoons salt in Dutch oven or deep kettle. Simmer, covered, until meat is tender, about 3 to 4 hours. Remove chicken pieces; cool quickly. Remove skin, then meat from bones. Cut meat into bite-size pieces; return to skimmed cooking stock. Add remaining ingredients. Cover. Simmer, stirring occasionally, until mixture is thick, about 2 hours. Yield: 8 portions.

MRS. HOMER A. MCNEELY

COLONEL ED DUNLAP'S
BRUNSWICK STEW II

Step I:

5 or 6 pound fat hen   10 pounds pork loin (native)
5 pounds round steak

Cook together until the meat leaves the bones. Chop or run meat through meat grinder.

Step II:

2 cans tomatoes   1 can peas
1 can carrots   1 large can mushrooms
1 can butter beans   6 onions, chopped fine
6 Irish potatoes, chopped fine   3 green peppers, chopped fine
1 pound butter   2 red peppers
1 can corn   2 cloves garlic

Cook Step II ingredients together until thoroughly done, then mix with the ground meat in a large iron, copper, or porcelain boiler.

Step III: Add:

1 can pimientos   1 bottle chili sauce
½ bottle Tabasco   1 bottle Worcestershire
2 tablespoons Kitchen Bouquet   ½ box paprika
½ pint olive oil   Juice of 6 lemons
2 heaping tablespoons   Black pepper and salt to taste
   Gulden mustard

Cook the stew very slowly for not less than 2 hours, or until it becomes one uniform mass. Serve hot. Serves 25.

MRS. JAMES E. WALL, JR.

CHARCOALED CHICKEN

2 broilers, split   Worcestershire sauce
Soy sauce

Several hours before cooking, brush the chickens generously with a sauce made of equal parts soy sauce and Worcestershire. Marinate in refrigerator. Broil over a charcoal fire until the chickens are tender.

SARAH NORRIS

CERISE CHICKEN

3 2-pound chickens, halved or split
Paprika
1 teaspoon salt
6 tablespoons butter
1 tablespoon flour
1 teaspoon sugar
⅛ teaspoon ground allspice
⅛ teaspoon ground cinnamon

⅛ teaspoon dry mustard
2 cups canned red sour pitted
    cherries (water pack)
1 cup canned crushed pineapple
1 chicken bouillon cube
¼ teaspoon red food coloring
3 cups hot cooked rice

Season chicken with paprika and ½ teaspoon salt. Sauté chicken in butter until brown. Remove chicken. Blend flour, sugar, spices, and ½ teaspoon salt in butter remaining in skillet. Drain cherries and pour the liquid into the skillet. Return chicken to skillet. Add pineapple, bouillon cube, and food coloring. Cover; simmer for 30 minutes. Add cherries and simmer for 10 minutes. To serve, arrange chicken on a bed of rice. Spoon some sauce over chicken, and serve remaining sauce separately. Serves 6.

MRS. CLARE M. PHILLIPS, JR.

CHICKEN BREASTS IN WINE

8 to 10 chicken breasts
¼ pound butter
1 or 2 onions, chopped
1 clove garlic
Pinch of thyme
1 bay leaf

Pinch of oregano
5 or 6 sprigs parsley
2 slices bacon
Salt and pepper to taste
1 wine glass cognac or brandy
1 cup claret

Wash, salt, and flour chicken breasts. Sear in pan with butter. While bubbling away add chopped onions or pearl onions, finely chopped garlic, thyme, bay leaf, oregano, parsley and diced bacon. Grate in fresh pepper. Simmer all together. Remove chicken, put in casserole.

Pour a wine glass of brandy or cognac over chicken, light it. When blaze is out, pour rest of ingredients from pan over chicken. Pour a cup of claret over chicken. Cook until tender (about 1 hour) in 350° oven. Baste once or twice. (The cognac burning step can be omitted.) This recipe can be done ahead of time and popped into oven when guests arrive.

MRS. JOHN R. HIMES

CHICKEN ACOSTA

4 chicken breasts
½ pound chicken livers
1 bay leaf
4 strips of bacon
4 slices boiled ham or
    Canadian bacon

1 large dill pickle, sliced
4 strips pimientos
Flour
2 eggs, beaten

Cook chicken breasts and livers in 3 cups of salted water with the bay leaf, until tender. Reserve broth for sauce. Remove bones from chicken. On each strip of bacon, place a breast of chicken; over the chicken, a slice of ham, pickle, and a pimento strip. Bring bacon around chicken and secure with a toothpick. Dip each roll in flour, then egg, and fry in deep fat.

SAUCE:

1 small onion (minced)
½ cup imported olive oil
2 heaping tablespoons flour
1 cup chicken broth

1 cup imported sauterne
Parsley
Spanish paprika

Fry the onion until transparent in olive oil, add 2 tablespoons flour; then the chicken broth (add salt and pepper to taste). Cut up chicken livers in very small pieces; add to flour-broth mixture. Allow to cook about 15 minutes, then add the wine and cook a few seconds. Slice the chicken rolls and arrange attractively on toast triangles. Pour hot sauce over all, garnish with parsley and sprinkle with Spanish paprika. Serves 4.

LAS NOVEDADES RESTAURANT
TAMPA, FLORIDA

CHICKEN OR TURKEY DIVAN

1 2-pound package frozen broccoli
Sliced chicken or turkey breast
½ cup sherry wine

3 cups of rich cream sauce
½ cup grated Parmesan cheese

Cook broccoli in salted water until tender. Drain, spread out on large flat platter. Cover with sliced chicken or turkey breast; drizzle sherry wine over surface, and completely cover with cream sauce to which 4 tablespoons of cheese have been added. Sprinkle surface with remainder of Parmesan cheese, and put in oven until brown and bubbling. Sharp yellow cheese can be substituted for Parmesan if preferred. Serves 8.

MRS. GRACE LOGAN

CHICKEN AND BROCCOLI CASSEROLE

1 chicken, 4½ to 5 pounds
1 teaspoon salt
2 or 3 peppercorns
1 stalk celery
1 carrot
1 onion
½ cup flour
1 cup milk

2 cups chicken broth
1 cup mayonnaise
1 teaspoon lemon juice
½ teaspoon curry powder
1 bunch broccoli or 2 packages
    frozen
1 to 2 cups buttered crumbs

Cut up chicken, add 5 cups water, salt, peppercorns, celery, carrot and onion. Simmer until chicken is tender. Remove chicken. Strain broth. Cube meat. Prepare sauce as follows: blend flour and milk until smooth. Add broth and cook until thickened. Remove from heat; add mayonnaise, lemon juice, and curry powder. Cook broccoli until tender. Drain, break into pieces in greased shallow baking dish. Top with chicken, then sauce and crumbs. Bake in 350° oven until crumbs are brown—about 45 minutes. Makes 6 servings.

MRS. CLAUDE LOGAN, JR.

CHICKEN CACEROLA COLUMBIA

2½-pound fryer
4 tablespoons butter
Pinch of oregano
½ teaspoon garlic powder
½ teaspoon salt
2 tablespoons butter
½ medium onion, chopped
1 tablespoon chopped smoked ham

3 chicken livers, chopped
2 potatoes, cut Parisienne
¼ cup mushroom buttons
¼ cup sauterne
White pepper and salt
Petit pois
Parsley

Bake the dressed whole fryer in 4 tablespoons of butter for 30 minutes at 350° until chicken is brown. Season with oregano, garlic powder, salt. When chicken is taken from oven, strain gravy through a colander. Braise in a saucepan with 2 tablespoons butter, the onion, ham, and livers. Add strained gravy from chicken. As soon as onion is brown, remove from stove. Cut chicken into quarters (remove breastbone and thigh bones) and place in clay casserole. Add braised sauce with raw Parisienne potatoes, mushrooms, 2 tablespoons sauterne, and salt and pepper to taste. Bake 30 minutes at 350°. When done, add remaining 2 tablespoons sauterne. Garnish with petit pois and chopped parsley. Serves 4.

COLUMBIA RESTAURANT, TAMPA, FLORIDA

CHICKEN CON SALSA RUBIA

1 fryer or 6 chicken breasts
Salt
Pepper
½ cup lemon juice
Flour
¼ cup lard or oil

1 can beef consommé
¼ cup white wine
1 can or 1 package of fresh
  mushrooms
½ cup diced cooked ham,
  optional

Marinate chicken overnight or for 3 to 4 hours with salt, pepper, and lemon juice. Flour chicken very lightly, then brown in oil. Now make a gravy as follows: Brown in a cooking pot, 2 tablespoons of flour in 2 tablespoons fat in which chicken was browned. Add can of consommé, ¼ cup of wine, and the mushrooms (liquid and all). If fresh mushrooms are used, they must previously be sautéed in butter. Add ham and then add the chicken. Cook slowly for about 1 hour. If gravy thickens too much, thin by adding a small amount of water or consommé.

MRS. HAL HOLTSINGER

CHICKEN FRICASSEE, HOLLANDAISE

1 3-pound fryer
2 leeks
2 sprigs parsley
1 bay leaf
2 whole cloves
1 sprig thyme
1 blade mace
1 carrot, sliced
1 onion
1 quart boiling water

1 teaspoon salt
½ teaspoon pepper
4 tablespoons butter
4 tablespoons flour
3 cups chicken broth
1 small can sliced mushrooms
2 egg yolks, beaten
½ cup cream
Juice of ½ lemon, strained

Cut and wash chicken, place in kettle. Make a bouquet, tying together leeks, parsley, bay leaf, cloves, thyme and mace, and add to chicken. Add carrot, onion, water and seasonings. Cover and bring to boil. Simmer 40 minutes or until chicken is tender. Remove chicken to serving dish. Keep warm. Melt butter in sauce pan; add flour; blend. Gradually add chicken broth, then mushrooms; bring to boil, then simmer 10 minutes. Combine egg yolks and cream, stir in lemon juice; stir this mixture into broth. Pour sauce over chicken and sprinkle with chopped parsley.

MRS. BERT FETZER

CHICKEN-IN-A-BAG

2½ to 3 pound fryer	Paprika
Salt	Garlic Salt
Pepper	Celery Salt
Onion Salt	16-pound brown grocery bag

Wash chicken and dry with paper towel. Sprinkle chicken with seasonings, inside and out. Put in bag and twist end of bag tightly. Place on rack in preheated 400° oven with pan below to catch any drippings that leak through bag. Do not disturb for 1½ hours. Chicken will be tender and juicy with a brown, crisp skin.

MRS. W. CRUTCHER ROSS

CHICKEN IN SOUR CREAM

3 pound chicken	1 to 1½ cups sour cream
½ stick butter	½ teaspoon each of salt,
2 tablespoons hot sherry	pepper, and dry mustard
1 tablespoon flour	4 tablespoons Parmesan cheese,
1 teaspoon tomato paste	grated
¾ cup chicken stock	

Cut up chicken, as for frying, and brown slowly in butter. Pour hot sherry over chicken. Remove chicken from pan and add flour, tomato paste, and chicken broth to sherry mixture. Bring to a boil, stirring constantly. Bit by bit add sour cream, then salt, pepper, and mustard, then 2 tablespoons cheese. Return chicken to pan and simmer gently for 30 minutes or until tender. Arrange chicken in serving casserole, pour sauce over it, and sprinkle with 2 tablespoons cheese. If prepared in advance, reheat in 350° oven or under broiler until brown. Garnish with parsley. Serves 4.

MRS. E. P. TALIAFERRO, JR.

CHICKEN IN WINE SAUCE

1 2-pound fryer, cut up	½ teaspoon garlic salt
1 teaspoon salt	½ cup butter
½ teaspoon pepper	½ cup sauterne

Sprinkle chicken with salt, pepper, and garlic salt. Brown in butter until golden. Pour wine over chicken, cover and simmer until tender.

MRS. JAMES A. WINSLOW

CHICKEN INTERLAKEN

Sauté in ½ cup of olive oil until light brown:
1 2 to 2½-pound fryer, quartered,

Add:

2 onions, chopped
1 large green pepper, chopped
1 clove garlic, chopped

1 No. 2 can tomatoes
1 bay leaf

Cook in covered kettle for 15 minutes.

Add:

8 medium Irish potatoes
2 tablespoons Spanish saffron
(dry out and crumble)
1 4-ounce can mushrooms and juice

1 small bottle of capers (drained)
½ cup slivered almonds
1 cup stuffed olives (halved)
¾ cup seedless raisins
¾ cup dry white wine

Cook slowly on top of stove until potatoes are done and chicken is tender.

MRS. W. T. MORGAN, JR.

SCALLOPED CHICKEN SUPREME

6 cups cooked chicken
4 cups chicken broth
6 cups cooked rice
3 cups milk
4 tablespoons butter
¾ cup flour
1 tablespoon salt

⅛ teaspoon pepper
1 cup blanched almonds
or pecans
1 small can pimientos
2 medium cans mushrooms
Buttered bread crumbs and
paprika for decoration

Cut cooked chicken into 1-inch pieces. Pour 1 cup chicken broth over cooked rice. Make rich gravy by adding milk and melted butter to remaining broth thickened with flour. Add salt and pepper. Slice almonds and cut pimientos very fine. Slice mushrooms and sauté until slightly browned. Butter a large shallow casserole, cover bottom with rice. Place a layer of chicken over rice and add a generous amount of gravy. Dot with almonds, pimientos, and, mushrooms. Repeat with a second layer of each. Sprinkle buttered crumbs over the top, then the paprika. Bake 45 minutes in 350° oven in two 8-inch casseroles or one very large casserole. Serves 12 to 16.

MRS. FRANK P. McMICHAEL

CHICKEN LANDETA

6 chicken breasts

2 Spanish sausages (Chorizos)

½ pound smoked ham, cut in strips

1 No. 2 can tomato sauce

1 large onion, quartered

3 carrots

3 ounces cooking sherry

Halve chicken breasts. Remove all bone from chicken breasts, cut Spanish sausages in thirds, and stuff chicken breasts with ham and Spanish sausages. Mold each piece to resemble a ball. Place in baking pan; add tomato sauce, onion, and carrots and bake in 370° oven for 30 minutes. Remove chicken breasts from pan and strain sauce through colander or food mill, then add sherry and pour over chicken. Serves 6.

SPANISH PARK RESTAURANT,
TAMPA, FLORIDA

CHICKEN LOAF

2 cups chopped cooked chicken

2 eggs

1 cup milk

1 cup bread crumbs

2 tablespoons chopped green pepper

2 tablespoons chopped
  pimientos

¼ cup chopped celery

½ teaspoon salt

¼ teaspoon paprika

Beat eggs and add the milk. Add remaining ingredients and pour into a buttered loaf pan. Bake in moderate oven 30 minutes. Cut into squares and top with mushroom sauce. Makes 8 small servings.

MUSHROOM SAUCE:

1 cup fresh or canned mushrooms

2 tablespoons butter

3 tablespoons flour

1½ cups milk or stock or
  combination

½ teaspoon salt

⅛ teaspoon nutmeg

Pepper to taste

1 tablespoon lemon juice

2 beaten egg yolks

Brown mushrooms in butter, add flour and blend. Add milk, salt, nutmeg, pepper. Cook until thick. Add lemon juice to beaten egg yolks. Slowly stir egg mixture into sauce. Cook 2 minutes.

MRS. ONAN WHITEHURST

CHICKEN MARENGO

1 fryer, 3 to 3¼ pounds
2 tablespoons butter
2 tablespoons olive oil
½ cup flour
¼ teaspoon salt
1 large onion, chopped

1 large clove garlic, minced
⅔ cup dry white wine
3 teaspoons tomato paste
Water
4 ounce can drained mushrooms

Cut chicken in 8 pieces. Heat butter and oil in large frying pan. Roll chicken pieces in flour, seasoned with salt, and brown on all sides. Add onion and garlic. Sauté gently for 2 minutes, then add wine and simmer 3 minutes. Add tomato paste and enough water to make a thin sauce, but not enough to cover chicken. Cover and cook over low heat 15 to 20 minutes. Add mushrooms and continue cooking additional 10 minutes. Serves 4.

MRS. JAMES L. BUDD

PIERRE JACQUET CHICKEN

2 fryers (2½ pounds each) cut up
1 tablespoon salt
1 teaspoon freshly ground pepper
½ cup flour
½ stick butter
½ cup olive oil

¼ cup chopped onion
1 clove garlic
2 3-ounce cans small whole mushrooms
1½ cups white wine
Chopped parsley

Season chicken lightly with salt and pepper, dip in flour and brown in butter and olive oil. Cook in covered dish in 400° oven until tender. Meanwhile in butter and oil remaining in pan sauté onion and garlic. Add mushrooms and wine and boil briskly about 3 minutes. Add meat sauce, mix well and let cook for 5 minutes or until all ingredients are blended and creamy. Serve chicken on platter, pour sauce over it, and sprinkle with chopped parsley.

MEAT SAUCE:

2 tablespoons suet
3 tablespoons flour

2 cans beef consommé, heated

Melt suet and remove. Blend in flour and mix well with wire whisk. Bring to slow boil and cook until flour is brown. Add hot consommé and keep stirring with whisk. Bring to a boil, reduce heat and simmer for an hour. Before using sauce, remove fat and film from top.

MRS. LAMAR SPARKMAN

CHICKEN IN SHERRY SAUCE

2 broilers, halved	½ green pepper, chopped
1 teaspoon salt	2 tablespoons bacon drippings
¼ teaspoon pepper	2 cans consommé
Butter	2 teaspoons curry powder
1 large onion, chopped	1½ to 2 cups sherry
4 carrots, sliced round	1½ cups brown or wild rice

Salt, pepper, and butter chicken. Brown under broiler· Sauté onion, carrots and green pepper in bacon drippings. When brown add consommé and curry powder. Simmer 10 minutes. Pour sauce over chicken in roasting pan. Bake covered 1½ hours in 350° oven. Add sherry for last ½ hour of baking. Serve on rice. Serves 4.

MRS. JULIEN PATE, JR.

COUNTRY CAPTAIN

2 2½-pound fryers cut up	2 teaspoons curry powder
1 teaspoon salt	2 cans tomatoes
½ teaspoon white pepper	½ teaspoon chopped parsley
2 onions, chopped fine	½ teaspoon thyme (powdered)
2 chopped green peppers	3 tablespoons currants
1 garlic clove, minced	Almonds for garnish

Remove skin from chicken; salt and pepper. Fry in fat ½ inch deep. After removing from pan pour off half the fat. In remaining fat sauté onions, pepper, garlic, and curry powder. After onion mixture is browned add tomatoes, parsley and thyme. Cook down slightly.

Put fried chicken in roaster and pour mixture over it. Add water to cover if necessary. Place top on roaster and cook in oven for 45 minutes at 400°.

Cook and steam 2 cups white rice. When chicken is done put in center of platter with rice around it. Pour gravy over rice and sprinkle blanched almonds and currants over this. Garnish with parsley. Serves 8 to 10.

MRS. G. WILLIAM GRAY

CHICKEN SHORTCAKE NATCHEZ

4 cups cooked white meat of
   chicken (cut in medium-size
   pieces)

2 cups canned mushrooms
4 cups cream sauce

Blend chicken, mushrooms and cream sauce. Slice squares of southern style cornbread (no sugar) through the center. Ladle chicken mixture over half of cornbread, top with another slice of cornbread and put more chicken mixture over this, shortcake fashion. Sprinkle with paprika. Serves 6.

CREAM SAUCE:

3 cups rich chicken stock
1½ cups flour
¼ pound margarine
5 ounces evaporated milk
¼ teaspoon salt

¼ teaspoon monosodium
   glutamate
1 or 2 drops yellow food
   coloring

Strain stock. Add flour to melted margarine, stirring constantly. When smooth add the stock gradually. Then add milk, salt, monosodium glutamate and food coloring. Stir well, and cook until thickened.

WEDGWOOD INN, ST. PETERSBURG, FLORIDA

FLORINA'S FRIED CHICKEN

2 fryers, cut in pieces
Salt
2 cups flour for dredging

Bacon drippings
1 stick of real butter

Soak chicken in cold salted water for at least ½ hour. Drain, and salt each piece separately. Put flour in a large paper bag and shake in it a few pieces at a time to coat with flour.

Cover the bottom of a large skillet with bacon drippings to the depth of ½ inch. When grease is hot, but not smoking, put in chicken, reduce heat to medium, and cook chicken until golden brown on both sides, turning only once. When the first pieces of chicken are put in the skillet, add 1 teaspoon of the butter. At intervals add the remaining butter, piece by piece. When done, drain the chicken on paper towels or brown paper. The chicken can be fried a little ahead and run under the broiler at the last minute to regain its heat and crispness.

If an electric skillet is used, the 380° setting is ideal.

MRS. KATHERINE MORGAN

DUTCH KITCHEN CHICKEN

1 5-pound hen
2½ cups flour
1⅔ cups milk
2 eggs

2 teaspoons baking powder
½ teaspoon salt
Hot fat, for deep frying

Chicken must be left whole. Place in pot with water sufficient to cover hen. Boil until drumsticks are very tender. Do not stick fork into breast which tears very easily. Allow hen to cool in broth; this prevents shrinkage and insures nice juicy meat. When chicken is cool remove from broth and gently cut or pull meat from bones in suitable pieces for serving. Make a batter of the flour, milk, eggs, baking powder and salt. Have a pan of hot fat ready. Dip portions of chicken in batter and drop into hot fat. Fry to a golden brown; turn occasionally. Drain on paper towels; serve at once.

MRS. JOHN P. CORCORAN, JR.

HAWAIIAN CHICKEN

1 broiler
½ cup butter
1 teaspoon cornstarch
1 teaspoon grated lemon peel
¼ cup lemon juice

⅓ cup pineapple syrup
2 tablespoons finely chopped onion
1 teaspoon soy sauce
¼ teaspoon thyme

Place in broiler chicken which has been halved, quartered, or preferably cut in pieces. Broil. Melt butter; blend in cornstarch. Add remaining ingredients. Cook 5 minutes over low heat, stirring constantly. Five minutes before chicken is done, place pineapple slices, peach halves, and maraschino cherries on broiler with chicken. Brush sauce on chicken and fruits. Cook 5 minutes longer. Serve with rice to which a dash of cinnamon, almonds, and butter have been added. Makes enough sauce for 2 to 3 broilers.

MRS. MANUEL CORRAL, JR.

YELLOW RICE AND CHICKEN

1 fryer	2 tablespoons salt
4 ounces lard or ½ pint olive oil	1 pound rice
1 onion	Pinch of saffron
2 cloves garlic	1 green pepper, chopped
6 ounces tomatoes	1 2-ounce can petit
1½ quarts water	pois (small size)
1 bay leaf	2 pimientos

Cut chicken in quarters and fry in oil with onion and garlic; when done, add tomatoes and water. Boil for 5 minutes. Add bay leaf, salt, rice, saffron and green pepper. Stir thoroughly and place in moderately heated oven for 20 minutes. Garnish with petit pois and pimientos.

VALENCIA GARDEN RESTAURANT,
TAMPA, FLORIDA

Turkey

TURKEY MORNAY WITH BROCCOLI

1 package frozen broccoli, or 1 bunch fresh	½ cup sauterne
¼ cup butter	Worcestershire sauce (½ to 1 teaspoon)
¼ cup flour	Salt and pepper
1 cup turkey stock or canned chicken broth	2 cups cooked turkey, sliced
½ cup light cream	Grated Parmesan cheese

Cook broccoli until tender. Drain, and arrange on bottom of greased casserole. Melt butter and stir in flour. Add turkey stock and cream. Cook, stirring until blended and then add the wine and seasonings. Arrange the turkey on top of the broccoli. Pour on the sauce. Sprinkle the top *lavishly* with the grated cheese. Bake in a moderately hot oven (400°) for 20 minutes, or until brown and bubbly. Serves 4.

MRS. HARRY A. MacEWEN

TURKEY SOUFFLÉ

1 cup minced turkey or chicken
1½ cups thick white sauce

3 eggs, separated

Mix turkey with white sauce and beaten egg yolks. Fold in beaten egg whites. Bake in 325° oven for 1 hour.

MRS. ALONSO REGAR

SMOKED TURKEY CASSEROLE

2 cups hot cream sauce
2 cups diced smoked turkey
1 hard-boiled egg, chopped
1 cup chopped mushrooms
1 tablespoon chopped green pepper

1 tablespoon chopped pimiento
Dash of Worcestershire sauce
½ to 1 cup wild rice, cooked
    as directed on package

To the cream sauce add turkey, egg, mushrooms, green peppers, pimiento, and Worcestershire. Pour over wild rice. Heat in slow oven before serving.

MRS. H. L. CULBREATH

Turkey Stuffing

CORNBREAD ALMOND STUFFING

3½ cups chopped celery
5 tablespoons minced onion
1½ cups butter
1 tablespoon poultry seasoning
2 teaspoons savor salt
½ teaspoon salt
½ teaspoon black pepper

8 cups white bread cubes
4 cups whole wheat bread cubes
4 cups corn bread cubes
2 eggs, lightly beaten
1 cup slivered toasted almonds
4 chicken bouillon cubes
2 cups water

Sauté celery and onion in butter. Sprinkle poultry dressing, savor salt, salt and pepper over bread cubes. To celery and onion mixture add eggs and almonds. Toss.

Dissolve bouillon cubes in water and pour over bread mixture, tossing lightly until blended. Stuff bird and put remaining stuffing in casserole and bake, covered, at 300° for 40 minutes. Remove cover and let brown. Stuffs 10 to 12 pound turkey plus extra casserole.

MRS. LEM BELL, JR.

MEAT STUFFING FOR TURKEY

2 pounds beef, ground	½ cup raisins
1 pound ham, ground	½ cup almonds
1 pound veal, ground	1 8-ounce can tomato sauce
2 onions, chopped	1 egg
½ green pepper, chopped	¼ cup bread crumbs
1 4-ounce can mushrooms and juice	½ teaspoon garlic salt
½ cup olives, halved	

Combine beef, ham, and veal. Sauté onions and green pepper. Add meat mixture and brown. Add remaining ingredients. Combine well and stuff in turkey cavity. This amount will stuff one large turkey.

MRS. MANUEL CORRAL, JR.

Game

CORNISH GAME HENS COOKED IN WINE

4 Cornish game hens	½ cup sherry
Salt and pepper	1 tablespoon flour
1 lemon	1 8-ounce can mushrooms
¼ pound butter	

Have butcher split birds in half with electric saw. Sprinkle both sides with salt, pepper and lemon juice. Place skin side up in baking pan. Dot with butter, add sherry, cover and cook until tender at 325° about 1 hour. Baste occasionally with drippings. If liquid cooks out add a little water. When tender, brown under broiler. Remove hens, mix flour with pan drippings, add mushrooms and juice to make a gravy. Serve on platter with gravy poured over all. Serves 4.

MRS. W. E. SUMNER

WILD DOVE OR QUAIL

4 small birds	Salt and black pepper
¼ lemon	4 slices of bacon
4 quarters raw apple or 4 small onions	¼ cup red wine

Rub birds with lemon. Stuff with apple or onion, season with salt and pepper, and wrap one piece of bacon round each bird. Put birds in the pressure cooker; add ¼ cup of wine. Cook 10 to 12 minutes at 15 pounds pressure, then reduce pressure gradually.

MRS. W. F. TOM LENFESTEY

ROAST WILD DUCK WITH APRICOT SAUCE

3 ducks	Salt
1 cup butter	Celery leaves
Black pepper	½ cup red wine

Scrub ducks inside and out with a detergent solution. Rinse thoroughly. Rub the ducks inside and out with ½ cup butter, salt, and pepper. Put bunch of celery leaves in each duck. Roast duck, breast side up, in hot oven 450° for 20 minutes. (These ducks will be rare; increase roasting time for preferred doneness, basting every 5 minutes with combination of the remaining butter, melted, and wine.) Carve, keeping warm over boiling water. Save juices for apricot sauce.

APRICOT SAUCE:

1 No. 2 can apricots	6 tablespoons butter
2 teaspoons grated orange rind	3 duck livers
2 cups red wine	Duck juices
Black pepper	

Drain apricots and run through coarse sieve into saucepan. Add orange rind, wine, pepper, and butter, and bring to a boil. Cook 5 minutes, then place pan over boiling water. Put duck livers (uncooked) through coarse sieve and add to duck juices. Stir into sauce. Continue cooking, stirring constantly until hot. Pour over carved duck and serve immediately.

Mrs. Richard T. Farrior

ROAST PHEASANT WITH BRANDY AND CREAM

3 pheasants	½ cup brandy
6 slices bacon	2 cups chicken stock
4 tablespoons butter	½ teaspoon freshly ground
8 shallots thinly sliced, or 2	black pepper
tablespoons minced onion	1 teaspoon salt
1 garlic clove, crushed	1 pint heavy cream
	¼ cup prepared horseradish

Cover breast of pheasant with bacon slices and tie up so they will not lose shape. Brown in iron frying pan with butter, shallots, and the crushed garlic. After birds are browned, place in baking dish with juices from pan. Pour heated brandy over birds and light with match. When flame dies add chicken stock, pepper, and salt. Roast uncovered in 375° oven for ½ hour, basting frequently. Add cream and horseradish to sauce, continue roasting 15 minutes, still basting frequently. Serve birds on heated platter with sauce around them. Serve with currant jelly and popped wild rice.

Mrs. R. T. Farrior

QUAIL IN CHAFING DISH

8 birds	4 tablespoons Worcestershire sauce
1 stick butter (or almost)	2 tablespoons flour
3 ounces sherry	1 cup cream
Juice of 1½ lemons	

Split birds (or leave whole, if you wish), salt well and pepper. In a Dutch oven on top of the stove, brown birds lightly in butter, breast down, with teaspoon of butter on each. When lightly browned, add enough water to keep birds from burning, cover and cook for about 1 hour. When almost done add sherry, lemon juice, and Worcestershire sauce. Cook about 20 minutes longer, then remove birds. Add blended flour and cream to the gravy, stir and let thicken. Put birds and gravy in a chafing dish and let stand until ready to serve, then light dish to reheat. These can be cooked early in the afternoon and set aside to be reheated for about ½ hour before serving. Serves 8. Doves cooked this way are as delicious as quail.

Mrs. Harry A. MacEwen

DESSIE SMITH'S ROUND STEAK SUPREME

Most game is strange-tasting to the average person, and as it is always on our menu in season many different ways to modify the taste were tried. It is sliced thin so not so much is wasted if the first taste does not satisfy. Venison, antelope, elk or beef may be used from shoulder, hind quarter or loin. If a more delicate flavor is desired, trim off *all* fat.

2 pounds of steak	1 tablespoon butter
1 tablespoonful olive oil	1 cup commercial mushroom sauce
	⅓ cup dry Burgundy wine

Slice steak ¼ inch thick. If necessary, use tenderizer sparingly. Let stand 2 hours. Place olive oil and butter in medium hot pan. Sear steak on both sides and remove to deep hot platter. Add commercial mushroom sauce and dry Burgundy wine to fry pan. Stir until hot and pour over meat. Serve with wild rice or brown rice.

If preparing game for freezing, remove all fat, or it will be too strong-flavored.

Withlacoochee River Lodge,
Inglis, Florida

ROAST LEG OF VENISON

Have butcher lard venison well with salt pork. Rub generously with salt, pepper, and Worcestershire sauce. Roast in 325° oven, allowing about 25 minutes per pound. When roast is done make thickened gravy from pan drippings. There should be about 1½ cups of gravy. Mix gravy with the following sauce:

2 tablespoons preserved citron, cut in Julienne strips
2 tablespoons glacé cherries
1 tablespoon white Sultana raisins

1 cup port wine
½ cup currant jelly
2 tablespoons shredded almonds

Soak the citron, cherries, and raisins in wine overnight or at least 2 hours. Cook for 5 minutes. Add currant jelly and as soon as the jelly is melted stir in the 1½ cups of gravy. At serving time add the shredded almonds.

Mrs. B. J. Skinner

Mr. John's Fish House on Indian Rocks Bay

CHAPTER XI

Fish

Fish from a beach, a boat, a bridge, or a bank. It doesn't matter. On this lovely West Coast, wherever you drop a line, you'll catch a fish. In the Gulf where the waters alternate in bands of bright blue and aquamarine, fish for snapper, grouper, kingfish, pompano, or trout. In the cool dark lakes throw your line for bass, bream, or catfish. Float down the crystal rivers which run to the Gulf and see the schools of mullet swimming serenely along, safe from the lure of bait but liable to be caught in a fisherman's net. Wherever you are, you're in heaven if you like to catch or eat fish.

The best way to cook and eat fish is right in the boat. Rent a wooden rowboat on a limpid stream. Take along a one-burner camp stove, a frying pan, a can of shortening, a box of cracker meal, a loaf of bread, a jar of marmalade, a jar of pickles, and a box of salt. Fish the cool green bank until two or three bass are swimming along by the boat on a stringer, then tie the boat in the shade of a low-hanging hardwood tree, and fry the fish. While they are smoking hot, eat the fish. Civilization was never like this.

When we were children, the Gulf beaches were a lonely outpost where the white shell roads were rippled like washboards, and one drove to neighboring towns for groceries, ice, and drinking water. But Indian Rocks Beach was Tampa's particular island which was colonized annually from June through August. The strip of bay which separated the island from the mainland was edged with thickets of mangrove bushes that formed miniature coves and inlets for children's games of pirates and explorers. Built out over the mangroves on rickety wooden stilts was Mr. John's fish house where one waited after the games were done for the day's output of smoked mullet. This is a delicacy which remains as fine and rare in the present as it was in memory. The shiny silver fish were split and smoked over a slow wood fire until they were a deep mahogany hue, and the meat lifted away from the bones revealing a tender underside of a fragile peach shade. Then, as now, one of our favorite beach suppers was smoked mullet, avocado and tomato salad, and steaming grits running with melted butter. Smoked mullet is also wonderful broken into small pieces and served with saltines as snacks.

BAKED FILLET OF FISH

4 or 5 fish fillets	Swiss cheese
Pepper	½ pint sour cream
Salt	

Select a flat 8 x 10-inch casserole suitable for serving; butter it well. Place fillets across dish; do not overlap. Sprinkle lightly with pepper and salt. Place a slice of Swiss cheese over each fillet; grind over a bit more pepper. Cover all with sour cream. Bake in 300° oven about 30 minutes. (large fillets require 5 to 10 minutes longer). Serves 4 or 5. This is good with any fish, but is especially good with kingfish.

MRS. JACK D. PETERS

TOMATO KING

1 kingfish	1 6-ounce can tomato paste
¾ teaspoon salt	½ lemon
½ teaspoon pepper	¼ teaspoon Worcestershire
1 large onion	2 tablespoons olive oil or
½ clove garlic	¼ stick margarine
1 medium green pepper	

Clean kingfish. Slice lengthwise to remove backbone. Salt and pepper kingfish. Place on large pan in middle of oven. Chop finely onion, garlic, and green pepper. Dilute tomato paste with an equal volume of water. Add Worcestershire and lemon. Brown onion, garlic and green pepper in oil until soft, then simmer in tomato mixture until onion and pepper are done. Pour over kingfish ½ hour before broiling. Broil 30 minutes until done; do not turn. Serve hot! Serves 6.

MRS. BALLARD S. CARTE

MULLET PAPILLOT

2 mullet, halved and boned	¼ teaspoon ground nutmeg
1 cup white sauce	½ teaspoon salt
½ pound chopped raw shrimp	

Brush salad oil on one side of four aluminum foil squares (about 10 inches square). Salt both sides of mullet and lay 1 piece on each foil square. Mix other ingredients and divide among the 4 servings of mullet. Fold foil over mullet and seal each foil package. Bake in 325° oven for 20 minutes or until well done. Serves 4.

JAMES E. WALL

ESCABECHE
(Spanish Pickled Fish)

1 kingfish	Olive oil
½ cup olive oil	Vinegar
½ cup salad oil	1 small jar stuffed green olives,
1 large onion	sliced or tiny Spanish olives
1 large green pepper	2 pimientos, cut into strips
1 clove garlic, chopped fine	3 sprigs parsley
Salt and pepper	

Slice kingfish in ½-inch slices, discarding less attractive darker parts. Sauté fish slowly in olive oil and salad oil in frying pan until brown. Remove fish from pan. To same oil add thinly sliced onion, green pepper sliced in thin rings, and garlic. Cook slowly until tender. Place layers of fish and vegetables alternately in a large glass jar or casserole with cover, sprinkling each layer lightly with salt and pepper. A heavy sprinkle of paprika may be added if desired. Add 1 part olive oil, 1 part white vinegar to cover all. Add olives, pimientos and parsley. Serve cold on lettuce leaf as appetizer, or hot as main dish.

MRS. PHILLIP L. SMOAK

FRIED KINGFISH

Cut kingfish steaks about 1 inch thick and freeze. Then take a sharp knife and cut four rounds from each piece, leaving skin and bones intact. Drop rounds into batter and then into hot deep fat and fry until golden brown. When all have been fried, drop the whole amount back into fat again for a few minutes. This allows each piece to be crisp and hot at the same time.

MRS. ERNEST A. UPMEYER

MOTHER VAN'S BATTER:

1 cup flour	1 tablespoon olive or salad oil
1 teaspoon salt	1 egg white, beaten stiff
1 cup water	

Sift together dry ingredients. Mix water and oil, add gradually to dry ingredients. Add stiffly beaten egg white. This batter was originally made for onion rings but is delicious for any kind of fish.

MRS. R. L. VANDERVORT

FILLET OF POMPANO NAPOLITAIN

6 fresh fillets of pompano
3 outside stalks of celery, chopped
1 small carrot, chopped
1 medium onion, chopped
1 bay leaf
1½ cups dry sherry
6 shallots, chopped fine
6 medium mushrooms,
  chopped fine

6 chopped shrimp
1 chopped Florida lobster tail
¼ pound Florida crabmeat
½ cup flour
1 tablespoon chopped parsley
Salt and pepper to taste
Hollandaise sauce

Place fillets in pan. Sprinkle chopped celery, carrot, onion over pompano. Add bay leaf and 1 cup dry sherry. Sauté shallots and mushrooms in butter over slow fire. Do not color or burn. Add shrimp, lobster tail, and crabmeat. Sprinkle flour over this mixture and stir well with wooden spoon. Keep stirring about 5 minutes to cook flour. Add ½ cup dry sherry. Continue stirring for 1 minute.

Lift pompano fillets out of broth; remove vegetables that might be stuck to fillets; place fillets in shallow heat-proof dish. Strain broth that pompano was cooked in and slowly add to shrimp, crabmeat, and lobster mixture. Keep stirring and cook 5 more minutes. This mixture should be like a paste. Add parsley, salt, and pepper to taste. Cover pompano fillets evenly with this paste. Now cover with a layer of Hollandaise sauce. Bake in oven at 400° until golden brown.

MISS NELL TRICE

RED SNAPPER ALICANTE

1 onion, sliced
1 pound red snapper steaks
¼ cup Spanish olive oil
½ teaspoon salt
Pinch of white pepper
½ cup brown gravy

½ cup white wine
12 almonds
4 rings breaded fried eggplant
Parsley

Spread 3 onion slices in bottom of clay casserole. Top with snapper steaks. Over the fish pour olive oil, salt, white pepper, brown gravy, wine, grated amonds and green pepper rings. Bake at 350° for 25 minutes. Garnish with breaded fried eggplant rings. Serves 2.

COLUMBIA RESTAURANT, TAMPA, FLORIDA

POMPANO PAPILLOT

1 onion, chopped fine	Dash of Tabasco sauce
1/4 pound butter	1 ounce sauterne
1 cup flour	1/2 pound shrimp, chopped
1 pint boiled milk	1/2 pound crawfish, chopped
2 eggs	Pompano steaks
Dash of nutmeg	Salt

Sauté onion for 5 minutes in melted butter. Slowly add flour to form paste, and slowy let cook dry. Add milk and cook to a thick cream sauce. Beat eggs with nutmeg, Tabasco, sauterne, and fold into cream sauce. Add chopped boiled shrimp and crawfish. Add salt to taste.

On buttered piece of French paper spread part of the cream sauce, then place a slice of skinned pompano steak. Spread more cream sauce, then another slice of pompano. Spread over top remaining sauce. Fold paper to form a bag with crimped edges. Brush melted butter over paper and bake 30 minutes at 350°. Serves 4.

COLUMBIA RESTAURANT, TAMPA, FLORIDA

SEA-TROUT CHEF FARFANTE

6 speckled trout (1 pound each)	6 egg yolks
6 large shrimp, cooked	6 fillets of anchovies
1/2 pound cooked lobster meat	1 pound cracker meal
1 large onion	6 eggs, beaten
1/4 pound toasted almonds	1/4 pound butter
10 ounces milk	4 ounces cooking sherry
1/4 cup flour	1 lime

Take fillets from each trout, being careful to remove all bones and skin. Chop shrimp and lobster meat in small pieces. Chop onion in small pieces, as finely as posible. Wrap almonds in cloth and beat until almonds are in fine pieces. Boil the milk; in a separate pan fry onion in 2 tablespoons butter until golden brown, then add chopped shrimp, lobster and flour. Add boiling milk and stir until creamy; add egg yolks and keep stirring until mixture thickens. Divide this mixture into 6 parts, and add 1 anchovy fillet to each part. Place mixture between 2 fillets of trout; roll in cracker meal, then in beaten eggs, and again in cracker meal. Place fish in pan and bake for 20 minutes in 350° oven, 10 minutes on each side. Melt 1/4 pound butter in wine, then add lime juice and crushed almonds; keep hot and pour over fish when ready to serve.

SPANISH PARK RESTAURANT,
TAMPA, FLORIDA

TROUT MARGUERY

4 fillets of trout (about
  1½ pounds)
1 8-ounce package shelled and
  deveined frozen shrimp (or ½
  pound fresh shrimp, shelled
  and deveined)
3 tablespoons butter
1 cup water
1 cup pale dry sherry
1 tablespoon lemon juice
1 2-ounce can button mushrooms
½ teaspoon salt

8 or 9 peppercorns
1 slice of onion
1 bay leaf
1 tablespoon flour
⅛ teaspoon paprika
¼ teaspoon nutmeg
1 egg, slightly beaten
3 or 4 dashes Tabasco
½ cup mayonnaise
¼ cup heavy cream, whipped
Parmesan cheese

Melt 1 tablespoon of the butter in a skillet. Cut the fillets in half and lay in skillet. Add raw shrimp, water, sherry, lemon juice, mushroom liquid, salt, peppercorns, onion and bay leaf. Bring to boil, reduce heat and simmer gently about 8 minutes. Carefully lift out fillets; drain and place in well-buttered shallow baking dish. Drain shrimp and place on top of fillets. Add the drained mushrooms. Boil the fish stock vigorously until reduced to 1¼ cups.

Melt remaining butter in small pan. Stir in flour, paprika and nutmeg and cook until bubbly. Strain the fish stock and stir into butter-flour mixture. Cook over low heat, stirring constantly, until mixture comes to a boil. Stir a little of the hot mixture into beaten egg, then return this to the sauce. Stir over low heat until the mixture thickens, being careful not to boil. Fold in Tabasco, mayonnaise and whipped cream. Pour the sauce over fillets and shrimp. Sprinkle generously with Parmesan cheese. Place in broiler about 5 inches under heat and brown lightly. Serve immediately. Serves 6.

This dish may be prepared in advance except for the broiling process. If it is prepared early in the day, bake in a 300° oven about 15 minutes to heat through before turning on broiler.

MRS. LOUIS SAXTON

FILLET OF RED SNAPPER AMANDINE

6 fillets of red snapper
Salt and pepper
Flour for dredging
1½ cups butter

1 cup almonds, bleached and
    sliced
1 lemon

Wipe fillets with a damp cloth. Sprinkle with salt and pepper and dredge in a little flour. Sauté in ½ cup melted butter until done but not too brown. Place fillets in a pan.

AMANDINE:

Mix almonds and 1 cup melted butter in a skillet. Heat until almonds are light brown. Pour almond mixture over red snapper fillets and sprinkle with lemon juice. Place in 375° oven for 3 to 5 minutes or until nicely browned. Serves 6. This amandine sauce is excellent with other fish.

ROLLANDE & PIERRE RESTAURANT
ST. PETERSBURG, FLORIDA

TROUT, RUSSIAN STYLE

6 to 9 trout, filleted
½ teaspoon salt
¼ teaspoon white pepper
2 eggs, well beaten
¼ cup milk
1½ cups toasted bread crumbs,
    pulverized

2 tablespoons corn or peanut oil
¼ pound butter, soft
2 eggs, hard-cooked, chopped fine
⅓ cup parsley, finely chopped
2 tablespoons pimiento, finely
    chopped
2 lemons, sliced thin

Salt and pepper the trout. Mix raw eggs and milk. Dip trout in mixture, then roll gently in bread crumbs. Heat oil on grill to medium heat (if using electric fry pan, heat to 300°). Use just enough oil to keep fish from sticking. Make a paste of the butter, hard-cooked eggs, parsley and pimiento.

Cook trout on grill until golden color, about 5 or 6 minutes on each side. Place on heated platter. Spread butter paste over each piece and top each with 2 or 3 slices of lemon. Serve immediately.

VALENCIA GARDEN RESTAURANT,
TAMPA, FLORIDA

FISH RUSSIAN STYLE

3 trout
Olive oil to cover
Salt and fresh ground pepper
  to taste

¼ pound butter or margarine,
  browned
Pepperidge Farm bread crumbs,
  rolled fine

Fillet 3 "good size" trout (about 1 pound each) or use 12 small fillets. Marinate 1 hour in olive oil to cover, placing fillets in large oven-proof dish in single layer. Drain off oil; lightly sprinkle fillets with salt and fresh ground pepper; add browned butter or margarine. Bake 10 minutes at 400°. Turn fillets, sprinkle generously with bread crumbs, and bake 10 minutes more, basting occasionally. Garnish with grated hard-boiled egg, finely chopped pimiento, and minced parsley. Serve in the baking dish, with lemon wedges. Serves 6.

Mrs. Richard S. McKay

HERB BAKED FISH

1 pound snapper, grouper,
  haddock, or halibut
1 tablespoon butter
1 teaspoon salt
½ teaspoon garlic salt
¼ teaspoon oregano
¼ teaspoon thyme

Dash of pepper
1 small bay leaf
½ cup thinly sliced onions
  (seperated into rings)
½ to ¾ cup light cream
Paprika

Place fish in 10 x 6 x 1½-inch baking dish. Dot with butter and sprinkle seasonings; add bay leaf and arrange onion rings over top of fish. Pour cream over all and sprinkle with paprika. Bake uncovered in 350° oven about 30 to 35 minutes. Yields 4 servings·

Leisure House, Tampa Electric Company

COD FISH CAKES

1 10½-ounce can Gortons
  cod fish cakes
1 small onion, grated fine
1 egg
Dash of Tabasco

1 teaspoon prepared horseradish
½ teaspoon salt
1 teaspoon baking powder
  (omit for hors d'oeuvres)

Mix together all ingredients, and shape into 2-inch patties. Fry in hot fat, about 1½ inches deep, until golden brown. Makes 8 patties. Serve for breakfast, topped with poached egg and bacon.

They can be seasoned more highly with onion and Tabasco, shaped into small balls and deep fried for hors d'oeuvres. Makes approximately 2 dozen.

Mrs. E. P. Taliaferro, Jr.

FISH FILLETS IN LEMON DRESSING

4 fillets of trout or flounder
  or any non-oily fish
2 tablespoons grated onion
1 tablespoon finely chopped
  celery (optional)
4 tablespoons melted butter
  or margarine

3 or 4 slices toasted bread
  broken in small pieces
1 tablespoon chopped parsley
Juice of 1 lemon
Grated rind of ½ lemon
1 teaspoon salt
¼ teaspoon pepper
⅛ teaspoon nutmeg

Sauté onion and celery in butter. Add broken bread pieces. Add remaining ingredients. To this mixture fold in any one of the following: 2 chopped hard-boiled eggs, ½ cup crabmeat, ½ cup chopped shrimp. Grease baking dish. Place 2 fillets of fish in bottom of dish. Spread dressing over fish. Place other 2 fillets of fish on top of dressing. Squeeze juice of ½ lemon over all. Dust lightly with paprika and dot with butter or margarine. Bake at 375° about 40 minutes.

HELEN ALLEN

Sponge Boats at Tarpon Springs

CHAPTER XII

Shellfish

Morning on the Gulf of Mexico is a time of exquisite peace. The Gulf, as far as you can see, is as smooth as a pond, with only a gentle lacing of waves on the clean white beach to foretell the surge of breakers which afternoon will bring. Morning is cool shadows of Australian pines cast on sand by the rising sun; blue-gray horizon stretching to the shores of Mexico; translucent green water, still and refreshing. Morning is a time for the crab fisherman to make his leisurely way along the shallows, dipping up blue-green crabs in his net, filling his pail for a noontime feast. The crabs must be boiled immediately in a kettle of sea water, and when the tender white meat is picked from the shell and made into salad, or deviled crabs topped with buttered breadcrumbs, there is no way to describe the delicacy of the flavor.

There are still a few oldtimers who have the will and the way to make coquina soup. This is made from a tiny shellfish no bigger than a fingernail. The minute, clam-shaped coquina, striped in sunset tones, burrows in the firm sand at the edge of the water, and must be scooped from its bed as the receding waves rush back to sea. The coquinas are sieved in water until they are free of sand, then pail after pail of them are boiled in lightly salted water until the shells pop open. The broth is strained and added to minced onion which has been lightly sautéed in butter and flour. When fresh black pepper is added to taste, a culinary triumph has been realized. Some cooks use coquina broth as a base for chowder made with tomatoes and vegetables. Take your pick, it's all delicious.

The bays of this region abound with scallops and oysters, there for the harvesting. Early explorers were amazed at the low-growing mangrove bushes which low tide revealed covered with oysters at their roots. But the Gulf is really most famous for its shrimp. Tampa is home port for a great shrimp fleet which fishes the waters from here to Mexico. In recent years a new shrimp bank was found which yielded individual shrimp six to eight inches long, and the meat was just as delicate and sweet as that of the smaller variety. This was a boon beyond compare to those who liked shrimp but hated the shelling. Last but not least, stone crabs yield a claw meat unmatched by any but that of Maine lobsters. For those who appreciate the wonders of shellfish, this West Coast of Florida is a Mecca.

Crawfish and Lobster

CRAWFISH CONGA

½ pound cooked crawfish meat, cut in bite-size pieces
Salt and pepper
Juice of half lime
2 ounces melted butter

1½ ounces cream cheese
½ ounce Roquefort or bleu cheese
2 fillets of anchovies
Aluminum foil 12 inches square

Place crawfish meat in center of foil, add salt and pepper and lime juice (you may rub foil with garlic if you desire). Blend together butter and both kinds of cheese and pour over crawfish. Place fillets of anchovies on top, then fold aluminum foil, and place in 400° oven for 10 minutes, and serve. Serves 1.

SPANISH PARK RESTAURANT,
TAMPA, FLORIDA

PLAIN OL' CRAWFISH

1 crawfish per person
(or more)
Butter

Salt and pepper to taste
Lemon wedges

Have the market split and clean *raw* crawfish. Wash and turn down to drain. Line broiler pan with foil and arrange crawfish on rack. Slather with butter. Bake at 300° for 30 to 40 minutes, then broil for about 5 minutes until delicately brown. Add salt and pepper to taste. Serve with lots of melted butter and wedges of lemon.

MRS. LOUIS SAXTON

LOBSTER NEWBURG

1 cup diced cooked lobster meat
2 tablespoons butter
¼ cup dry sherry wine

3 egg yolks
1 cup light cream
1 teaspoon Worcestershire

Heat lobster meat in butter in top of double boiler. Add sherry and cook 1 minute. Combine egg yolks, cream and Worcestershire and add to lobster. Cook mixture slowly until thick. Serve on toast points. Serves 2 to 3.

MRS. WALTON HICKS

LOBSTER (OR CRAWFISH) THERMIDOR

2 large Florida crawfish tails
4 tablespoons butter
2 4-ounce cans mushrooms, drained
4 tablespoons flour
1 teaspoon dry mustard
1 teaspoon salt
⅛ teaspoon Cayenne
⅛ teaspoon nutmeg

1 cup milk
1 cup light cream
2 egg yolks, slightly beaten
1 tablespoon lemon juice
3 tablespoons sherry
½ cup bread crumbs
2 tablespoons grated Parmesan cheese
2 tablespoons melted butter

Boil crawfish tails, if not already cooked. Remove meat and dice. Melt 4 tablespoons butter in saucepan; add mushrooms and sauté until brown. Blend in flour, mustard, salt, Cayenne, and nutmeg. Gradually add milk and cream. Cook over medium heat, stirring constantly, until mixture thickens and comes to a boil. Stir small amount of hot mixture into egg yolks; add to sauce. Remove from heat. Stir in lemon juice, sherry, and crawfish meat. Place in buttered casserole. Combine bread crumbs, cheese, and 2 tablespoons melted butter; sprinkle over crawfish. Bake in hot oven (400°) about 15 minutes, or until crumbs are brown. May be served over thin toast. Serves 6 to 8.

MRS. ROD SHAW, JR.

Crabmeat

CRAB AU GRATIN

½ pound butter
1 cup flour
2 quarts milk
1½ pounds Cheddar cheese
   (grated or cubed)
1¾ pounds claw crabmeat

1½ tablespoons salt
1 tablespoon onion
¼ tablespoon Tabasco
1 teaspoon Worcestershire
1 teaspoon pepper

Make a white sauce with first 3 ingredients, then add cheese and seasonings. Stir until smooth. Fold in crab. Turn into buttered casserole and bake at 325° for 30 minutes. Serves 8 to 10.

MRS. HARLAN LOGAN

BAKED CRABMEAT

1 pound crabmeat	1 teaspoon Worcestershire
4 tablespoons butter	1 teaspoon chopped parsley
2 tablespoons flour	Dash Cayenne pepper
1½ cups milk	¼ teaspoon celery salt
¼ teaspoon salt	2 eggs, well-beaten
Juice of one small onion	Buttered bread crumbs
Juice of ½ lemon	

Pick crabmeat carefully to remove all bits of shell. Melt butter in heavy saucepan. Blend in flour; add milk and stir constantly over low heat until thickened. Add all seasonings. Add beaten eggs; stir but do not let boil. Mix sauce with crabmeat. Pour into glass baking dish. Top with buttered crumbs. Bake at 350° for 30 to 40 minutes.

MRS. PRENTISS HUDDLESTON

CRAB BISQUE

½ cup butter	3 bay leaves
½ cup chopped onion	¼ teaspoon Tabasco
1 cup chopped green onion	3 pounds redfish, scamp or
4 cups chicken stock	similar fish
4 carrots cut in small bits	4 cups milk
1 cup of parsley, chopped	⅓ cup flour
2 cups chopped celery	4 cups heavy cream
3 teaspoons salt	1 pound cooked, cleaned and
½ teaspoon white pepper	chopped shrimp
½ teaspoon powdered mace	1 pound lump crabmeat
½ teaspoon thyme	½ teaspoon paprika

In large pot melt butter. Add onion and green onion and cook slowly until tender. Add chicken stock, carrots, parsley, celery, salt, pepper, mace, thyme, bay leaves, Tabasco, and fish. Simmer for 45 minutes, adding additional stock or water if necessary.

Add 1 cup of milk to the flour, slowly, mixing until smooth. Stirring constantly, slowly add remaining milk and the cream to the pot. Continue stirring over medium heat until smooth and thick.

Reserve 3 tablespoons shrimp. Add remaining shrimp and crabmeat. Continue stirring and cook for 10 minutes more. Serve in large ramekins or soup bowls. Garnish with chopped shrimp and paprika. Serves 14.

JACK WILSON

AVOCADO-CRAB IMPERIAL

½ stick butter
¼ cup flour
2 cups milk
1 cup mild cheese, grated
1 tablespoon grated onion
2 tablespoons sherry

1 teaspoon salt
¼ teaspoon pepper
1 pound crabmeat
4 avocados
Lime juice
Bread crumbs

Melt butter, blend in flour; slowly add milk, stirring constantly. Cook over low heat until thickened. Add cheese, stir until melted. Remove from heat, add onion, sherry, salt, pepper, and crabmeat; mix well. Pile into 8 avocado halves that have been sprinkled with lime juice; sprinkle with fine bread crumbs. Bake 15 minutes in 350° oven.

MRS. NORMAN STALLINGS

CRAB CAKES

1 pound white crabmeat, picked
  and flaked
1 egg, beaten
1 medium onion, chopped fine
1 tablespoon Worcestershire sauce

2 tablespoons mayonnaise
½ teaspoon Tabasco
1 teaspoon dry mustard
1 teaspoon salt
Juice of ½ lemon

Combine all ingredients and form into 8 patties 2 inches in diameter. Better if chilled a few hours. Fry in deep fat until golden brown.

MRS. GEORGE KAMPS

HOT CRAB CROQUETTES

3 tablespoons margarine
3 tablespoons flour
1 cup milk
1 teaspoon salt
⅛ teaspoon pepper
¾ teaspoon dry mustard

¼ teaspoon Worcestershire
1 tablespoon finely grated onion
2 cups crabmeat
1 cup crumbs
2 eggs lightly beaten

Make a thick cream sauce of the margarine, flour and milk. Add seasonings, onion and crabmeat. Mix this well and chill. Make into balls; roll in crumbs, then in egg and again in crumbs. Fry a few at a time in deep fat until golden brown. Serve hot.

MRS. RAY C. BROWN

DEVILED CRAB I

1 pound crabmeat	1 egg
2 tablespoons chopped parsley	1 cup mayonnaise
2 tablespoons onion, optional	½ cup sherry
2 teaspoons mustard	Dash Tabasco
1 tablespoon Worcestershire	Buttered bread crumbs
1 tablespoon water	

Mix all ingredients. Put in small greased custard cups, crab shells, or casserole. Top with buttered bread crumbs which have been made by adding crumbs to melted butter. Bake at 350° until light brown.

MRS. JOHN HUNNICUTT

DEVILED CRAB II

3 cups crabmeat	1 beaten egg yolk
¼ teaspoon mace	½ cup sherry
¼ teaspoon mustard	Salt and pepper to taste
¼ teaspoon powdered cloves	1 egg white beaten stiff
1 tablespoon melted butter	Cracker crumbs

Flake crabmeat in a mixing bowl and season with mace, mustard and cloves. Stir in melted butter, beaten egg yolk, sherry, salt and pepper. Fold in stiffly beaten egg white. Turn the crab mixture into six buttered individual ramekins and sprinkle with cracker crumbs. Bake in a moderate oven (350°) for 30 minutes until mixture is heated through and topping is brown.

MRS. REGAR HICKMAN

CRAB ENCHILADA

1 dozen crabs or 2 to 3 cups crabmeat	2 teaspoons McCormick's powdered seafood seasoning (more if you like it hot)
1 green pepper, chopped	⅛ teaspoon thyme
2 large onions, chopped	⅛ teaspoon oregano
2 tablespoons olive oil	Salt to taste
1 No. 2½ can tomatoes—solid pack or tomatoes and purée (not too watery)	

Clean raw crabs and crack claws. Sauté pepper and onions in oil until tender but not brown. Add tomatoes and simmer 20 minutes. Add crabs (or crabmeat) and seasonings. Bring to a boil and simmer 20 minutes. Aprons should be provided for all hands when served. Serves 4 to 6.

MRS. ISABELLE DELCHER

CRABMEAT FONDANT

1 can condensed asparagus soup
1 can condensed cream of
   mushroom soup
1 cup light cream
1 pound of crabmeat, flaked
2 teaspoons Worcestershire

¼ teaspoon Cayenne pepper
1 ounce of cognac, brandy or sherry
½ cup grated Gruyere cheese
1 teaspoon anchovy paste
Rusk or Melba toast

Use a chafing dish. Place the pan over water basin. Be sure that the water in the basin is hot. Turn in the soups and add cream slowly, stirring all the while to remove lumps. Add the crabmeat, the seasonings, and the cognac. Mixture should have a very sharp flavor. When it's all really hot, stir in the cheese and anchovy paste. Give it a quick stir or two until the cheese melts, and then serve over rounds of rusk or thin slices of Melba toast. Chow mein noodles may be used too, allowing 1 can for 2 servings. Serves 6.

MRS. VICTOR B. YEATS

CRAB LOUIS

1½ pounds crabmeat
Shredded lettuce
6 tomatoes

6 hard-cooked eggs
1 avocado
Crab Louis sauce

Get as large pieces of crab as possible. Pick over crab carefully to remove all shell and tissue. On each of six salad plates arrange a bed of lettuce. In center of each place a mound of crabmeat. Surround with wedges of tomatoes, hard-cooked eggs and avocado. Serve well chilled with the following sauce.

CRAB LOUIS SAUCE:

1 cup mayonnaise
2 tablespoons grated onion
   (or 1 tablespoon onion and
   1 tablespoon chopped chives)
1 tablespoon lemon juice

1 teaspoon minced green pepper
½ cup chili sauce
1 teaspoon Worcestershire
Dash of Cayenne
Salt and pepper to taste

Mix well and chill.

MRS. PRENTISS HUDDLESTON

CRAB GUMBO

1 piece ham hock
¾ cup flour
4 cups chopped onions
4 cloves garlic
2 tablespoons bacon drippings
1 cup chopped green pepper

1 cup chopped celery
1 tablespoon salt
4 bay leaves
1 tablespoon crab boil
½ pound chopped fresh okra
1 pound shrimp (or more)
1 pound crabmeat (or more)

Boil ham about 2 hours in 3 quarts of water. Brown flour, onions, and garlic in bacon drippings, stirring constantly. Add 2½ quarts of water, then green pepper and celery. Add salt, bay leaves and crab boil. Boil slowly 1½ to 2 hours. During last hour of cooking add okra and at least 2 quarts of water from ham hock. (Skim off excess grease.) When nearly ready to serve, add shrimp and crabmeat and boil 15 minutes. Be sure to cover with liquid. Serve with rice. Serves 6 or 8.

MRS. CHARLES M. DAVIS

CRABMEAT IMPERIAL

5 pounds crabmeat
½ cup capers
6 hard-boiled eggs, diced fine
½ cup pimientos, diced
15 slices bread, diced fine
1½ tablespoons salt
¾ tablespoon white pepper
½ teaspoon Tabasco sauce

1 tablespoon Worcestershire sauce
1 teaspoon monosodium glutamate
1 cup butter
½ cup chopped parsley
½ cup lemon juice
1 cup cream sauce
12 egg whites, beaten stiff
1 cup mayonnaise

Combine all ingredients except egg whites and mayonnaise and place in a casserole. Blend stiffly beaten egg whites and mayonnaise and spread on top. Bake in 350° oven 15 minutes or until heated through. Serves 25. Coquille or clam shells may be used, but reduce baking time.

GASPARILLA INN, BOCA GRANDE, FLORIDA

CREAMED CRABMEAT ON TOAST

4 tablespoons butter
4 tablespoons flour
½ pint cream
4 tablespoons sherry

Salt and pepper to taste
1 pound white crabmeat
  (cooked or canned)
¾ cup sharp grated cheese

Make cream sauce in top of double boiler from the butter, flour, and cream. Add sherry and salt and pepper. Remove from heat and add crabmeat. Put in chafing dish to keep warm and add grated cheese. Mix thoroughly so cheese will melt. This may be made ahead of time, refrigerated, then heated at the last minute. It is very important not to overcook, however. Serve on Melba toast. Serves 4.

MRS. JIM WINSLOW

ORIGINAL RECIPE FOR YBOR CITY DEVILED CRAB

(As sold on the streets of Tampa's Latin Quarter.)

CROQUETTE DOUGH:

3 loaves stale American bread

1 loaf stale Cuban bread (grind very fine and sift)

1 level tablespoon paprika

1 teaspoon salt

Remove crust from 3 loaves bread and discard crust. Soak remainder of bread in water 15 minutes. Drain water and squeeze until almost dry. Add the sifted Cuban bread gradually until you have dough. Add paprika and salt and mix thoroughly. Form dough into ball and put in the refrigerator for approximately 2 hours.

CRABMEAT FILLING:

5 tablespoons oil

3 onions, finely chopped

½ red or green bell pepper, finely chopped

4 cloves garlic, mashed or chopped fine

1 level teaspoon crushed red hot pepper (Italian style)

2 bay leaves

½ teaspoon sugar

1 level teaspoon salt

1 6-ounce can tomato paste

1 pound can fresh crabmeat (claws), picked over and shredded

Fry very slowly in oil, the onions, bell pepper, garlic, crushed hot peppers for 15 minutes. Add bay leaves, sugar, salt, and the tomato paste. Stir, then cover and cook 15 minutes at low heat. Add crabmeat and cook for 10 minutes, uncover, put on platter in refrigerator for 2 hours.

Take about 3 tablespoons of the bread dough and press in your hand; put in a tablespoon of crab filling, then seal like a croquette with two pointed ends. Dip into the following mixture: 2 eggs, well beaten with ½ cup milk, salt, and dash of black pepper. Mix 1 cup cracker meal and ½ cup flour. Roll croquettes first in the cracker-flour mixture, then in the eggs, and again in the cracker-flour mixture. Put in refrigerator for 2 hours. Fry in deep fat until brown. Make miniature size for parties.

COLUMBIA RESTAURANT, TAMPA, FLORIDA

Oysters and Scallops

DEVILED OYSTERS

4 dozen small oysters (1 pint)
1 onion, minced
1 clove garlic
2 tablespoons butter
2 egg yolks, well beaten
¾ cup cream
1 tablespoon flour
1 bay leaf (optional)

3 full stalks parsley, minced
3 tablespoons chives, minced
½ teaspoon salt
Black pepper
Worcestershire sauce (optional)
Tabasco (optional)
Cracker crumbs
Butter

Cook oysters slightly in their own liquor. Drain and cut into small pieces. Sauté onion and garlic in butter. Beat egg yolks and add to cream. Add flour, cream and bay leaf to mixture of onion and garlic. Cook slowly 10 to 15 minutes, and add parsley, chives, salt and pepper, Worcestershire and Tabasco to taste. Remove bay leaf and add oysters. Fill shells or casserole and dust with cracker crumbs. Put pat of butter on each and bake 10 to 15 minutes in a 350° oven. This dish, which serves 2, may be made early and baked at the last minute.

MRS. H. L. CROWDER, JR.

MINCED OYSTERS

3 pints oysters
1½ boxes of soda crackers
2 small onions
Juice of 1½ lemons

¼ teaspoon paprika
1 tablespoon Worcestershire sauce
2 tablespoons butter, melted
Salt to taste

Scald the oysters in their own juice, drain and chop. Save liquor for seasoning. Roll crackers, but not too fine. Set aside. Chop onions fine, and add remaining ingredients. Combine oysters, crackers, and seasonings, mixing well with oyster juice. Be careful not to get mixture too soft. Place in shells and dust top lightly with fine cracker crumbs. Melt additional butter (8-10 tablespoons) so that you have enough to put about a tablespoon over the top of each shell. Bake in oven 8 to 10 minutes or until heated through, then run under the broiler until slightly browned. Serves 8 to 10.

MRS. JOE F. GRABLE

OYSTER PATTIES

1 quart oysters (save liquid,
   if needed later)
½ cup flour (more if needed)
3 tablespoons shortening
1 medium onion, chopped fine

1 bunch shallots, chopped fine
1 small clove garlic
1 tablespoon finely chopped parsley
Salt and pepper to taste

Drain oysters in colander, removing all particles of shell, saving water. Brown flour in fat to make roux, then add chopped onion with white part of shallots, and cook about 10 minutes. Add garlic, parsley, green parts of shallots, and oysters. Cook until desired thickness; if too thick, add oyster liquid. Add salt and pepper to taste. Fills 12 large patty shells.

MRS. JAMES P. VAN PELT

POACHED OYSTERS ON TOAST

4 strips lean bacon (breakfast
   style)
1 pint small oysters with liquid

1 lemon
6 slices of crisp toast

Fry bacon in skillet until crisp. Remove and drain. Leave about 2 teaspoons bacon fat in skillet. Add oysters and liquid to skillet and cook over medium heat until edges begin to curl. Mix lemon juice with oysters. Serve on toast with bacon crumbled over each serving. Serves 6.

JACK WILSON

SCALLOPED OYSTERS

1 pint oysters
½ box soda crackers, crumbled
Salt
Pepper

Butter
1 cup milk
1 egg

In a casserole put a layer of crackers. Alternate crackers with a thick layer of oysters, salt, pepper and butter. Sprinkle a little oyster liquor over each layer. Finish with crumbs on top. At end pour over all 1 cup of milk with egg beaten in it. Bake in covered dish 35 minutes at 325°. Brown top after cover is removed. Serves 6.

MRS. M. E. WILSON

OVEN SCALLOPS

4 tablespoons butter   1 pound scallops
2 or 3 tablespoons lemon juice   Salt and pepper to taste

Mix butter and lemon juice in heavy skillet. Add scallops; place in 400° oven. Shake occasionally; bake until brown, tender, and "glazed" (about 5 to 7 minutes). Sprinkle with salt and freshly ground pepper. Serves 3 to 4.

MRS. J. BROWN FARRIOR

Shrimp

BAKED GARLIC SHRIMP

12 small cooked shrimp   3 tablespoons melted butter
½ to 1 teaspoon minced fresh garlic   Paprika
Crushed cracker crumbs

Place shrimp in an individual oven-proof casserole, top with garlic (according to taste). Cover with cracker crumbs and pour over the melted butter. Sprinkle with paprika and bake at 375° for 12 to 15 minutes. Serves 1.

WEDGWOOD INN, ST. PETERSBURG, FLORIDA

BAKED STUFFED SHRIMP

2 4-ounce packages Ritz crackers   1 cup finely chopped pecans
4 ounces (1 stick) butter   ½ teaspoon Worcestershire
1 egg   3 tablespoons water
                                         3 dozen large shrimp

Roll the Ritz crackers until fine. Add other ingredients except shrimp and mix until sticky. Use approximately 5 or 6 shrimp per serving, depending upon size of shrimp. Peel and split raw shrimp leaving the tails. Stuff each shrimp with the above mixture and place on a buttered tray (or in two baking dishes, approximately 11 x 7-inches). Put tray under the broiler until the stuffing is browned, then remove from the broiler. Place tray or baking dishes in larger broiler pan and surround with boiling water to finish cooking on top of stove. Cook 3 to 4 minutes, or until shrimp are done. Serve on lettuce leaves with garlic butter sauce. Serves 6.

PINK ELEPHANT DINING ROOM
BOCA GRANDE, FLORIDA

MINCED BAKED SHRIMP IN SHELL

1 pound shrimp, cooked and cleaned
2 hard-boiled eggs, chopped
1 stick butter (melted)
1 teaspoon chopped parsley
1 tablespoon lemon juice

1 tablespoon onion juice
1 tablespoon Worcestershire sauce
1 teaspoon dry mustard
Salt and Tabasco to taste
Cracker crumbs

Grind the cooked shrimp and add the eggs. Add the other ingredients except cracker crumbs and mix together. Fill sea shells with this mixture. Sprinkle well with cracker crumbs. Place shells in a pan of hot water and bake in moderate oven until mixture is hot. This serves 4 to 6 depending upon the size of the sea shells.

MRS. BLACKBURN LOWRY

BOILED SHRIMP WITH BUTTER SAUCE

This is strictly a "taste and add a little more" recipe, but this is a beginning point.

BUTTER SAUCE:

2 sticks butter, melted
¼ teaspoon turmeric
⅛ teaspoon curry
¼ teaspoon dry mustard

2 tablespoons lemon juice
Salt
Few drops of Tabasco
Dash of Worcestershire

Combine. This will serve 4 people. (One-half stick of butter per person when served this way.)

BOILED SHRIMP:

Season boiling water with following:

Salt
Garlic
Bay leaves
Pickling spices

Lemon
Onion
Vinegar

Add washed, unpeeled shrimp (½ pound per person). Do not peel before adding, or at all, as they are served on a plate wth cup of butter sauce in do-it-yourself, peel-and-dunk fashion. Cook the shrimp 10 minutes, then drain.

MRS. CHARLES T. HEALY

SHRIMP 'N BEER

10 pounds unpeeled large shrimp
8 cans flat beer (or judge amount
   of beer according to size pot
   you use to cook the shrimp)

2 boxes Zatarains crab boil,
   in bags
½ box (4 ounces) monosodium
   glutamate
½ bottle Tabasco

Bring beer to a boil. Add seasonings, leaving crab boil in the bags. Add shrimp and bring to boil. Cover and simmer for 10 minutes or until tender. Serve hot or cold with a good seafood sauce and let your guests peel their own.

BILL SAVAGE

ITALIAN BROILED SHRIMP

2 pounds jumbo shrimp
¼ cup flour

½ stick butter
¼ cup olive oil

Shell and devein shrimp, leaving tails on. Wash and dry. Dust on flour. Put butter and olive oil in large baking dish (9 x 14-inches), heat until butter melts. Place shrimp in single layer in dish, and put in 400° oven for 8 minutes. Pour sauce over shrimp, mix until all are coated. Place shrimp under broiler for 2 to 3 minutes. Serve immediately. Serves 4 to 6.

SAUCE:

4 tablespoons butter
2 tablespoons flour
Juice of 1 lemon
½ teaspoon fresh ground pepper

1 cup hot water
2 tablespoons finely chopped garlic
4 tablespoons finely chopped
   parsley

Melt butter, add flour, mix in lemon juice, pepper, water and bring to boil, stirring constantly. Cook 5 minutes, remove from heat, add garlic and parsley; mix.

MRS. NEIL MCMULLEN

SHRIMP CASSEROLE I

2 pounds raw shrimp
⅓ cup finely chopped onion
⅓ cup celery
2 tablespoons butter or margarine
1 or 2 cloves garlic
1 cup raw rice
1 No. 3 can tomatoes
2 cups chicken bouillon or
   canned consommé

1 bay leaf
3 tablespoons chopped parsley
½ teaspoon ground cloves
½ teaspoon marjoram
1 teaspoon chili powder
Dash Cayenne
1 tablespoon salt
⅛ teaspoon pepper

Shell and clean raw shrimp. Brown onion and celery in butter or margarine with garlic cloves. Into a casserole that holds at least 2½ quarts, put the onion, celery, garlic, shrimp, raw rice, tomatoes and chicken bouillon or canned consommé. Add remaining ingredients and stir. Cover tightly and cook 1½ to 2 hours at 350°. Stir once with a fork during cooking period so that all flavors are blended more fully. Serves 6.

Mrs. Victor B. Yeats

CURRIED SHRIMP I

¼ cup butter or margarine
1 large onion, chopped
1 large apple, chopped
1 cup chopped celery
6 teaspoons curry powder
4 tablespoons flour
2½ cups chicken stock

1 tablespoon lemon juice
1 cup cream
½ teaspoon salt
Pepper
2 cups cooked shrimp
¼ cup seedless raisins
2 tablespoons chutney

Melt butter in heavy skillet. Add onion, apple and celery and cook gently about 5 minutes. Do not allow onion to brown. Sprinkle curry powder and flour over mixture gradually until it is all blended. Remove skillet from heat and gradually add chicken stock and lemon juice. Add cream and mix well. Return to fire and cook until thick. Add salt to taste and dash of pepper. Add shrimp, raisins and chutney. Cover and simmer 15 to 20 minutes to blend flavors. If not serving immediately, turn heat off and leave skillet covered. Do not overcook or celery and apples will be mushy. Serve over rice. Accompany dish with generous bowls of chopped cooked bacon, ground peanuts, coconut, chutney, hard-cooked chopped eggs, chopped spring onions. Serves 4.

Mrs. Robert T. Cozart

CURRIED SHRIMP II

1 cup coconut milk and coconut
  water
2 large onions, chopped, and garlic
  (optional)
¼ cup oil
2 large tomatoes, chopped

2 tablespoons curry powder
2½ pounds raw shrimp, shelled
2 raw chopped apples
2 raw unpeeled potatoes, chopped
Salt and pepper
Worcestershire sauce

Drain off and save liquid inside coconut (this is the water). Grate coconut and set gratings to steep in liquid where they will get warm, not hot. Put them in a heavy cloth and squeeze all the juice you can. Put the gratings back in a bowl, pour boiling water over them, steep again, wringing out resulting juice. The flavor is delicious (this is the milk).

Sauté onions in oil gently about 5 minutes until delicately golden, not brown. Add tomatoes and cook 2 minutes. Mix curry powder (more according to taste) with coconut milk. Add to tomatoes and onions and blend thoroughly. Add shrimp, apples and potatoes, season to taste with salt, pepper and Worcestershire. Simmer for 20 minutes (coconut milk must *never* boil). If not serving immediately, turn heat very low and leave skillet covered. Don't overcook or apples and potatoes will be mushy.

Accompany with generous bowls of curry accessories. First and foremost, of course, is rice. Next comes chutney. Then come the fascinators: grated peanuts, slivered almonds, grated coconut, chopped eggs (chop yolks and whites separately), and chopped cooked bacon. These are sprinkled over the mound of curry and rice.

Mrs. Eliot C. Fletcher

FRIED SHRIMP

1 pound shrimp
¼ cup flour
1 teaspoon curry powder

1 teaspoon paprika
1 egg beaten with 1 tablespoon
  water
Cracker crumbs

Shell and devein shrimp. Dry thoroughly. Mix flour, curry powder and paprika in a small grocery bag. Put shrimp in bag and shake well. Then dip shrimp in egg mixture and roll in cracker crumbs until well-coated. Fry in deep fat heated to 380° to 390° until golden brown. Don't overcook. It takes just a few minutes.

Mrs. Prentiss Huddleston

CATHERINE ATKIN'S SHRIMP

½ cup butter
5 tablespoons flour
2 tablespoons curry powder
1 teaspoon salt
½ teaspoon paprika
½ teaspoon nutmeg
½ teaspoon monosodium glutamate

3 cups light cream
2 ½ pounds shrimp, cooked and cleaned
2 tablespoons lemon juice
2 tablespoons sherry
1 teaspoon onion juice
2 teaspoons Worcestershire sauce

Melt butter. Blend in flour, curry, salt, paprika, nutmeg and monosodium glutamate. Stir in cream. Cook until it thickens. Add remainder of ingredients and heat thoroughly. Serve from chafing dish over rice that has been cooked in 3 parts water, 1 part orange juice, and 1 tablespoon grated orange peel. We serve toasted flaked coconut and mango chutney in side dishes.

MRS. JACK ECKERD

SHRIMP COQUILLE

2 to 2½ pounds shrimp (cleaned but not cooked)
¼ stick (2 tablespoons) butter
1 pint mayonnaise
1 pint chili sauce
1 teaspoon Worcestershire sauce
1 teaspoon Escoffier sauce*

1 pinch Cayenne pepper
¼ teaspoon curry powder
¼ teaspoon powdered English mustard
Salt and pepper to taste
Small can of grated Parmesan cheese

Spread shrimp with butter in large flat pan. Cover with sauce made by mixing remaining ingredients, except cheese. Top with grated Parmesan cheese. Bake in middle of oven with broiler on until brown (15 to 20 minutes). Serve over the rice. Serves 4 to 6. This recipe can also be used with crab or lobster.

*Available at food specialty stores.

MRS. ROBERT T. COZART

SHRIMP WITH DILL

2 tablespoons butter
1 tablespoon chopped shallots
1 pound raw shelled shrimp

¼ cup dry white wine
1 ½ cups medium white sauce
½ tablespoon chopped fresh dill

Melt butter in sauce pan. Add shallots, shrimp and wine. Cover and simmer 5 minutes. Add white sauce and dill and simmer 5 minutes more. Serves 4.

MRS. BLAINE HOWELL

HARINA CON CAMARONES

1 cup yellow corn meal	1 chili pepper, chopped
6 cups water	1 clove garlic, chopped
1 teaspoon salt	1 tablespoon tomato paste
2 tablespoons olive oil	1 pound raw shrimp, peeled
1 onion, chopped	and deveined

Bring corn meal and water to boil. Add salt. Cook slowly. Put olive oil in skillet; add onion, pepper and garlic, and sauté slowly until onion is tender. Add tomato paste and shrimp, then simmer for a short time. Add this to the corn meal mixture and simmer over low heat until it thickens—about 1 hour. Serves 4. Serve in soup bowls.

MRS. JAMES E. WALL

SCALLOPED SHRIMP PIQUANT

3 cups cornflakes	1 teaspoon grated onion
1 cup mayonnaise	2 hard-boiled eggs, finely chopped
⅓ cup white table wine	½ teaspoon salt
½ teaspoon Worcestershire	⅛ teaspoon pepper
2 cups cooked, cleaned shrimp	6 thin slices lemon
½ cup finely diced celery	Dash of paprika

Crush cornflakes into fine crumbs. Combine mayonnaise, wine, and Worcestershire sauce. Cut shrimp into bite-size pieces. Add 2 cups cornflakes crumbs, celery, onion, eggs, mayonnaise mixture, salt, and pepper. Spoon into baking shells or individual casseroles. Sprinkle remaining cornflakes crumbs over shrimp mixture. Top each serving with a lemon slice; sprinkle with paprika. Bake in 400° oven about 20 minutes or until bubbly or lightly browned.

MRS. GLEN EVINS

SHRIMPS DE JONGHE

1 large clove garlic, grated	Paprika
1 teaspoon salt	4 tablespoons chopped parsley
¾ cup butter	¼ cup good sherry
1 cup bread crumbs	3 pounds boiled shrimp
Cayenne	

Mix garlic and salt. Cream butter; add garlic and salt, bread crumbs, seasonings, parsley, and sherry. Place alternate layers of shrimp and the bread crumb mixture in a buttered baking dish or individual shells. Bake in a hot oven 20 to 25 minutes. Serves 6 to 8.

THE CHATTERBOX, ST. PETERSBURG, FLORIDA

SHRIMP FLORIDAN EN PAPILOTE

2 pounds 21-25 count shrimp,
  or 4 dozen (this means 21-25
  to the pound)
8 ounces cream cheese
8 ounces bleu cheese
8 ounces sour cream

2 tablespoons finely chopped
  fresh garlic
4 tablespoons finely chopped
  fresh parsley
½ cup sauterne wine
6 wedges of lemon
6 pieces of 12 x 12 inch foil

Cook, peel, and clean shrimp and let cool. Blend together the cheeses and sour cream, being careful to get a smooth and even mixture. Add the chopped garlic and parsley, and mix in well. Add the wine. A bit more or less wine may be required to get the desired thickness of the mixture. Cheese sauce will thin with cooking, so do not thin too much. Place about 4 ounces of the mixture on a piece of foil; add 8 shrimp, or more if you so desire, and top with a piece of lemon. Fold over 2 sides of the foil, then the ends, so that a tight package is formed to prevent leaking. Bake the packages in the oven at 350° for about 10 minutes. Serves 6. Serve with baked potatoes as the cheese sauce from the shrimp is delicious on the potato.

THE GARDEN SEAT INN
CLEARWATER, FLORIDA

ARMSTRONG'S SHRIMP CREOLE

½ cup chopped white bacon
2 cloves chopped garlic
⅔ cup chopped celery
1 large onion
1 medium bell pepper
½ cup olive oil
1 large can Spanish tomatoes
2 6-ounce cans tomato paste

1 cup water
1½ teaspoons sugar
2 teaspoons Worcestershire sauce
½ teaspoon Tabasco
½ teaspoon monosodium glutamate
Salt and pepper to taste
2½ pounds raw cleaned shrimp

In a large heavy pan fry the bacon, garlic, celery, onion and bell pepper in the olive oil until the onion begins to turn (do not brown). Then add the rest of the ingredients except the shrimp. Let mixture come to a good boil, then simmer for 3 hours. Add shrimp and boil for 10 minutes. Must be served with rice. Serves 6 to 8.

MRS. HENRY HOLMES

CUBAN SHRIMP CREOLE

3 cloves garlic	1 small can brown gravy
2 onions	Salt to taste
2 green peppers	Dash of hot sauce
2 bay leaves	Dash of Lea and Perrins sauce
1 cup olive oil	1 1/2 pounds shrimp, cooked and
1 8-ounce can tomato sauce	cleaned

Chop fine the garlic, onions, green peppers and bay leaves. Sauté in olive oil. When browned add the tomato sauce, brown gravy, salt, hot sauce, and Lea and Perrins sauce, and let brown a little longer. Add shrimp and cook another 15 minutes. Serves 4. Serve over yellow rice in individual casseroles. Garnish with large French fried onion rings.

LAS NOVEDADES RESTAURANT
TAMPA, FLORIDA

SHRIMP WITH CANTONESE SAUCE

2 tablespoons shortening or	2 pounds raw shrimp (cleaned)
cooking oil	1/4 cup cornstarch (diluted with
1 clove garlic	1/4 cup water)
1/2 pound ground pork	3 teaspoons monosodium glutamate
1 teaspoon salt	3 eggs, well beaten
2 teaspoons cooking sherry	1 scallion

Heat shortening in 12-inch frying pan. Add crushed garlic, ground pork, and salt. Sauté 1/2 minute. Add sherry, shrimp, 4 cups water, and cook covered for 5 minutes. Add cornstarch and monosodium glutamate and mix well. When gravy thickens, add eggs and chopped scallion. Let simmer 1 to 2 minutes and blend well. Serve with boiled rice.

LAMAS SUPPER CLUB, TAMPA, FLORIDA

PINK ELEPHANT SAUTÉED SHRIMP

8 ounces (2 sticks) butter	1/2 teaspoon pepper
4 dozen shrimp, shelled and deveined	2 teaspoons paprika
1 teaspoon salt	3 teaspoons garlic salt
	1/3 cup good cooking sherry

Melt butter in saucepan. Sauté the shrimp and seasonings until almost done then, add sherry wine. Simmer until shrimp are done. Serve over toast points. Serves 6.

PINK ELEPHANT DINING ROOM
BOCA GRANDE, FLORIDA

SHRIMP WITH GREEN PEPPERS

6 tablespoons flour	1 clove garlic, diced
2 tablespoons grated cheese	½ cup olive oil
1½ teaspoons salt	6 medium green peppers
1 pound raw shelled shrimp	¼ cup dry white wine

Mix flour, cheese and 1 teaspoon salt in a paper bag. Add shrimp and shake until well-coated. In a skillet, crush garlic to a paste with ½ teaspoon salt, add olive oil and heat. Fry shrimp 5 minutes or until done, stirring frequently, and remove them. Stem and seed peppers and tear them into coarse chunks. Add peppers to the oil in which the shrimp were fried and brown over medium heat about 5 minutes. Lower heat, cover pan and cook for 20 minutes or until the peppers are completely soft. Add the shrimp and wine and bring to a boil. Serve to 4, with rice or spaghettini.

MRS. BLAINE HOWELL

PIERRE JACQUET'S SHRIMP LAMAR

2½ pounds shrimp	¼ stick sweet butter
½ pound fresh mushrooms	Flour
½ stick sweet butter	½ teaspoon salt
1½ ounces Scotch whiskey	¼ teaspoon Worcestershire
1 pint heavy cream	Tabasco (dash)

Boil shrimp, then shell them (Pierre does not de-vein the shrimp and it is better that way). Sauté shrimp and mushrooms in ½ stick of butter (in an electric skillet 350°). Add whiskey and light it. Add cream and stir while heating, but do not boil. Make paste of softened ¼ stick butter and flour and add with the remaining ingredients. Cook for 5 minutes.

MRS. HARLAN LOGAN

SHRIMP PIE

3 slices of bread cut ½ inch thick	½ teaspoon Worcestershire
1 cup milk	2 tablespoons sherry
2 cups peeled cooked shrimp	Mace and nutmeg to taste
2 tablespoons butter	(about ¼ teaspoon each)
¼ teaspoon black pepper	

Shrimp are cooked best when shelled, cleaned and put raw into a small amount of salted water to which a little powdered seafood seasoning has been added. Cook for 5 minutes. Soak the bread in the milk and mash with a fork. Add shrimp, butter and seasonings. Bake in a buttered casserole about 20 minutes in a 375° oven.

MRS. HENRY ROBERTSON, SR.

PORTUGUESE SHRIMP

2 cloves garlic, diced

1 teaspoon salt

6 peppercorns

1 pound raw shelled shrimp

2 bay leaves

2 tablespoons vinegar

Boiling water

2 tablespoons olive oil

Crush the garlic with salt and peppercorns. Add the shrimp, bay leaves and vinegar and marinate 10 minutes. Pour on enough boiling water to cover the shrimp and simmer gently 5 minutes or until done. Remove the shrimp and boil until the liquid evaporates, leaving only the pan scrapings. Add the oil to the pan, mix with the scrapings and when hot, fry the shrimp 5 minutes or until done, stirring frequently. Pour the sauce over. Serve 2.

MRS. BLAINE HOWELL

SHRIMP STUFFED EGGPLANT

2 4½-ounce cans deveined shrimp

½ cup chopped onion

¼ cup chopped green pepper

½ cup chopped parsley

2 cloves garlic, finely chopped

⅓ cup shortening

1 large eggplant

1 cup canned tomatoes

2 whole bay leaves

1 teaspoon salt

¼ teaspoon pepper

½ teaspoon crushed whole thyme

⅔ cup shrimp liquid

3 tablespoons butter or margarine, melted

¾ cup dry bread crumbs

Drain shrimp. Save liquid. Sauté onion, green pepper, parsley and garlic in shortening until tender. Wash and cut eggplant in half lengthwise and scoop out pulp, leaving about ¼-inch thickness around shell. Turn shells upside-down in a pan of cold water to prevent discoloration. Chop pulp. Add tomatoes, seasonings, shrimp liquid and chopped eggplant to onion mixture. Cover and simmer 10 minutes, or until eggplant is tender. Remove bay leaves. Add shrimp. Combine butter and crumbs. Fill shells with alternate layers of shrimp mixture and crumbs. Place in baking pan, adding a little hot water to prevent sticking. Bake in a hot oven (400°) for 35 to 40 minutes or until brown. Serves 6.

MRS. R. R. DUKE

SHRIMP WITH YELLOW RICE

½ cup Spanish olive oil
2 cloves of garlic
1 small Spanish onion
1 green pepper
1 pound peeled and deveined
raw shrimp

¾ cup whole tomatoes
1 pinch of saffron
1 tablespoon salt
½ teaspoon yellow coloring
2 cups seafood broth or water
1 cup of Valencia rice

Heat olive oil, sauté the chopped garlic, onion and green pepper in it; when half-done add the raw shrimp. When shrimp turn pink, add the tomatoes, saffron, salt, coloring and seafood broth or water. When mixture starts boiling, add 1 cup of Valencia rice. Bake in oven at 350° for 15 minutes. Garnish with peas, pimiento and parsley leaves. Serves 2.

COLUMBIA RESTAURANT, TAMPA, FLORIDA

Shellfish Combinations

BAKED CRAB AND SHRIMP

1 medium green pepper,
chopped fine
1 medium onion, chopped fine
1 cup celery, chopped fine
1 pound crabmeat

½ pound shrimp, cooked and cut up
½ teaspoon salt
⅛ teaspoon pepper
1 teaspoon Worcestershire
1 cup mayonnaise

Mix all ingredients together and place in shells. Bake or broil until slightly brown on top and thoroughly heated. Buttered bread crumbs may be placed on top before baking, if desired. Serve in individual large scallop shells. Serves 8.

COLUMBIA RESTAURANT, TAMPA, FLORIDA

SEAFOOD CRUNCH

1 10-ounce can frozen condensed
cream of shrimp soup
¼ cup mayonnaise
1 cup crushed potato chips
1 6½-ounce can crabmeat
(drained and flaked)

1 cup diced celery
½ cup diced onion
½ cup diced green pepper
1 teaspoon Worcestershire

Thaw shrimp soup and mix well with mayonnaise. Add ¾ cup crushed potato chips and remaining ingredients. Stir well. Turn into greased casserole and top with remaining ¼ cup crushed potato chips. Bake in 350° oven for 45 minutes. Makes four servings.

MRS. T. N. HENDERSON, JR.

NEW ORLEANS GUMBO FILÉ

1 large hen	1 dessert spoon salt
½ pound sliced ham	½ teaspoon pepper
1 tablespoon butter or lard	4 quarts water
1 tablespoon flour	2 pounds raw shrimp
1 large onion, chopped	½ pound claw crabmeat
Small bunch of parsley, chopped	1 pint oysters
Juice of 1 tomato or ½ cup	
tomato juice	

Clean and cut up hen. Cut ham into small pieces. Blend butter and flour in skillet. Add chicken and ham, brown for 10 minutes; add onion and parsley, tomato juice, salt and pepper. Cover with 4 quarts of water, and simmer for 2 hours. Cool, remove chicken from bones and return to soup. About half an hour before the meal, add raw shrimp, peeled and washed. About 5 minutes before serving, add crabmeat and oysters. Serve with boiled rice, letting each person sprinkle filé powder to his own taste

MRS. EUGENE MURPHY

SEAFOOD CASSEROLE I

1 pound fish (flounder, etc.)	1 pimiento, diced
6 tablespoons butter	Salt and pepper
1 pound shrimp, peeled and deveined	⅛ teaspoon thyme
½ pound crabmeat	⅛ teaspoon oregano
½ pint oysters	1 cup medium white sauce
½ pint scallops	Bread crumbs
1 can mushrooms	Parsley, chopped

Simmer flounder 5 minutes. Remove from bone. Sauté the other seafoods one at a time, each in a tablespoon of butter. In a large bowl mix mushrooms, pimiento, salt, pepper, thyme, oregano, and seafoods. Place ½ of mixture in large casserole and cover with ½ cup white sauce. Add remainder of mixture, then white sauce. Cover with bread crumbs, dot with butter. Place in 325° oven until crumbs are browned lightly. Sprinkle with parsley. Serve hot. Serves 6 to 8.

MRS. CHARLES C. BEVER, JR.

SEAFOOD CASSEROLE II

3 pounds shrimp
3 pounds lobster or crawfish
1 pound crabmeat
1 small carrot
1 small onion
2-inch piece celery stalk

Enough cheesecloth to tie up
vegetables and bay leaf
½ cup boiling water
1 bay leaf
1 teaspoon salt
⅛ teaspoon pepper

Shell and remove vein from shrimp. Place in ½ cup boiling water with cheesecloth bag of seasonings and simmer for 10 minutes. Remove from heat and allow to cool in liquid. Drop crawfish or lobster in large pot of boiling water to which 1 teaspoon of salt has been added. Boil for 10 minutes. Drain and allow to cool. Go through crabmeat carefully and remove any shell. Remove meat from lobster and cut into small pieces. Drain shrimp and cut into small pieces. Combine lobster, shrimp and crabmeat. Mix well. (Discard cheesecloth bag of seasonings.)

SAUCE:

4 tablespoons butter
⅓ cup flour
2 cups milk
1 cup light cream
½ pound Cheddar cheese, diced

½ to ¾ cup sherry wine
1 teaspoon salt
⅛ teaspoon pepper
⅛ teaspoon rosemary

Melt butter in 1½ quart sauce pan. Add flour. Remove from heat and mix thoroughly. Add milk and cream slowly, stirring constantly. Return to heat and continue stirring until sauce is thickened. Add cheese, sherry, and seasonings. Pour sauce over seafood and blend well. Put in 2 quart casserole and bake for 30 minutes in 350° oven. Serve hot. If casserole is made the day before, refrigerate until ready to bake, allow 40 minutes for baking. Serves 8.

MRS. VICTOR H. KNIGHT, JR.

SEAFOOD MORNAY

Line a shallow casserole with any cooked seafood—oysters, shrimp, crabmeat or flaked fish. Cover with Mornay Sauce. Broil in hot oven until the sauce blisters. Then serve in all its glory.

MORNAY SAUCE:

5 tablespoons butter
3 tablespoons flour
½ teaspoon salt
1 cup milk
½ cup white wine

½ cup sharp cheese, grated
3 dashes Tabasco
Dash of garlic powder
Pepper to taste
2 egg yolks

Melt butter. Blend in flour and salt. Add milk, wine, and cheese and cook until mixture thickens. Remove from heat; add seasonings and egg yolks. Beat well. Pour over seafood.

MRS. G. PIERCE WOOD, JR.

SEAFOOD DELIGHT

1 cup minced onion
3 tablespoons butter
3 tablespoons flour
1 teaspoon dry mustard
½ teaspoon oregano
¼ cup chopped chives (optional)
1 teaspoon salt
½ teaspoon pepper

½ teaspoon Tabasco sauce
1 teaspoon garlic powder
1 cup milk
1 cup cream
1 cup pre-cooked celery
1 pint oysters
1 pound boiled shrimp
1 pound crabmeat

Sauté onion in butter. Remove from heat and blend in a mixture of flour, mustard, oregano, chives, salt, pepper, Tabasco, garlic powder, milk and cream. Add celery. If more liquid is needed, use water in which celery was cooked. Heat oysters until the edges curl, then stir into mixture with shrimp and crabmeat. Place in clam shells or a large casserole and top with bread crumbs heated in butter. Bake 25 to 30 minutes in 350° oven. Serves 10.

MRS. WALTON N. HICKS, JR.

SHRIMP CASSEROLE II

6 hard-boiled deviled eggs
2 cups boiled or steamed shrimp
2 cups thin cream sauce
½ pound sharp yellow cheese
1 teaspoon salt

½ teaspoon pepper
1 teaspoon Worcestershire
½ teaspoon Tabasco
Buttered bread crumbs

Line greased casserole with eggs. Add shrimp· Cover with mixture of cream sauce and grated yellow cheese. Add salt, pepper, Worcestershire and Tabasco. Top with buttered bread crumbs and bake 30 minutes in 350° oven. Optional: Casserole may first be lined with cooked noodles or Chinese noodles. Serves 6.

MRS. J. E. McELMURRAY

CHAPTER XIII

Vegetables

In this area, where for twelve months a year fresh vegetables are only minutes away from the market, cooks are inclined to exchange fancy and elegant recipes because simple cooking of vegetables seems too easy to mention. Yet simple cooking is in a way our best. Who could ask for more than garden fresh, smooth yellow baby squash steamed in lightly salted water and dressed with butter and pepper? Or tender, young, green cabbage chopped and cooked the same way? Or tiny, olive-green pods of okra prepared exactly the same except for the addition of a dash of vinegar to the cooking water? What is better than fresh steamed broccoli dressed with lemon and butter?

Our way with beans and greens is the ultimate in simplicity. A one or two-inch square of salt pork is scalded, then cooked in boiling water for about an hour. Then a little salt is added along with the string beans, or field peas, or collard greens, or mustard greens, or turnip greens. Since the pork is already done, the vegetable need only be cooked until it is tender. We do not worry about limiting the amount of water to avoid loss of vitamins because we savor the "pot liquor" as much as the vegetable itself. It is our practice to serve these vegetables as side dishes and to dip up the juices with crisp, golden slices of hot, homemade cornbread. It is simple fare but utterly delicious.

LUNCHEON ASPARAGUS

3 tablespoons butter	1 3-ounce can button mushrooms, drained
3 tablespoons flour	1 14-ounce can asparagus spears, drained
1 cup warm milk	4 toasted English muffins
1 cup grated cheese	8 pieces crisp bacon
Salt and pepper	1/4 cup sherry, optional
1 onion, sliced thin	

Melt butter in double boiler. Add flour, blend, and cook for several minutes. Add milk gradually, stirring until thickened. Add cheese and allow to melt. Salt and pepper to taste. Add onion and mushrooms. Put asparagus on muffins. Pour sauce over this and sprinkle with bacon pieces. Sherry may be added to sauce before serving. Serves 4.

MRS. ROBERT COZART

ALCACHOFAS
(Artichokes)

4 artichokes
½ cup water
1 cup bread crumbs
2 cloves garlic

2 tablespoons grated cheese
2 sprigs fresh parsley
2 tablespoons olive oil

Wash and drain artichokes. Set aside. Mix all other ingredients thoroughly and sprinkle over and between leaves of artichokes. Place in frying pan and cover. Steam for 1 hour over low heat.

MRS. NORMAN GIOVENCO

KITTY'S HARVARD BEETS

5 tablespoons tart vinegar
6 tablespoons sugar
½ teaspoon salt
½ cup beet juice

1 or more tablespoons of
  lemon juice
2 rounded tablespoons flour
2 tablespoons butter
1 No. 2 can small whole beets

Mix vinegar, sugar, salt and juices and stir. Blend flour in melted butter and stir into liquid. Let simmer a few minutes before adding beets.

MRS. LAMAR SPARKMAN

SPARACHI
(Asparagus in sauce)

1 pound fresh or wild asparagus tips
2 eggs
1 cup bread crumbs
2 tablespoons grated Parmesan
  cheese
2 onions
3 cloves garlic

3 tablespoons olive oil
1 small can tomato paste
1½ cups water
1 large can tomatoes, strained
1 teaspoon salt
1 teaspoon sugar
Pepper to taste

Cut off tenderest tips of asparagus. Boil in salted water. Drain and chop. Mix with eggs, bread crumbs, and 1 tablespoon of grated Parmesan cheese. Put aside.

Sauté onions and garlic in olive oil in a large pot. Add tomato paste and ½ cup of water and cook, stirring frequently, for 15 minutes. Add strained tomatoes, rest of water, salt, sugar, and pepper, and the other tablespoon of grated Parmesan cheese. Cook for ½ hour, uncovered, and 1 hour, covered, at low heat. Stir periodically.

Meanwhile make patties of asparagus mixture, fry them in deep fat until golden brown and add sauce for last hour of cooking. May be served on spaghetti.

MRS. NORMAN GIOVENCO

BLACK BEANS

1 pound black beans (Blue Jay Brand, if possible)	½ cup olive oil
½ gallon water	¼ ham bone
1 large onion	3 bay leaves
3 green peppers	1 tablespoon salt
1 clove garlic	1 ounce white bacon
	½ cup vinegar

Wash beans thoroughly and soak overnight in water. Use this water for cooking. Fry slightly onion, green pepper and garlic in olive oil; combine all ingredients, except the vinegar which is added a few minutes before beans are ready to serve. Cook with slow fire until beans are tender and the liquid is of thick consistency.

VALENCIA GARDEN RESTAURANT,
TAMPA, FLORIDA

FEIJOADA COMPLETA

This is a traditional Brazilian dish which is served in the finest or most humble homes in Brazil.

3 cups dried black beans	2 garlic cloves, minced
1 pound hot sausages in casing	1 tablespoon salad oil
1 pound smoked tongue	1 teaspoon chili powder
1 pound dried beef cut in cubes	Salt and pepper to taste
¼ pound whole bacon	

Wash beans; place in pot; cover with cold water and let stand overnight. Cook beans in same water until they are tender (about 2 hours). Prepare meats by cutting tongue in large pieces, pricking sausages with a fork and placing them together with dried beef and white bacon in one large pot. Simmer the meats in a little water for about 2 hours and drain. Add meats to the beans. Brown garlic in oil. Add chili powder and 1 cup of cooked beans which have been mashed. Add this to the pot of meat and beans; simmer for 15 minutes.

To serve, meat may be taken out and put on a platter, while beans are served over fluffy rice. To complete the meal one can serve fresh orange sections, shredded greens and mandioca flour. The latter is sprinkled over all the food if desired. (If the dried beef is not available in your locality it may be omitted or corned beef may be substituted). This serves 8.

MRS. VERNER C. JORDAN, JR.

BLACK BEANS AND MEAT SAUCE

1 pound dried black beans	3 cloves garlic
1¾ teaspoons salt	1 cup olive oil
3 green peppers	1 can tomato soup
4 onions	2 pounds ground round steak

Wash beans thoroughly in plenty of water. Cover with water and ¼ teaspoon salt, to soak overnight. Next morning bring to boil, cook very slowly for 5 hours. Grind or chop fine the peppers, onions, and garlic. Place in frying pan with the olive oil, cover and sauté slowly. When beans have cooked 4½ hours, add half the pepper-onion mixture to the beans and simmer 30 minutes more. To other half of pepper-onion mixture add the tomato soup, meat and remaining teaspoon and a half of salt. Cover and cook slowly about 20 minutes or until meat is thoroughly done. Serve over rice, cooked very dry, and top with generous helpings of sauce. Amounts of green pepper, onion and garlic may be varied according to taste.

MRS. MARGARET KNAUF

BORDER BEANS
(For West Bend electric bean pot)

1 small package pinto beans	¼ teaspoon oregano
¼ pound salt pork, cubed	15 chili pequins crushed with the
10 large cloves garlic, thinly	end of a spoon (Spice Islands)
sliced	Salt to taste

Wash and pick over beans. Cover with 2 quarts of cold water and bring slowly to a boil on the stove; simmer for 45 minutes. Place bean pot on its hot-plate and plug in. Transfer beans to pot. Cook 1 hour (hot water should just cover beans) then add salt pork. Cook 1 hour, then add garlic. Cook 1 hour and add oregano and chili pequins. Cook about 11 more hours or until beans are bursting. Add salt 30 minutes before serving. I cook the beans for 24 hours. Serve in side dishes or miniature bean pots. Delicious with barbecue or picnic fare.

HARLAN LOGAN

BRUSSELS SPROUTS IN ONION CREAM

1½ pounds Brussels sprouts	2 tablespoons butter
½ cup chopped onion	1 pint sour cream

Steam Brussels sprouts for 15 minutes, or until tender. Sauté onion in butter until rich brown. Stir in sour cream and heat, stirring constantly. Add Brussels sprouts and mix well. Serves 6.

MRS. CLARE M. PHILLIPS, JR.

BAKED GARBANZO BEANS

2 large Spanish onions, sliced thin
2 tablespoons olive oil
2 16-ounce cans garbanzo beans
1 16-ounce can tomatoes

⅛ teaspoon salt
⅛ teaspoon pepper
2 tablespoons brown sugar
2 tablespoons flour

Sauté onions in oil until transparent. Add garbanzos, tomatoes, salt and pepper. Bring to a boil and stir in brown sugar. Thicken with flour which has been mixed smooth with some of liquid. (Should be very thick.) Put in 2-quart baking dish and bake for 1½ hours at 300°. Serves 8.

MRS. W. E. SUMNER

SPANISH BEAN POT

2 No. 2 cans red kidney beans
2 tablespoons bacon fat
1 large clove garlic, minced
⅛ teaspoon English thyme
⅛ teaspoon rosemary
1 small bay leaf
2 whole cloves
1 teaspoon salt
2 teaspoons dry mustard

¼ teaspoon Cayenne pepper
2 tablespoons strong cider vinegar
½ cup juice from pickled peaches,
    pears, or any canned fruit
    (not too sweet)
4 slices bacon
1 onion sliced thin
¼ cup strong black coffee
1 jigger brandy

Put beans in bean pot (pottery preferred). Mix together all other ingredients except bacon, onion, coffee, and brandy. Pour over beans, stir, and bake 1 hour in a 275° oven. Cover beans with onion, then bacon. Bake for 15 minutes longer in 400° oven. Add coffee and bake a few minutes more until the bacon is crisp. Add brandy and leave in hot oven until brandy is thoroughly heated. Serve piping hot. Serves 8 to 10.

MRS. MARY BROCKMAN

BROCCOLI DELUXE

1 large bunch broccoli or
    2 packages frozen
2 tablespoons butter

2 tablespoons sauterne
or other white wine

Steam broccoli until just tender. Drain. Add butter and wine and toss lightly. Serve immediately. This always tender broccoli has a hauntingly different flavor. Serves 4.

MRS. A. M. CROWELL, JR .

PRISCILLA'S RED CABBAGE

1 small head red cabbage
1 pint of water
½ cup fresh or canned seedless
   grapes
2 cooking apples, pared and sliced

1 small onion, chopped
2 tablespoons brown sugar
¾ tablespoons butter
¾ tablespoons flour
¾ teaspoons salt
⅓ cup claret

Shred cabbage and boil in water until tender. Place cabbage and liquid in casserole. Add remaining ingredients. Bake covered for 1 hour at 350°.

MRS. A. C. LIGGETT

STEAMED CARROTS

1 bunch of carrots
Water
¼ teaspoon salt

½ teaspoon sugar
1 tablespoon butter
1 sprig fresh mint

In a heavy-bottomed saucepan cook carrots, cut in Julienne strips, in small amount of water until just tender. Drain; add salt, sugar, and butter. Toss until butter melts; add sprig of mint; cover. Carrots will absorb the mint flavor. Remove mint sprig just before serving. Serve with lamb.

MRS. HUGH MACFARLANE

ORANGE CARROTS

2 bunches carrots
2 tablespoons butter
½ teaspoon salt
¼ teaspoon powdered cloves
Grated orange rind

4 oranges
1 tablespoon butter
½ cup sugar
¼ cup water

Cook carrots until tender, drain, and mash. Add butter, salt, cloves and grated rind from tops of oranges. While carrots are cooking, cut tops from oranges ¼ way down. Scrape pulp from them, reserving pulp from 2. Fill shells with carrot mixture and dot with butter. Heat pulp of 2 oranges with sugar and water. Place shells in baking dish, pour hot orange syrup over them. Bake in 400° oven for 15 minutes, basting often with syrup from pan. Delicious with broiled ham and cornbread. Serves 4.

MRS. PRESTON GARRETT

LUCHOW'S RED CABBAGE

3 ¼ to 4 pound head red cabbage
1 large or 2 small apples
2 tablespoons butter
1 medium onion, sliced
2 cups water
½ cup red wine vinegar
½ cup sugar

½ teaspoon salt
¼ teaspoon pepper
2 cloves
1 bay leaf
Juice of ½ lemon
1 ½ tablespoons flour

Wash cabbage. Shred as for coleslaw. Peel and slice apples. Melt butter in large sauce pan and sauté apples and onion gently 3 to 4 minutes. Stir in water, vinegar, sugar, salt, pepper, cloves, bay leaf, and lemon juice. Bring to a boil. Add cabbage and mix well. Cover and simmer 45 minutes or until tender. Sprinkle flour over top. Cover and simmer 5 minutes. Mix well and cook 5 minutes longer. Serves 6 to 8.

MRS. JAMES T. COWART

FLORIDA CARROTS

2 tablespoons butter
4 cups shredded carrots
  (1 average bunch)
1 minced onion

½ cup sauterne wine
2 teaspoons sugar
¼ teaspoon salt
⅛ teaspoon pepper

Melt butter in saucepan. Add carrots, onion, wine, sugar, salt and pepper. Cover and cook 15 minutes or until tender, or bake in a casserole in a moderate oven (350°) 25 to 30 minutes. Serves 6.

MRS. JAMES C. HOPPE

BEULAH'S SOUTHERN CORN PUDDING

9 ears fresh corn, grated
1 pint milk
1 ½ teaspoons salt

1 tablespoon sugar
2 tablespoons melted butter
4 eggs, separated

Add corn, milk, salt, sugar and butter to beaten yolks of eggs. Fold in stiffly beaten whites. Put in greased baking dish and cook for 1 hour in preheated oven at 350°. Time the baking to serve immediately. Good with any game. Serves 6.

MRS. FRED J. WOODS

CAULIFLOWER AU GRATIN

1 large head cauliflower	1 cup sharp Cheddar cheese
6 tablespoons butter	4 tablespoons minced parsley
4 tablespoons flour	1 tablespoon grated sweet onion
Salt	¼ teaspoon monosodium glutamate
Pepper	Cornflakes
2 cups cold milk	Paprika

Break cauliflower into flowerets. Soak in cold water ½ hour. Cook in salted boiling water about 15 minutes. Do not overcook. Drain. Blend butter and flour, add salt and pepper to taste; add cold milk; cook and stir to a smooth sauce. Add 1 cup (or more) sharp Cheddar cheese, parsley, onion and monosodium glutamate. Pour a small amount of sauce in bottom of casserole; then a layer of cauliflower. Continue, alternating layers of sauce and cauliflower, making the last layer sauce. Crumble a small amount of cornflakes and sprinkle on top. Shake paprika over all and bake 20 to 30 minutes in 375° oven. Serves 6 to 8.

MRS. STEPHEN M. SPARKMAN

IMAN BAYILDI
(Eggplant)

¼ cup rice	½ cup minced parsley
1½ cups boiling water	¼ cup fresh mint or 1 teaspoon
½ teaspoon salt	dried mint
¼ cup olive oil	½ cup raisins
1 large eggplant, peeled	½ cup slivered almonds
¾ cup minced onion	1½ cups canned tomatoes or 2 cups
½ cup minced green pepper	fresh tomatoes
1 clove garlic (minced)	Salt and pepper

Boil rice in 1½ cups boiling salted water about 15 minutes. Heat olive oil; add chopped egg plant, onion, green pepper, and garlic. Cook until tender. Add parsley, mint, raisins, nuts, and tomatoes. Combine with rice, salt and pepper. Put in greased casserole. Bake in 375° oven 40 to 60 minutes. Serves 6 or 8.

MRS. LARRY N. BOYD

ROASTED CORN

At the market place ask for unshucked fresh yellow corn. You can plan on 2 ears apiece, but I think some men will eat 3 or 4 ears. Pull outside leaves of corn down; take out silk; rinse well. Put plenty of butter on corn, pull up leaves and wrap heavy-duty aluminum foil tightly around corn.

This can be put on charcoal before meat is to be roasted and then put aside while meat is cooking; it will remain hot in foil.

My husband says the corn should be cooked a couple of minutes to each quarter of corn, which means to turn it every 2 minutes of cooking it, approximately 8 minutes in all. Be sure corn is placed in the charcoal.

Serve with plenty more butter and salt to hungry people.

MRS. M. LEO ELLIOTT, JR.

EGGPLANT CASSEROLE

½ medium onion, chopped
½ green pepper, chopped
3 stalks celery, chopped
2 tablespoons cooking oil
1 16-ounce can tomatoes, sieved

½ teaspoon Worcestershire sauce
½ teaspoon salt (or to taste)
⅛ teaspoon pepper
1 large eggplant
¼ pound Cheddar cheese, grated

Sauté first 3 ingredients in cooking oil until onion is golden. Add tomatoes, Worcestershire, salt, and pepper. Simmer. Peel and cube eggplant and cook in salted water until almost done but still firm. Drain and add to tomato mixture. Simmer about 5 more minutes. Turn into a buttered casserole, mix in ¾ of the grated cheese, and sprinkle the remaining cheese over the top. Dot with butter and bake about 15 minutes in a 350° oven or until the cheese is melted and bubbly. This may be prepared ahead and refrigerated until time to pop in the oven. Serves 6 or 8.

MRS. ROGERS MORGAN

HARVARD BEETS BURGUNDY

1 No. 2 can julienne beets
1 tablespoon cornstarch
½ cup sugar
⅛ teaspoon powdered cloves

Few grains of salt
½ cup Burgundy or claret wine
¼ cup wine vinegar
2 tablespoons butter or margarine

Drain beets, reserving ¼ cup liquid. Mix cornstarch, sugar, cloves, and salt in a saucepan; gradually add wine, wine vinegar, and ¼ cup beet liquid, stirring until mixture is completely smooth. Stir over medium heat until mixture is thickened and clear. Add butter and drained beets. Remove from heat, cover, and let stand 30 minutes to blend flavors. Serves 4 to 5.

MRS. ROBERT FOSTER

KAPOK TREE INN CORN FRITTERS

1 cup all-purpose flour, sifted
1½ teaspoons baking powder
1 tablespoon sugar
1 scant teaspoon salt

1 egg
¼ cup milk
½ cup whole kernel corn
Fat for deep frying

Resift flour, baking powder, sugar and salt together. Add egg, milk and corn. Stir until blended. Drop batter into fat a teaspoonful at a time. Maintain fat at 350° and fry until golden brown, turning once with a spoon to cook evenly. Remove fritters from fat and drain on paper towel. Serve piping hot on a warm platter. Sprinkle fritters with confectioners sugar before serving.

THE KAPOK TREE INN
CLEARWATER, FLORIDA

DEVILED EGGPLANT

1 eggplant
4 eggs
2 cups milk
1½ teaspoon salt
1 teaspoon sugar
Dash of pepper
⅓ cup pimientos, diced

⅓ cup onions, chopped
⅓ cup green pepper, chopped
2 cups bread crumbs
½ cup melted butter
2 teaspoons baking powder
Paprika

Peel and cook eggplant until tender. Drain and cool. This makes 1 quart of cooked eggplant. Beat eggs, add milk, salt, sugar, and pepper. Combine eggplant with pimientos, onion, green pepper. Add the egg mixture, fold in bread crumbs. Add butter and baking powder. Mix well. Pour into greased baking dish. Top with melted butter, sprinkle with paprika. Bake 20 to 30 minutes in 350° oven.

MRS. GEORGIA DIXON DUNLAP

GREEN LIMAS AND MUSHROOMS

1 package frozen baby Lima beans
1 3-ounce can sliced mushrooms
¼ cup chopped onion

½ teaspoon sugar
½ teaspoon salt
Dash of pepper
½ cup sour cream

Place Limas in saucepan. Drain mushrooms. Save liquid and add water to make ½ cup. Add to beans with onion, sugar, salt and pepper. Cover and bring to a boil. Then simmer 20 minutes. Uncover and cook until most of the liquid is gone. Add mushrooms and cream. Serves 4.

MRS. J. H. WILLIAMS, JR.

STUFFED EGGPLANT

1 large eggplant	2 tablespoons melted shortening
1 tablespoon minced onion	1 egg, well beaten
1 tablespoon minced green pepper	1 teaspoon salt
2 tomatoes (fresh or canned), diced	½ teaspoon pepper
	1 cup ground ham

Cut off stem end of eggplant. Boil whole eggplant 10 minutes or until tender. Split lengthwise and scrape out insides; mash and combine with all other ingredients. Replace in shells, sprinkle with buttered bread crumbs (½ cup crumbs, 1 tablespoon melted butter). Bake at 350° for 45 minutes.

MRS. HAROLD GREEN

STUFFED MUSHROOMS

1 pound large fresh mushrooms	1 clove garlic, chopped fine
2 tablespoons butter	½ teaspoon celery salt
¼ cup onion, chopped fine	¼ teaspoon freshly ground black pepper
¼ pound ground raw veal	1 tablespoon chopped parsley

Clean mushrooms; remove and chop stems. Melt butter in heavy skillet. Add mushroom stems, onion, veal, and garlic; brown lightly. Stir in seasonings, mixing well. Fill mushroom caps; place in greased shallow baking dish. Bake 20 to 25 minutes at 375°. Serves 5 or 6 as main dish, with sauce spooned over mushrooms.

SAUCE:

2 tablespoons butter	½ teaspoon celery salt
¼ cup onion, chopped fine	1 teaspoon Worcestershire sauce
1 clove garlic, chopped fine	1 tablespoon lemon juice
1½ tablespoons flour	½ cup sauterne (or other white wine)
¼ teaspoon dry mustard	½ cup commercial sour cream
½ teaspoon marjoram, crushed	

Melt butter, add onion and garlic, and brown lightly. Blend in flour, seasonings, and then wine. Cook over low heat, stirring, until thickened. Add sour cream just before serving. (To serve stuffed mushrooms on toast, add ½ cup milk to sauce to make it thinner.)

MRS. JOHN B. L'ENGLE, SR.

STUFFED VEGETABLES
(Fela)

1 head of cabbage	1 tablespoon salt
4 small yellow squash	1 teaspoon pepper
3 small tomatoes	1 tablespoon dried mint leaves
3 small green peppers	1 tablespoon dried parsley
1 pound ground beef	2 tablespoons lemon juice
4 tablespoons olive oil	3 slices bacon or slice of fat
4 tablespoons butter	from beef roast
2 onions, chopped	18 grape vine leaves (bought in
4 cloves of garlic	bottles)
⅔ cup rice (uncooked)	3 cups boiling water

Remove the core from a head of cabbage and place in a pot of boiling water. Cook for 5 minutes or until leaves separate. Cool cabbage and cut the larger leaves in 2 pieces, removing the heavy vein when necessary. Cover the bottom of a large kettle with the unused cabbage leaves. Cut off the thin part of the squash and the small stem end. Cut a small slice from the bottom of the tomatoes. Cut slice from top of peppers and remove the seeds. Carefully remove the pulp from the tomatoes and the squash; chop and add to the ground beef. Heat the oil and butter in a skillet and sauté the onions for 5 minutes. Add to the meat. Add the rice, salt, pepper, mint, parsley and lemon juice, mixing well with hands to blend. Carefully fill the tomatoes, squash and peppers with the meat mixture, replacing the slice of tomato when filled. Place the bacon or fat on top of cabbage in kettle and arrange the stuffed vegetables in the kettle, open end up. Using 1 tablespoon of the meat mixture for each leaf, fill about 12 cabbage leaves, by placing the meat on one end of leaf, turning in the sides and rolling into fingers. Place in the kettle with open end down, between the other vegetables. Wash the grape leaves in hot water, drain and fill as for cabbage leaves starting at the stem end of the leaf with the rough side in. If leaves are small, use two. Cover vegetables with remaining cabbage and vine leaves; weight down with a heavy plate; add 3 cups water and cover. Bring to a boil then simmer for about 1 hour or until the rice is tender. Drain off the liquid and add enough water to make 3 cups for lemon sauce. Serve assorted vegetables with hot lemon sauce.

LEMON SAUCE:
(Avogolemono Sauce)

2 eggs	1 teaspoon cornstarch
1 tablespoon water	3 cups liquid
¼ cup lemon juice	

Beat eggs well with rotary or electric beater adding water, lemon juice and cornstarch while beating. Slowly add the hot liquid from the cooked vegetables, stirring all the time. Cook over low heat, continuing to stir until thick.

Louis Pappas Restaurant,
Tarpon Springs, Florida

MUSHROOMS IN SOUR CREAM

1 pound fresh mushrooms
1 medium onion, minced
6 tablespoons butter
1 teaspoon salt
¼ teaspoon pepper

1 to 2 tablespoons flour
1 cup sour cream
½ teaspoon Worcestershire sauce
Chopped parsley

Wash mushrooms well; peel, chop stems. Sauté slowly with onion in butter until onion is transparent and golden. Season with salt and pepper, sprinkle lightly with flour. Stir gently to avoid bruising mushrooms. Cover and cook 5 minutes. Blend in sour cream and Worcestershire. Heat slowly. Serve at once. Garnish with parsley. Serves 4.

Mrs. Norman Stallings

RESIN BAKED POTATOES

Resin baked Idaho potatoes are excellent with charcoal broiled steaks. Your own outside barbecue grill is a perfect place to boil the resin for these potatoes.

Fill a large pot, can or bucket with resin (as you would fill a deep fat fryer with oil). Bring to a boil over low coals, being careful that it doesn't boil over! Tightly wrap medium-sized potatoes with heavy aluminum foil. Carefully drop into boiling resin. They will float when they are done, usually in about 35 or 40 minutes. Do not stick with fork to test. (You may want to cook one extra potato to test with fork). Serve these fluffy, mealy, delicious potatoes with whipped butter, sour cream, or your favorite sauce. After resin cools, it will harden. Leave in same pot or can, to be used over and over again. Resin can be purchased in most hardware stores.

Leo's, The House of Steaks
Tampa, Florida

OKRA AND TOMATOES

2 tablespoons salad oil
1 medium onion, chopped
¼ bell pepper, chopped (optional)
1 pound can tomatoes

1 tablespoon vinegar
Salt and pepper
2 pounds okra, sliced crosswise

In a skillet brown the onion and pepper in oil over medium heat until the onion is clear. Add tomatoes, vinegar, and salt and pepper to taste. Cover and simmer about 5 minutes. Add okra, cover and cook until tender.

MRS. E. C. DePURY

ONION PIE

4 large onions, chopped
2 tablespoons butter
3 eggs, slightly beaten
½ teaspoon salt

¼ teaspoon paprika
1 pint milk
1 unbaked 9-inch flaky pie shell

Sauté onions in butter until transparent. Put into pie shell. To slightly beaten eggs add salt, paprika, and milk. Pour mixture over the onions. Bake in 375° oven 15 to 20 minutes or until pie is golden brown. Good hot or cold. Serves 8 as hors d'eourves or 6 as main course.

MRS. W. E. ROBERTSON

CHEESE ONION BAKE

6 cups thinly sliced onion
   rings (about 6 medium onions)
¼ cup butter or margarine
¼ cup enriched flour
2 cups milk

½ teaspoon salt
⅛ teaspoon pepper
½ teaspoon monosodium glutamate
2 cups shredded sharp processed
   American cheese (½ pound)

Place onion rings in 1½-quart casserole. Melt butter in saucepan; blend in flour. Gradually stir in milk. Cook, stirring constantly, until thick. Stir in salt, pepper, monosodium glutamate and cheese. Pour over onions. Bake uncovered in 325° oven aboout 35 minutes. Serves 4 to 6.

MRS. ALONZO REGAR

FRENCH PEAS

4 tablespoons butter   ½ small head lettuce, shredded
1 onion, finely chopped   ½ cup bouillon or stock
2 pounds fresh peas

Melt 3 tablespoons butter in bottom of saucepan. Sauté onion in butter until soft. Add peas, shredded lettuce and stock. Cover peas closely and simmer for 10 to 15 minutes. Add remaining tablespoon of butter and serve.

Mrs. E. B. Bradford

PAPAS RELLENAS
(Stuffed Potatoes)

POTATO MIXTURE:

2 cups mashed potatoes (mash   1 egg
   with very little milk and some   1 cup bread crumbs
   butter)   Salt and pepper to taste

MEAT FILLING:

1 onion, chopped   1 small can tomato paste
1 clove garlic, crushed   1 cup water
1 small green pepper, chopped   ½ teaspoon salt
2 tablespoons olive oil   ½ teaspoon sugar
1 pound ground beef   1 8-ounce can tomato sauce

Set aside mashed potaoes. Put egg in deep dish and beat it. Put bread crumbs on platter with some salt and pepper and set aside.

For filling, sauté onion, garlic, and green pepper in olive oil until tender. Stir in meat and cook until no longer red. Add tomato paste and ½ cup of the water with salt and sugar. Cook, stirring frequently, for 15 minutes. Add can of tomato sauce and rest of water. Cook for 15 minutes uncovered, then for ½ hour covered. Cool.

When ground meat filling is cool, scoop a mound of mashed potatoes in hand and press to form indentation. Fill scoop with 1 to 1½ tablespoons of ground meat filling. Cover with another flattened mound of mashed potatoes (forms rounded potato with filling inside). Roll in beaten egg then in bread crumbs and fry in deep fat.

Mrs. Norman Giovenco

FRIED ONION RINGS

2 large onions	1 cup flour
1 egg	1 teaspoon salt
1½ cups milk	¼ teaspoon pepper

Mild sweet onions are best for frying. Slice onions crosswise in thin slices, separate into rings. Beat egg slightly, add milk. Add salt and pepper to flour, mix thoroughly. Dip onion rings into milk mixture, then in flour. Fry in deep hot fat (360° to 375°) until lightly browned. Drain on absorbent paper. Sprinkle with salt. This amount of milk and flour mixture will dip at least four large onions, but a smaller amount makes dipping difficult.

A. M. CROWELL, JR.

SCALLOPED POTATOES A LA JIFFY

6 medium potatoes (about 2 pounds)	1 teaspoon salt
2 tablespoons butter	⅛ teaspoon black pepper
⅓ cup chopped onion	½ cup (about 2 ounces) grated
1 cup thick sour cream, commercial	sharp Cheddar cheese

Wash potatoes, cook, covered, in boiling salted water to cover 25 to 35 minutes, or until tender. Drain the potatoes and shake in the pan over low heat. Peel and cut into ¼-inch slices. Arrange potato slices in neat, close layers in a buttered 1½-quart casserole. Heat butter in saucepan over low heat. Add onion and cook until tender. Blend onion with sour cream, salt, and pepper. Spoon sour cream mixture over potatoes in casserole. Top with grated cheese. Bake at 350° for about 35 minutes. Serves 6.

LEISURE HOUSE, TAMPA ELECTRIC COMPANY

SPINACH PARMESAN

3 pounds spinach	1 teaspoon salt
6 tablespoons Parmesan cheese	⅛ teaspoon pepper
6 tablespoons minced onion	½ teaspoon monosodium glutamate
6 tablespoons heavy cream	½ cup buttered bread crumbs
5 tablespoons melted butter or margarine	

Cook the spinach until tender. Drain thoroughly. Add other ingredients except crumbs. Arrange in shallow baking dish and top with buttered crumbs. Bake in hot oven (450°) 10 to 15 minutes. Serves 6.

MRS. ALONZO REGAR

BAKED POTATOES STUFFED WITH TUNA

6 baking potatoes
1 cup milk
½ stick butter or margarine
2 7-ounce cans tuna
1 onion, finely chopped

1 small green pepper
  (finely chopped)
Salt and pepper
½ cup sharp Cheddar cheese

Bake potatoes; scoop out of shell and whip with milk and butter as for mashed potatoes. Mix in flaked, well-drained tuna, onion, and green pepper. Add salt and pepper to taste. Fill shells heaping full with potato-tuna mixture and bake 30 minutes. Remove from oven and top with grated cheese. Return to oven until cheese is thoroughly melted. Serve piping hot. May be prepared ahead and heated at the last minute. Salmon or crab may be substituted for the tuna. Yields 8 to 10 servings.

MRS. ROBERT MAURAIS

SWEET POTATO PUDDING

2 eggs
1 cup sugar
2 cups grated sweet potatoes

½ stick of butter
1 cup sweet milk
½ teaspoon nutmeg

Beat eggs and sugar until light and creamy. Add other ingredients and pour into a buttered pan or glass baking dish. Cook 45 minutes in a moderate oven (350°). When it browns on top, stir and let brown again. This is an excellent dish served with ham. Serves 6.

MRS. ANSLEY WATSON

SQUASH CASSEROLE I

2 pounds squash
½ cup chopped onion
½ cup chopped bacon (cooked)
  or ham

1 cup grated American or
  Cheddar cheese
1 teaspoon salt
½ teaspoon pepper
¾ cup bread crumbs

Clean and slice squash. Cook squash in enough water to cover for 15 minutes. While squash is cooking, fry bacon. Sauté onion in bacon fat until soft, not brown. Drain fat off. Drain and mash squash and combine with onion, bacon, and cheese. Salt and pepper to taste. Cover with bread crumbs. Bake in 350° oven for ½ hour before serving. Serves 8.

MRS. JERRY FOGARTY, JR.

SQUASH CASSEROLE II

3 pounds yellow squash
Butter to taste
Salt and pepper to taste

1 cup grated imported Swiss cheese
1 ½ cups Cuban bread crumbs
Slivered almonds

Cook diced squash in small amount of salted water until barely tender. Drain; add butter, salt, pepper, cheese, and bread crumbs. Mix all ingredients lightly. Top with almonds. Bake 1 hour at 300°.

MRS. LEE WARD

ZUCCHINI CASSEROLE

1 cup red Italian onion rings
1 cup green pepper strips
¼ cup butter
2 cups zucchini, cut in 1-inch slices

4 tomatoes, peeled and
    cut in wedges
Salt and pepper
Parmesan cheese

Sauté onion rings and pepper strips in butter. When vegetables begin to take color add zucchini and sauté about 5 minutes longer. Add tomatoes and cook until tomatoes are soft (about 5 minutes). Season with freshly ground black pepper and salt. Turn the vegetables into a casserole and sprinkle with Parmesan cheese. Just before serving time, bake the casserole in a moderately hot oven (375°) until topping browns and vegetables are hot.

MRS. REGAR HICKMAN

SWEET SOUR GREEN BEANS

2 pounds green beans
¼ cup water
1 tablespoon fat
2 tablespoons onion, grated

½ cup vinegar
2 tablespoons sugar
½ teaspoon salt
¼ teaspoon pepper

Wash and trim ends from beans. Cut into Julienne strips and place in 2-quart saucepan with ¼ cup water. Cook 25 to 30 minutes or until beans are tender. Melt fat in a separate pot, add grated onion, vinegar, vegetable liquid (drained from beans), sugar and seasonings. Bring to a boil and pour over green beans.

Variation: Use 1 tablespoon bacon drippings for the fat and crumble bacon on top of beans just before serving. Serves 6.

MRS. J. P. CORCORAN

STRING BEANS JULIENNE
A LA FRANCOIS

1 pound fresh string beans
2 tablespoons butter
½ teaspoon salt

½ teaspoon chervil
½ cup water

Wash and string beans. Cut into narrow lengthwise strips. Combine ingredients and steam in a covered pot over low heat for 30 minutes.

Mrs. Guy R. Webb

BAKED STUFFED TOMATO

8 tomatoes
1 large onion, minced
2 tablespoons butter
1 cup sliced mushrooms

1 cup chicken livers
1 cup cooked wild rice
Bread crumbs
Parsley

Scoop out tomatoes and save pulp. Cook onion in butter until tender. Add mushrooms and livers. Cook 5 to 10 minutes. When done chop chichen livers. Add pulp that has been scraped out of tomatoes. Cook until softened, add rice and simmer until most of moisture has been cooked away. Stuff in tomatoes. Cover top with crumbs. Put in pan with a little hot water. Bake 15 to 20 minutes in moderate oven. Decorate top with parsley buds.

Mrs. Grace Logan

SCALLOPED CHEESE TOMATOES

½ cup Pepperidge Farms Stuffing
1 No. 2 ½ can tomatoes
1 tablespoon butter
1 tablespoon bacon drippings
¼ teaspoon garlic salt

½ teaspoon Lawry's salt
2 teaspoons sugar
¾ cup grated Cheddar cheese
1 cup thinly sliced onion
¼ teaspoon oregano

Place a layer of stuffing in a buttered shallow baking dish. To the tomatoes add the butter, drippings, salts and sugar. Cover stuffing with a layer of tomatoes, then a layer of cheese, then onion. Repeat, ending with cheese on top. Sprinkle with oregano. Bake for half hour at 350°.

Mrs. Louis M. Saxton

STRING BEANS SPECIAL

2 10-ounce packages frozen
French-style green beans
2 tablespoons butter
½ cup minced onion
6 ounces slivered almonds
2 tablespoons flour
2 teaspoons salt

½ teaspoon pepper
½ teaspoon dry mustard
1 teaspoon Worcestershire sauce
Garlic powder (optional)
1 cup milk
1 cup thick sour cream
4 ounces sharp Cheddar cheese,
about 1 cup grated

Cook beans until just tender. Melt butter in a saucepan. Add onion and almonds and cook over medium heat, stirring occasionally. Cook until onion is transparent. Remove from heat and blend in flour, salt, pepper, mustard, Worcestershire sauce and garlic powder. Heat until mixture bubbles. Remove from heat and gradually add milk and sour cream, stirring constantly. Cook over low heat, stirring constantly, 2 or 3 minutes longer. Do not boil. Drain beans and add to sauce. Toss gently until well-coated with sauce. Turn into baking dish. Sprinkle with the grated cheese. Bake at 350° 10 to 15 minutes. Serve piping hot. Serves 6 to 8.

MRS. WALTON HICKS, JR.

SUPREME VEGETABLE CASSEROLE

1 5-ounce box fresh mushrooms
¼ cup butter (extra butter will be
needed for browning almonds)
1 small onion, grated
3 tablespoons flour
2 cups warm milk
4 ounces sharp Cheddar cheese, cubed
1 teaspoon soy sauce

½ teaspoon salt
¼ teaspoon pepper
½ teaspoon monosodium glutamate
½ cup slivered almonds
2 packages cooked frozen
French green beans
1 3-ounce can water chestnuts
(drain and slice)

Wash mushrooms, separate caps and stems; sauté mushrooms in butter, add grated onion. Cook slowly 10 minutes or until mushrooms are tender, stirring constantly. Remove from pan. Add flour to the butter; cook, stirring until well-blended, and add 2 tablespoons more butter if necessary. Add warm milk gradually. Cook to consistency of cream sauce. Add to sauce: cheese, soy sauce, salt, pepper, and monosodium glutamate. Blend in well.

Sauté slivered almonds in butter until light brown. In casserole dish put layer each of cooked French beans, mushrooms, water chestnuts, and sauce; repeat until all are used. Top with slivered almonds. Cook in 350° oven for 30 minutes or until it bubbles. Tabasco, ¼ to ½ teaspoon, may be added if desired. Serves 4 to 6.

MRS. WHITING PRESTON

VEGETABLE SURPRISE

Per Serving:

1 medium potato, quartered
1 large onion slice
1 slice bell pepper
1 tomato, cut in large wedges

1 carrot, quartered
2 tablespoons butter
Salt and pepper to taste

Place vegetables neatly on a sheet of foil. Add butter, salt and pepper. Wrap in foil, making each package air tight, so that the vegetables will steam in their own juices. Place in oven and bake 1 hour at 400°. When cooked, open top of package and serve in the foil, one package per person. Especially good with barbecue or charcoal broiled steaks.

MRS. O. W. FOSTER

HERBED ROASTING EARS

6 ears sweet corn, husked
¼ cup soft butter
1 teaspoon dried rosemary
  or 1 tablespoon fresh

½ teaspoon dried marjoram or
1½ teaspoons fresh
1 small head romaine lettuce,
  freshly rinsed

Spread corn with mixture of butter with herbs. Wrap each ear in 2 or 3 leaves romaine; place in shallow baking dish. Cover tightly with foil. Bake in oven at 450° for 20 to 25 minutes.

LEISURE HOUSE, TAMPA ELECTRIC COMPANY

HOME BAKED BEANS

2 12-ounce packages Great
  Northern Beans
1 large onion, peeled
1 pound white bacon

1 level teaspoon black
  pepper (use it all)
½ cup brown sugar
½ cup white sugar
½ teaspoon dry mustard

Wash beans and cover generously with water to soak overnight. Cook in the same water, add onion, white bacon, and pepper. When the beans and pork are tender, but still juicy, season with sugars and mustard. Add salt to taste. Pour in large casserole. Thinly slice the white bacon and spread over top of beans. Sprinkle white sugar over the bacon. Bake at 300° for at least 2 hours, the longer the better. Add water as necessary to keep moist.

MRS. ELIZABETH L. SAXTON

CHAPTER XIV

Desserts

Practically everyone has an old cookbook in the family which was handed down from mother to daughter for several generations. When we began to compile this book we found these old notebooks a mine of information. The majority of recipes pertained largely to desserts, cakes, and pies because these were, naturally, the more complicated recipes. As the recipes came in to us, it was amazing to see the varied origins of them and the many ways they had been adapted to make use of the native products.

Sherbet recipes called for mangoes, oranges, lemons, and limes. Shortcakes were made with oranges and grapefruit as well as the more familiar strawberries and peaches. Still, strawberry shortcake is a particular delicacy of the region because the little town of Plant City, only 25 miles from Tampa, is a strawberry growing center. In December and January the large, luscious berries are ripe and ready for the markets. For a small fee you can pick your own berries in the fields and lay in a store of jellies and jams for the year. Fresh strawberry ice cream can be made and eaten at once or packed in the freezer for enjoyment in the hot summer months. It's a joy to have fresh fruits when the weather is cool, and the urge and energy to cook are strong within you.

Be sure to try the Spanish recipe for Flan de Leche which is smooth, rich egg custard molded on a caramel base. It is served upside down with the creamy caramel uppermost. A satiny treat.

Desserts

APPLE CRISP

4 to 6 apples	¾ teaspoon salt
1 cup flour	1 unbeaten egg
1 cup sugar	⅓ cup melted butter
1 teaspoon baking powder	Cinnamon

Peel and core apples. Slice thin and place in a 6 x 10-inch greased baking dish. Sift together flour, sugar, baking powder, and salt. Mix with unbeaten egg. This forms a crumb mixture. Spread over apples; then pour melted butter over the top. Sprinkle with cinnamon. Bake in 350° oven 30 to 40 minutes.

MRS. GARRETT W. JUDY

ENGLISH TOFFEE SQUARES

1 cup of rolled vanilla wafers
1 cup chopped pecans
1 cup powdered sugar
½ pound butter

3 eggs separated
1½ squares bitter chocolate,
 melted
½ teaspoon vanilla

Roll vanilla wafers into crumbs and mix with chopped pecans. Using half of this mixture, cover bottom of buttered 9 x 9-inch pan. Cream butter and sugar. Add beaten egg yolks to cooled melted chocolate and vanilla. Fold in beaten egg whites. Pour in pan and spread remaining wafer-nut mixture over top. Refrigerate overnight and serve with whipped cream topping. This makes 8 generous servings.

MRS. GRACE LOGAN

CANDIED ORANGE CREAM

2 3-ounce packages cream cheese
1 pint heavy cream
1 teaspoon sugar

3 tablespoons chopped, candied
orange peel

Mash cream cheese. Add a little heavy cream to soften, then add remainder of 1 pint cream and whip until thick. Add sugar, continue beating and when stiff, add chopped candied orange peel. Serve with fresh strawberries or raspberries, or with pears poached in grenadine.

MRS. PRESTON GARRETT

SPANISH CUSTARD
(Flan de Leche)

3 cups of sugar
½ cup water
6 eggs
1 teaspoon vanilla

¼ teaspoon anisette, scant
Pinch of salt
1 pint of boiling milk

Boil 1 cup of sugar and ½ cup of water until brown, then pour the caramel into 6 molds. Beat eggs, add 2 cups of sugar, vanilla, anisette, salt and beat again. Add boiling milk little by little, then strain through cloth or china colander. Pour mixture into custard cups, put cups in water-filled pan and bake for 30 minutes in 350° oven (don't let water boil, or custard will be filled with holes). Cool in refrigerator. When ready to serve, press edges of custard with spoon to break away from mold, then turn upside down. The caramel then tops the custard. Serves 6.

COLUMBIA RESTAURANT, TAMPA, FLORIDA

GRANDMOTHER'S BOILED CUSTARD

2 quarts sweet milk
8 egg yolks, beaten

2 scant cups sugar
4 teaspoons vanilla or brandy
    to taste

Pour milk into double boiler and place over boiling water. Beat egg yolks until spongy and slowly add the sugar, beating well. Add a small amount of the hot milk to the mixture and mix until smooth. Slowly add this to the rest of the milk, stirring constantly until it is as thick as desired. Do not let the mixture boil at any time. When cool add vanilla or brandy. Serve in punch or eggnog cups.

MRS. LINUS W. HEWIT

GRAPEFRUIT SHORTCAKE

2 grapefruit   2 tablespoons sugar

Section grapefruit. Place in earthen or glass bowl, and sprinkle with just enough sugar to sweeten (about 2 tablespoons). Set aside until ready to use.

DOUGH:

2 heaping tablespoons sugar
3 cups Bisquick

Sweet milk, ½ to ¾ cup
Butter

Add sugar to Bisquick. Add enough sweet milk to make a soft dough. Do not roll out, but spread in well-greased baking pan so that thickness of dough when baked will not exceed 1 inch. Dot with butter. Bake in 450° oven until brown, or about 20 minutes.

SAUCE:

1 cup sugar
1 rounded tablespoon flour
    or cornstarch
1 heaping tablespoon butter

2 cups boiling water
1/16 teaspoon salt
½ teaspoon nutmeg

Over low heat blend thoroughly sugar, flour, and butter. Slowly add 2 cups boiling water. Remove from heat; add salt and nutmeg.

Split each serving of cake into layers. Put grapefruit between layers and on top. Spoon over the sauce. Serves 6 and is good either hot or cold.

MRS. W. F. EDWARDS

MERINGUES

2 egg whites
3 drops vinegar
½ teaspoon water

⅛ teaspoon salt
½ cup granulated sugar
½ teaspoon vanilla

Beat whites until stiff. Add vinegar, water, and salt. Beat slightly, then add sugar very gradually. Add vanilla. Beat until stiff but not dry. Drop spoonfuls of meringue on a greased cookie sheet, shaping with spoon to depress center and build up sides. Cook for 1 hour at 250°. Cool slowly. Serve filled with ice cream or fruit. This makes 6 to 8 meringues. They keep well in an airtight tin.

MRS. JAMES H. KENNEDY

MERINGUE FILLING

5 Heath bars

½ pint whipping cream

Thoroughly chill 5 Heath bars. Break in pieces and put into electric blender one at a time. Add whipping cream to blended Heath bars in blender and mix to consistency of whipped cream. This makes enough filling for 8 large or 40 teaspoon-size meringues. This will freeze well.

MRS. W. BRAXTON SCHELL

ORANGE SOUFFLÉ

3 tablespoons butter
3 tablespoons flour
¾ cup milk
½ cup granulated sugar
Dash of salt

¼ cup fresh orange juice
1 tablespoon grated orange rind
4 eggs, separated
Sugar

Melt butter in a saucepan over low heat; add flour and stir until smooth. Slowly add milk, stirring constantly, until smooth and thickened. Add sugar, salt, orange juice and grated orange rind; blend well and cook 3 to 4 minutes longer. Remove from heat; cool slightly. Beat egg yolks until light and lemon-colored. Stir into mixture. Beat egg whites until stiff but not dry; fold into mixture. Pour mixture into an ungreased 1½ quart casserole or baking dish. Set baking dish in pan of warm water and bake at 350° for 45 to 50 minutes. Five minutes before cooking is completed, sprinkle a little granulated sugar over soufflé.

MRS. STANLEY CAMPBELL

INDIAN RICE

1½ cups rice	2 cloves
3 cups water	2 tablespoons raisins
¼ teaspoon whole saffron or	2 tablespoons unsalted pistachio
⅛ teaspoon ground saffron	nuts
½ teaspoon salt	2 tablespoons cashews, Brazil nuts,
1 cup sugar	or filberts
2 cups water	2 tablespoons blanched almonds
¾ cup butter or margarine	1 tablespoon lemon juice

Boil rice in 3 cups of water with saffron and salt for 10 minutes. Drain. Boil sugar in 2 cups of water for 1 minute, stirring constantly. Set aside. Melt butter in heavy saucepan. Add cloves and simmer for 10 minutes. Add rice and 1½ cups sugar syrup. Mix well. Simmer for 10 minutes, stirring frequently. Add remaining ingredients and simmer for 15 minutes, or until rice is done, stirring once or twice. If mixture becomes too dry, add remaining syrup. Remove from heat, cover, and let stand for 15 minutes. Serve warm or cold. If desired, serve with whipped cream. Serves 6.

MRS. CLARE M. PHILLIPS, JR.

ORANGE TROPICALE

6 large oranges	½ cup dried figs, chopped
1 cup sifted cake flour	6 marshmallows, diced
1 teaspoon baking powder	3 tablespoons chopped almonds
¼ teaspoon salt	or cashew nuts
3 tablespoons butter	3 tablespoons chopped, shredded
4 tablespoons sugar	coconut

To make orange cups, wash oranges and cut a 2-inch thick slice off bud end. Carefully remove all pulp and juice from cups. Measure out 1 cup juice. Save pulp for other uses. To make filling, sift together flour, baking powder and salt. Sift again. Work butter and sugar together until fluffy. Beat in flour mixture alternately with ⅓ cup of the orange juice. Fold in figs, marshmallows, nuts and coconut. Fill each orange shell half full of batter. Set orange cups in a baking dish and bake in a moderately hot oven (375°) about 45 minutes, or until centers puff. Meantime, chill the remaining ⅔ cup of orange juice. Remove orange cups from oven; spoon chilled juice over hot filling. Serve while warm.

MRS. CLARE M. PHILLIPS, JR.

SAUCY CHEESE CAKE DESSERTS

⅓ cup sugar	1 8-ounce package cream cheese
2 tablespoons cornstarch	2 eggs
¼ teaspoon salt	½ cup sugar
1½ cups unsweetened pineapple juice	¼ teaspoon salt
	½ cup milk
¼ teaspoon grated lemon peel	½ teaspoon vanilla
1 tablespoon lemon juice	⅓ cup sliced pecans

Mix sugar, cornstarch and salt; add pineapple juice and cook, stirring until thick and clear. Add lemon peel and lemon juice. Pour mixture into dessert-size baking dishes. To softened cream cheese add eggs one at a time and beat until smooth after each addition; add sugar and salt. Stir in milk and vanilla. Spoon this mixture over the mixture in dessert dishes. Sprinkle with sliced pecans. Bake at 325° until set. Cool before serving. Serves 6.

MRS. BERNARD WILSON

SHERRIED BANANAS IN WINE SAUCE

6 bananas	Few grains of freshly grated nutmeg
Juice of 1 or more lemons	
2 egg yolks	2 egg whites
¼ cup sugar	Dash of salt
¼ cup sherry	¾ cup cream, whipped
Grated rind of 2 lemons	

Diagonally slice bananas in ½-inch slices and arrange in an attractive pattern in shallow serving casserole. Squeeze a generous amount of lemon juice over them and let stand for 30 minutes. Beat egg yolks thoroughly, adding sugar and sherry. When quite smooth, add grated rind and nutmeg. Fold in egg whites, which have been beaten stiff but not dry, with salt. Fold in whipped cream and pile mixture on top of bananas. Bake at 325° for 30 minutes. Serve from casserole and pour over sauce.

SAUCE: Cream together;

½ cup butter	Dash of salt
½ cup powdered sugar	3 tablespoons sherry

Top with freshly grated nutmeg. Spoon over casserole. Serves 6.

MRS. CHARLES LYLES

SWEDISH APPLECAKE WITH VANILLA SAUCE

4 tablespoons butter	1 ⅓ cups apple sauce
2 cups zwieback crumbs or stale Swedish limpa, grated	

Melt butter in skillet, add crumbs and stir until nicely browned. Butter baking dish or 8-inch pie pan. Alternate layers of crumbs and apple sauce, placing crumbs on top. Bake in moderate oven (375°) 25 to 35 minutes. Cool before unmolding and serve with Vanilla Sauce.

VANILLA SAUCE:

3 egg yolks	2 teaspoons vanilla
2 tablespoons sugar	1 cup whipped cream
1 cup cream, heated	

Beat egg yolks and sugar in top of double boiler. Add heated cream and cook until thick, stirring constantly. Remove from heat, add vanilla and cool, beating occasionally. When cooled, fold in whipped cream carefully and serve. This serves 6 to 8.

MRS. BENGT TJERNSTROM

BISHOP WHIPPLE PUDDING

½ cup sugar	1 cup dates, cut
⅛ teaspoon salt	⅔ cup flour
2 eggs	1 teaspoon baking powder
1 cup broken nut meats	1 teaspoon vanilla

Add sugar and salt to beaten eggs. Add nuts, dates and flour, sifted with baking powder to mixture. Add vanilla. Spread in greased and floured 8 x 10-inch pan. Bake at 350° 30 to 35 minutes.

SAUCE:

¾ stick butter	1 tablespoon hot water
1½ cups dark brown sugar	4 tablespoons evaporated milk
Pinch of salt	1 teaspoon vanilla

Melt butter. Add sugar and salt. Stir over low heat until dissolved. Add hot water and stir until thoroughly dissolved. Remove from heat, cool slightly. Slowly add milk and vanilla. Cut pudding into servings. Split each piece and add 2 or 3 tablespoons of the warm sauce and top with generous helping of whipped cream. This serves 10 or 12.

MRS. STEPHEN M. SPARKMAN

CASSAVA PUDDING

4 cups of cassava which has been
   peeled, grated, soaked in water,
   and then drained
3 cups sweet milk
3½ cups sugar
1 teaspoon vanilla

1½ sticks butter
6 eggs
¼ teaspoon salt
2 cans evaporated milk
2 cans coconut

Mix all ingredients and bake at 350° for 30 or 40 minutes. If the mixture is divided in half it makes two 13 x 9-inch pans. Serve as a dessert or as a vegetable at a barbecue.

Mrs. J. Brown Farrior

DELICIOUS LEMON PUDDING

1 tablespoon melted butter
4 tablespoons sugar
2 eggs, separated

Grated rind and juice of 1 lemon
1 cup milk

Mix together butter, sugar, beaten egg yolks, grated rind and juice. Add milk and fold in beaten egg whites. Put in baking dish or custard cups and bake in pan of hot water about 30 minutes in 325° oven.

Mrs. Alonzo Regar

OLD-FASHIONED PUDDING

4 cups sweet potatoes
2 eggs
½ cup brown sugar
½ cup white sugar
½ cup milk

4 tablespoons butter
1 teaspoon ginger
½ teaspoon cinnamon
¼ teaspoon nutmeg
½ teaspoon salt

Grate or grind sweet potatoes. Add slightly beaten eggs, then add sugars, milk, butter and spices. Bake mixture in iron skillet in 325° oven about 2 hours. Remove frequently and stir from bottom until pudding is dark all through. Serve with hot lemon sauce or cream.

Mrs. Ben Corvette, Jr.

B A K L A V A

5 cups sugar
5 cups water
1 tablespoon honey
Juice of 1 lemon

1 pound blanched almonds,
    chopped fine
½ teaspoon grated nutmeg
1 pound pastry sheets (Phyllo)
½ pound butter, melted

Combine sugar, water, and honey, and boil about 20 minutes. Add lemon juice and boil another minute. While syrup is being made start putting Baklava together. Combine chopped almonds with nutmeg and mix well. Line a buttered 9 x 14-inch baking pan with 1 sheet of Phyllo (these may be bought from Greek bakery or delicatessen). Brush with melted butter and add 1 more sheet of pastry. Repeat this 1 more time. Now add 3 to 4 tablespoons chopped almonds (enough to form thin layer). Place 1 sheet on top of this layer, brush with butter and add another layer of almonds. Repeat until all ingredients are used, ending with 2 or 3 whole pastry sheets brushed with butter. When the top sheet is brushed with butter, take a sharp knife and score the top sheets in diamond shapes. Bake in 300° oven for 1 hour or until golden brown. Remove from oven and pour hot syrup gradually over Baklava. If syrup is not absorbed do not add more until it is. All the syrup doesn't have to be used. Cool. Cut the pieces through and allow time for the pieces to absorb the syrup before serving. Serves 24 to 30. This Greek dessert is very sweet. I like it cut in bite-size pieces and served at a coffee.

MRS. JOHN T. KARAPHILLIS

S T R A W B E R R Y   T O R T E

¼ teaspoon cream of tartar
6 egg whites
2 cups sugar
¼ teaspoon salt
¼ teaspoon vinegar

1 teaspoon vanilla
2 quarts strawberries
¼ cup sugar
1 pint whipping cream

Add cream of tartar to egg whites and beat until stiff. Add sugar a little at a time, sifting in gently and beating constantly until the mixture peaks. Add salt, vinegar and vanilla, beating well after each addition. Bake in two well-greased 9-inch cake pans for 40 minutes at 300°. Turn out on rack to cool. Cap berries, cut into halves, add ¼ cup sugar. Cover one layer with berries, then with whipped cream. Put other layer on top, cover with remaining berries. Ice entire torte with whipped cream. Garnish with whole berries. Serves 8 to 10.

MRS. MYRON GIBBONS

APPLE TORTE

1 egg	½ teaspoon cinnamon
¾ cup sugar	½ cup peeled, chopped tart apples
⅓ cup flour	½ cup chopped pecans
1¼ teaspoons baking powder	1 teaspoon vanilla
⅛ teaspoon salt	Whipped cream

Beat egg well; add sugar, beating until light and creamy. Sift together flour, baking powder, salt, and cinnamon. Add to egg mixture and blend well. Fold in apples, nuts, and vanilla. Pour into greased paper-lined 8-inch square pan. Bake in a 325° oven for 30 minutes. The meringue-like crust rises quite high, falls and cracks when cut—but it's supposed to. Serve warm or cold with whipped cream.

MRS. LOUIS SAXTON

Refrigerator Desserts

SHERRY CAKE

4 egg yolks	4 egg whites
½ cup sherry	½ pint heavy whipping cream
½ cup sugar	1 cup sugar
1 envelope plain gelatin	1 small angel food cake
⅓ cup milk	½ pint whipped cream

Beat egg yolks, sherry, and ½ cup sugar. Cook in double boiler until like a custard. Soak gelatin in milk and stir into hot sherry custard. Let cool. Whip egg whites stiff. Whip ½ pint cream with 1 cup sugar. Fold these into custard. Crumble angel food cake and place a layer of crumbs in bottom of greased 9-inch spring mold pan. Make several layers, alternating crumbs and mixture. Let stand in refrigerator 12 hours. Turn out and ice with ½ pint of plain whipped cream. Serves 8.

MRS. T. N. HENDERSON, JR.

LITTLE BIT OF HEAVEN

1 pound of marshmallows	¼ pound salted almonds
1 17-ounce can Royal Anne cherries, drained	1 pint whipping cream Sherry

Cut marshmallows and cherries into pieces. Chop almonds. Add these 3 ingredients to cream, after it has been whipped. Add sherry to taste. Place in refrigerator until ready to serve. Serves 8.

MRS. BLACKBURN LOWRY

CHOCOLATE POMPADOUR

This recipe was secured in Barbados. It's heavenly smooth and satiny.

1 6-ounce package semisweet chocolate bits	⅔ cup heavy cream, whipped
3 eggs, separated	4 to 6 tablespoons créme de menthe or créme de cacao

Melt chocolate over very low heat. Place in mixing bowl. Add egg yolks slowly, beating well as you mix. Mixture will be quite thick. Fold in whipped cream. Add liqueur to taste. Fold in stiffly beaten egg whites. Chill an hour or more. Yields 6 small servings. Can be doubled or tripled with ease.

MRS. HERBERT ROBSON

CHOCOLATE ICEBOX CAKE

2 1-ounce squares baking chocolate	½ cup butter
½ cup sugar	1 cup powdered sugar
¼ cup milk	1 teaspoon vanilla
4 eggs, separated	2 dozen lady fingers

Melt chocolate and add granulated sugar, milk and egg yolks. Stir constantly until thick, then let cool. Cream butter and powdered sugar and add to chocolate mixture. Add vanilla and fold in beaten egg whites. Line dish with lady fingers and pour in mixture. Let mixture stand in refrigerator 24 hours.

MRS. CHARLES T. LYLES

EASY FABULOUS DESSERT

1 pound macaroons (reserve 10 macaroons to toast and crumble for top)	Rum
	2 quarts Mocha ice cream
	½ pint whipping cream

Line sides and bottom of silver bowl with macaroons that have been thoroughly soaked in rum. Chill. When ready to serve dessert, fill bowl with ice cream. Top with whipped cream (lightly sweetened) and sprinkle with macaroon crumbs. Serves 10 to 12.

MRS. WILLIAM C. GILMORE, JR.

CHOCOLATE ICEBOX MOUSSE

4 cakes German sweet chocolate
4 tablespoons boiling water
8 eggs, separated
4 tablespoons powdered sugar

2 teaspoons lemon juice
2½ dozen lady fingers
½ pint whipping cream

Melt chocolate in boiling water, add beaten egg yolks, sugar, and lemon juice. Mix well. Remove from heat and fold in stiffly beaten egg whites. Line sides and bottom of 2-quart casserole or mold with wax paper. Put half of lady fingers on bottom and around sides. Pour in half of chocolate mixture, then add a layer of remaining lady fingers and remainder of chocolate. Refrigerate overnight. Unmold and ice with whipped cream. Instead of lady fingers you may use pound cake or angel food cake.

MRS. JAMES V. BUDD

CHRISTMAS MACAROON PUDDING

2 envelopes plain gelatin
1 cup cold water
3 eggs, separated
1 cup sugar
¾ quart hot milk

1 teaspoon vanilla
1 dozen almond macaroons
½ pint whipping cream
Small jar maraschino cherries

Dissolve gelatin in 1 cup cold water. Cream yolks of eggs and sugar. Pour gelatin into egg and sugar mixture and mix well; add hot milk and cook until slightly thickened. Set aside to cool. Add vanilla and well beaten egg whites to cooled mixture. Place moistened macaroons in bottom of serving dish and pour custard over the macaroons. Place in refrigerator until solid. When ready, top with whipped cream and garnish with cherry halves. Serves 8.

MRS. E. O. SAVITZ

DATE-MARSHMALLOW LOG

45 graham crackers
24 marshmallows, diced
1½ cups chopped dates

3 cups chopped pecans or walnuts
1½ cups heavy cream

Roll graham crackers to fine crumbs; combine marshmallows, dates, nuts; mix thoroughly with 2¾ cups cracker crumbs. Add cream (not whipped); mix thoroughly. Shape into roll (about 3½ inches in diameter); roll in remaining crumbs. Wrap well in wax paper and chill several hours in refrigerator. Cut in ¾-inch slices to serve. Top with whipped cream. Serves 12.

MRS. RUSSELL R. CURTIS

ENGLISH TOFFEE ICEBOX PUDDING

2 cups powdered sugar	2 large eggs, separated
2 tablespoons cocoa	1 cup chopped nuts
1/2 teaspoon salt	1 teaspoon vanilla
1/2 cup butter (1 stick)	1 3/4 cups vanilla wafer crumbs

Sift sugar once and then sift again with cocoa and salt. Cream butter and add sugar slowly. Add egg yolks, one at a time, beating after each addition; add nuts and vanilla. Fold in beaten egg whites. Line pan with wax paper and cover with vanilla wafer crumbs. Pour in mixture and top with remainder of crumbs. Let stand in refrigerator for 12 hours. Top with whipped cream, flavored with rum.

Mrs. K. I. McKay, Sr.

MINCEMEAT MOLDS

2 tablespoons plain gelatin	3 1/2 cups scalded milk
1/2 cup cold milk	1 teaspoon vanilla
4 eggs, separated	1 1/2 cups prepared mincemeat
1/2 cup sugar	2 tablespoons rum, brandy, or
1/4 teaspoon salt	sherry
2 tablespoons cornstarch	4 tablespoons sugar

Soften gelatin in cold milk. Set aside. Mix beaten egg yolks, 1/2 cup sugar, salt, and cornstarch. Add to scalded milk. Cook in a double boiler until mixture coats the spoon. Add softened gelatin and stir until dissolved. Chill until slightly thickened. Add vanilla. Fold in mincemeat and rum, brandy, or sherry. Whip egg whites until soft peaks form. Beat in 4 tablespoons sugar. Fold in mincemeat mixture. Mold. Makes 14 1/2-cup molds. Chill.

Mrs. Ralph Polk, Jr.

BISCUIT TORTONI

1 egg white	3 tablespoons of brandy
1/4 cup granulated sugar	(or more to taste)
1 cup heavy cream, whipped	1 tablespoon maraschino cherry
1/2 cup almond macaroon crumbs	juice
(1 dozen macaroons, dried in	
oven and finely crumbled)	

Beat egg white till stiff, gradually adding sugar. Fold in whipped cream, then crumbs. Reserve a little of each for garnish. Add brandy and cherry juice. Spoon into paper soufflé cup. Make swirl of cream on top and sprinkle with a few crumbs. Freeze uncovered until set, then wrap in foil until ready to use. Can be prepared well ahead. Serves 8.

Mrs. E. P. Taliaferro, Jr.

BANANA CREAM PUDDING

1 egg
2 tablespoons cornstarch
2 tablespoons sugar
2 cups milk

1 large box vanilla wafers
4 to 6 bananas
½ pint whipping cream

Beat egg; add cornstarch and sugar. Beat well and add milk. Cook in double boiler until consistency of whipped cream. Line dish with wafers, then a layer of sliced bananas, a layer of custard, a layer of whipped cream. Alternate in this order and end with a layer of cookies on top. This will fill a 2 quart casserole. Refrigerate for 4 or 5 hours.

MRS. ROBERT A. FOSTER

ORANGE CHARLOTTE

1 tablespoon plain, unflavored
    gelatin
¼ cup cold water
½ cup sugar or honey
¼ teaspoon salt

2 eggs, separated
1½ cups orange juice
2 tablespoons lemon juice
1 cup cream, whipped

Soften gelatin in cold water and dissolve over hot water. Add sugar or honey and salt to well-beaten egg yolks. Add ¾ cup of the orange juice and cook over hot water until mixture thickens. Add the remaining orange juice, lemon juice and gelatin and mix well. Chill and when mixture begins to thicken beat with rotary egg beater until light. Add egg whites beaten until stiff and beat thoroughly. Fold in whipped cream. Chill until firm (about 2 hours). If desired, garnish with additional orange slices.

MRS. PRESTON T. GARRETT

TRIFLE

Sponge cake, three 9-inch layers
    about 1½ inches thick
1 pint sherry wine
1 quart boiled custard
6 ounces blanched chopped almonds

1 pint strawberry preserves
1 dozen almond macaroons,
    crushed
½ pint heavy cream, whipped

Place one layer of cake in bottom of deep dish. Pour ⅓ of wine over layer; spread with ⅓ of boiled custard; sprinkle with ⅓ of almonds; spread with ½ of preserves; sprinkle with ⅓ of crushed macaroons. Repeat above procedure for second layer. Do same with third layer omitting preserves. Top with whipped cream. Chill in refrigerator. Can be made days ahead. Add whipped cream when ready to serve.

MRS. E. F. CARTER, JR.

ORANGE ICEBOX CAKE

1 cup sugar

2 cups cold water

4 envelopes gelatin

1 cup water

1 cup orange sections

1 cup orange juice

Juice of 2 lemons

½ pound marshmallows, cut up
   (or use miniature marshmallows)

1½ pints whipping cream

¾ pound or 1 cup almonds or
   pecans, broken

Shredded coconut

2 dozen lady fingers

Boil sugar and 2 cups water until syrup is formed. Add gelatin softened in 1 cup water. When cool add fruit and juices. Add marshmallows to 1 pint of cream and whip. Fold into fruit mixture and add nuts. Line large angel food cake pan with wax paper. Line with lady fingers and pour in mixture. Chill 4 or 5 hours or overnight. When ready to serve turn out on platter, ice with ½ pint whipped cream, and sprinkle with coconut. Serves 15 to 20.

MRS. A. S. MOFFETT

MARSHMALLOW ICEBOX CAKE

½ pound vanilla wafers,
   crushed to fine crumbs

½ cup soft butter

½ cup chocolate syrup

½ cup powdered sugar

½ pound marshmallows, chopped

½ teaspoon salt

1 teaspoon vanilla

1 cup chopped pecans

3 egg whites

Whipped cream

Spread half of vanilla wafer crumbs in bottom of an 8 x 10-inch greased pan. Mix butter, chocolate syrup and powdered sugar; add marshmallows, salt, vanilla and pecans. Fold this mixture into stiffly beaten egg whites. Carefully spread over crumbs in pan and cover top with remaining crumbs. Refrigerate and let chill for several hours or overnight. Top with whipped cream. Serves 10.

MRS. WHITFIELD PALMER

Frozen Desserts

FROZEN FRENCH PASTRY

½ cup butter
2 eggs
1 cup powdered sugar

2 3-ounce packages Nabisco
   Sugar Wafers, crushed
½ pint heavy cream, whipped

Melt butter over hot water. Beat eggs well, gradually add sugar. Add egg mixture to melted butter. Cook over hot water, stirring constantly until thickened to custard consistency. Roll wafers to crumbs and place a ¼-inch layer in bottom of buttered 8-inch square pan. Add alternate layers of custard and whipped cream. Top with remainder of wafer crumbs and freeze several hours or overnight. Cut into squares to serve (let stand at room temperature a few minutes before cutting). Serves 8.

MRS. J. A. MEIER

FROZEN LEMON CUSTARD

3 tablespoons (heaping) lemon
   gelatin
1 cup hot water
¾ cup sugar
4 eggs, separated

Juice of 1 lemon
½ pint heavy cream
1 small box vanilla wafers,
   crushed

Dissolve lemon gelatin in hot water; cool. Mix sugar, egg yolks, and lemon juice in double boiler until thick. Beat egg whites until stiff; whip the cream. Fold cooled sauce into gelatin mixture, then fold in whipped cream and last the egg whites. Sprinkle crushed vanilla wafers in bottom of refrigerator pan; add custard and top with remainder of vanilla wafer crumbs. Freeze. Serves 8.

MRS. ROBERT T. COZART

FROZEN RUM CREAM

8 egg yolks
8 tablespoons sugar
6 egg whites

3 cups heavy cream, whipped
1 cup rum

Beat egg yolks, gradually add sugar, and beat until the mixture is thick and pale in color. Fold in stiffly beaten egg whites; then fold in whipped cream. Stir in rum very gradually. Turn the cream into a deep refrigerator tray and freeze for about 8 hours. Serve in sherbet glasses. Serves 8.

MRS. REGAR HICKMAN

CHANTILLY

1½ dozen ladyfingers (double)	5 tablespoons sifted powdered
½ pint heavy cream	sugar
5 egg whites	½ teaspoon vanilla

Line bottom of 6 or 7 inch pan having at least 3-inch straight sides, with circle of wax paper. Stand ladyfingers on ends around sides of pan. Whip cream. Beat egg whites until stiff, slowly adding sugar and vanilla. Carefully fold egg whites into the whipped cream. Pour into mold, being certain that the ladyfingers remain standing. Freeze. To serve, turn out on serving dish and remove wax paper. This is an old Spanish recipe (pronounced Shän-tee-ee).

MRS. MANUAL CORRAL, JR.

ARABIAN ICE CREAM

1 pint milk	6 toasted almond macaroons,
¾ cup sugar	crushed fine
3 eggs	3 tablespoons honey
¼ teaspoon salt	½ teaspoon almond extract
	½ pint cream, whipped

Combine milk, sugar, eggs and salt and cook in double boiler until thick. The mixture should coat a spoon. Add crushed macaroons, honey and almond extract. When cool fold in whipped cream and freeze. If made in refrigerator stir within an hour.

MISS ISABELLE CLARK

CUSTARD ICE CREAM

1 tablespoon flour	2 cups scalded milk
1½ cups granulated sugar	4 cups light cream
1 teaspoon salt	1½ teaspoons flavoring extract
2 egg yolks	

Mix flour, sugar and salt and add slightly beaten egg yolks, stirring until smooth. Add scalded milk slowly. Cook in top of double boiler until mixture thickens. When cool, add cream and extract. Pour in old-fashioned freezer and freeze. Makes approximately 2 quarts.

MRS. W. FRANK HOBBS

MANGO ICE CREAM

2 cups mango pulp (about 3)
⅛ teaspoon salt
¾ cup sugar
Juice of 1 lime

2 teaspoons unflavored gelatin
2 tablespoons cold water
¼ cup hot water
1 pint heavy cream

Peel and cut mangoes into small pieces, then mash well with fork (or blend in blender). Add salt, sugar and lime juice. Soften gelatin in cold water, then dissolve in hot water. Mix into fruit; chill thoroughly. Whip cream stiff, fold in fruit; freeze in refrigerator set at coldest temperature until half frozen. Remove to chilled bowl, beat well, return to refrigerator. Remove and beat at least once more, then freeze hard.

MRS. NEIL MCMULLEN

MINT ICE CREAM

2 cups milk
1 cup chopped mint leaves
8 egg yolks

1 cup sugar
2 cups cream, whipped
Green food coloring

Scald milk. Remove from heat; add mint leaves and let stand for 20 minutes. Strain. Beat egg yolks until slightly thickened. Add sugar gradually, beating until thick and lemon-colored. Add scalded milk gradually. Cook over very low heat for 10 minutes, stirring constantly. Cool and stir in a few drops of green coloring. Fold mixture into whipped cream. Pour into freezing trays and freeze. Makes about 2 quarts.

MRS. CLARE M. PHILLIPS, JR.

PEACH MOUSSE

1 cup fresh peaches, mashed
1 teaspoon gelatin dissolved
   in 1 tablespoon of water
   (set in pan of hot water
   to dissolve thoroughly)

½ cup sugar
Few grains of salt
3 drops almond extract
½ pint cream

Mix thoroughly all ingredients except cream and place in refrigerator tray. Place in freezer. Stir and beat when it begins to thicken. Beat ½ pint cream until stiff; add the peach mixture gradually, beating constantly. Freeze for 3 hours or more.

MRS. DONALD M. LINS

OLD-FASHIONED ICE CREAM

You haven't lived unless you have an old-fashioned ice cream freezer in your home and all the children have had a turn at turning the crank and licking the dasher.

Uncooked Cream (like sherbet)

2½ cups sugar	2 cups sweet cream
4 eggs well beaten	1½ teaspoons vanilla
4 cups homogenized milk	

Add sugar to eggs and beat thoroughly, add milk and cream, stir well. Scald just before freezing. Flavor with vanilla. One teaspoon lemon extract may be substituted for vanilla. Freeze in old-fashioned freezer. Makes almost 2 quarts.

MRS. W. FRANK HOBBS

MILK SHERBET

1 quart milk	¾ cup lemon juice (about
2 cups sugar	3 lemons)

Scald milk, add sugar and cool. Add lemon juice after freezing has started.

MRS. CARLTON C. CONE

"WE THREE" SHERBET

3 cups water	1 flat can crushed pineapple
2 cups sugar	Juice of 3 lemons
3 bananas, crushed	Juice of 3 oranges

Heat water and dissolve sugar in it. Cool and then mix all other ingredients together. After mixture has frozen to a mush, stir and refreeze. Makes about 2 quarts.

MRS. OLIVER WALL KUHN

FRESH STRAWBERRY PARFAIT

22 marshmallows	1 cup whipping cream
1 lemon	1 cup fresh strawberries

Melt marshmallows in double boiler. Add juice of lemon and mix. Fold whipped cream into mixture. Fold in strawberries (and part of juice). Place in freezer tray. Serves 6 to 8.

MRS. HAROLD J. LEGGETT, JR.

APRICOT ICE

2 quarts apricots
1 6-ounce can frozen
   orange concentrate

3 large limes or 6 lemons
1½ cups sugar
14 ounces water

Use electric blender to make purée of apricots or put through a coarse sieve. Combine all ingredients in a 4-quart ice cream churn. Freeze according to churn instructions. Make about an hour before serving. Makes 4 quarts.

MRS. ANSLEY WATSON

Ice Cream Sauces

REGAL CHOCOLATE SAUCE

½ cup light corn syrup
1 cup sugar
1 cup water

3 1-ounce squares unsweetened
   chocolate
1 teaspoon vanilla
1 cup evaporated milk

Combine syrup, sugar and water. Cook to soft ball stage (235°) on candy thermometer. Remove from heat; add chocolate and stir until melted. Add vanilla and *slowly* add evaporated milk, mixing thoroughly. Store in refrigerator. Yield 2 cups.

MRS. LEFFIE M. CARLTON, JR.

GASPARILLA ICE CREAM

1 16-ounce jar pineapple
   and apricot preserves
1½ cups rum
3 quarts vanilla ice cream

1 package frozen pineapple
   (refrigerate 24 hours)
Fresh coconut, grated

Put preserves in top of double boiler. When melted add rum and heat. Put ice cream on platter. Dot with pineapple and coconut. Light sauce and pour over ice cream. May add almonds toasted in butter. The sauce can be nicely served from a chafing dish at the table. Serves 12.

MRS. ROBERT T. COZART

ALMOND PRALINE BALLS

1 quart vanilla ice cream
1 cup toasted slivered
  almonds or pecans
2 cups light cream (or half
  and half)

¼ cup butter
1½ cups light brown sugar
2 tablespoons corn syrup

Scoop 6 large balls of ice cream. Roll balls in toasted almonds and place in freezer to harden. To make sauce combine cream, butter, sugar, and syrup in heavy saucepan; cook over very low heat, stirring constantly, until mixture is smooth and has thickened slightly, about 5 to 10 minutes. Cool, stirring frequently. Serve over almond balls. Makes 6 servings.

KITCHEN CORNER

MOCHA BRANDY SAUCE

6 ounces sweet chocolate
½ ounce bitter chocolate

½ cup strong black coffee, hot
1 tablespoon brandy

Cut both sweet and bitter chocolate into small pieces and add to hot coffee, stirring constantly until melted. Add brandy and mix until the sauce is smooth. Serve hot over ice cream.

MRS. REGAR HICKMAN

TUTTI-FRUTTI

1 cup fresh fruit (use only
  strawberries, pineapple,
  peaches and/or bing cherries)

1 cup sugar
½ cup whiskey or brandy

To start your Tutti-Frutti, mix the fruit, sugar, and brandy in a large jar with a tight fitting lid. Stir every day until sugar is completely dissolved. Let stand on pantry shelf about 2 weeks before using. After this add only the sugar and fruit (as the fruit comes in season). The mixture "brandies" itself. You may add more than 1 cup of fruit and 1 cup of sugar at one time, just be sure to add equal proportions of each. Keep on hand to serve over ice cream. NEVER dip the ice cream spoon into the Tutti-Frutti jar. This spoils it, and it must be thrown out.

MRS. PAUL D. COCHRAN, JR.

PRALINE CRUNCH
(An Ice Cream Topping)

½ cup butter
1 cup brown sugar, firmly
    packed

½ cup chopped pecans
2¼ cups cornflakes

Place butter and sugar in sauce pan and bring to a boil. Boil just
2 minutes. Add the nuts and cornflakes and toss with fork to coat
with the syrup. Cool and serve on vanilla ice cream.

MRS. PAUL SMITH, JR.

University of Tampa, Built as a Luxury Hotel in 1891

CHAPTER XV

Cakes and Frostings

When Marie Antoinette said of the poor of France, "Let them eat cake.", she meant a flat patty of coarse meal on the order of Yankee Johnny Cake or Southern Hoe Cake. The poor lady was much misunderstood. But don't misunderstand us. When we speak of cake, we mean just that: fluffy golden cakes, rich dark chocolate cakes, tall airy angel food cakes, crunchy coffee cakes, frosty coconut cakes, heavenly tea cakes, buttery pound cakes with a hint of spice. They need no description. That knowledge is in the eating.

Cakes

BRAZO DE GITANO
(Gypsy's Arm)

6 eggs, separated	6 tablespoons cake flour
6 tablespoons sugar	Cinnamon, powdered sugar,
	glazed cherries, and almonds

Beat egg whites until stiff but not dry, add sugar slowly and continue beating until well mixed. Beat in 6 egg yolks. Fold in the flour. Line a jelly roll pan with wax paper that has been buttered. Spread batter in pan and bake at 350°, 20 to 25 minutes. Remove cake onto a board that has been sprinkled with granulated sugar to prevent cake from sticking. Spread custard on cake, sprinkle with cinnamon. Roll (like a jelly roll). Sprinkle with powdered sugar. Decorate with glazed cherries and almonds. Heat ½ cup water and ¼ cup sugar until sugar melts. Pour over cake to moisten.

FILLING:

6 egg yolks	1¾ cups milk
4 tablespoons sugar	1 cinnamon stick
2 tablespoons flour	

Beat egg yolks, add sugar, beat again until well mixed. Stir in flour, add milk and cinnamon stick. Put in double boiler and stir constantly until it becomes a thick custard.

MRS. HAL S. HOLTSINGER

A N G E L   F O O D   C A K E

1½ cups sifted sugar
1 cup sifted cake flour
1 teaspoon cream of tartar
½ teaspoon salt

12 egg whites
½ teaspoon vanilla extract
½ teaspoon lemon extract

Sift sugar, flour, cream of tartar and salt together 11 times. Beat egg whites until stiff but not dry. Fold in sifted dry ingredients very carefully, a small amount at a time, so as not to lose volume. Add flavoring. Bake in ungreased tube pan at 325° for nearly 1 hour. Be extremely careful in removing cake from pan, leaving it inverted until cold and ready to fall out with very little assistance.

MRS. WILLIAM C. BLAKE, JR.

F R E S H   A P P L E   C A K E

¼ pound butter
1 cup sugar
1 teaspoon vanilla
1 egg
1 cup all-purpose flour
¼ teaspoon salt

1 teaspoon soda
½ cup white raisins
1 cup black walnuts (pecans
   may be substituted)
½ cup shredded fresh coconut,
2 cups chopped raw apples

Cream butter and sugar. Combine vanilla and egg and add. Sift dry ingredients and add. Then add raisins, nuts, coconut and mix. Add apples last. Bake in 8½-inch square glass dish for 40 minutes at 350°. Best when served warm.

MRS. WALTON HICKS

M O T H E R ' S   C H E E S E   C A K E

5 egg whites
1 cup sugar
2 teaspoons vanilla

1½ pounds cream cheese
18 graham crackers
¼ stick butter (melted)

Beat egg whites until stiff; fold in sugar and vanilla. Beat cream cheese in an electric mixer, add egg whites and beat. Pour in pan lined with crushed graham cracker crumbs that have been mixed with melted butter. Sprinkle a few crumbs on top, or cover top with crumbs. Bake in an 8 x 11 x 2-inch glass baking dish for 25 to 35 minutes at 325°. Serves 8 to 10.

MRS. FRED L. WOLF

BUTTERMILK CAKE

1 cup butter
3 cups sugar
10 egg whites
4 cups flour (use 1 ⅓ cups
    White Lily and 2 ⅔ Swansdown)
1 ½ level teaspoons cream of
    tartar, sifted with the flour

1 cup buttermilk
Vanilla
¼ teaspoon salt
½ level teaspoon soda dissolved
    in 2 teaspoons tepid water

Cream butter and sifted sugar adding a little of the egg whites to make creaming easier. Beat well. Add beaten whites of eggs and flour alternately. Put in buttermilk just before the last of flour. Add flavoring and last of all pour in the soda water. Bake in a very slow oven for 1 hour. Put in oven at about 250° for 15 minutes, then increase heat to 300°—325°. Makes 3 large or 4 small layers. Frost with your favorite frosting.

MRS. WILLIAM J. BULLARD

CHEESE CAKE

20 graham crackers, crushed
½ cup melted butter

¼ cup sugar

STEP I:

Mix these 3 ingredients and line an 8-inch square pan or spring-form pan with this mixture. Bake at 350° for 5 minutes.

STEP II:

1 pound cream cheese, softened
½ cup sugar

3 eggs

Beat these 3 ingredients in electric mixer until soft and smooth. Pour into the crumb lined pan and bake at 350° for 15 to 20 minutes. Cool to room temperature.

STEP III:

2 cups thick commercial sour cream
1 ¼ cups sugar

1 teaspoon vanilla

Combine *very gently*. Pour over the cake, using a light touch. Sprinkle with blanched, sliced almonds and cinnamon. Bake at 350° for 10 minutes. Cool and chill for 24 hours before serving.

MRS. DONALD M. LINS

CHOCOLATE CAKE

½ cup butter
2 cups sugar
3 squares chocolate, melted
2 eggs
2 cups sifted flour
½ teaspoon salt

1 teaspoon soda
1 cup milk
2 teaspoons vanilla
Juice of ½ lemon
1 cup nuts

Cream butter and sugar. Add melted chocolate. Add slightly beaten eggs. Sift together flour, salt and soda. Add alternately with milk. Add vanilla, lemon juice and nuts. Pour into 2 greased 9-inch square pans. Bake 30 to 40 minutes at 375°.

FILLING and FROSTING:

¼ pound butter
3 squares baking chocolate
1 egg
Juice of ½ lemon

1 teaspoon vanilla
1 box confectioners sugar
1 cup nuts

Melt butter and chocolate. Do not cook. Add to beaten egg. Then beat in other ingredients.

MRS. EDWIN DUNN, JR.

THREE-LAYER CHOCOLATE CAKE

2 cups sugar
¾ cup butter
3 eggs
5 tablespoons cocoa
3 cups flour

1 cup buttermilk
1 teaspoon vanilla
¼ teaspoon salt
1 teaspoon soda

Cream the sugar and butter. Add unbeaten eggs and mix. Dissolve the cocoa in 2 tablespoons hot water and add to mixture. Add alternately the flour and buttermilk and mix. Add vanilla and salt. Add soda dissolved in 3 tablespoons hot water to mixture and bake in 3 layer-cake pans, 30 to 35 minutes at 350°. Frost with Mocha Cake Icing.

UNCOOKED MOCHA CAKE ICING:

½ cup butter
2 cups powdered sugar
3 tablespoons cocoa
2 tablespoons cold coffee

1 teaspoon vanilla
1 egg white
2 or 3 tablespoons sweet or
   sour cream (optional)

Cream the butter and sugar. Add cocoa and coffee, then vanilla. Next add unbeaten egg white. If this mixture is too thick, add a few tablespoons of thick sweet or sour cream. Spread on cake .

MRS. PETER TAYLOR

ORANGE COFFEE CAKE

2 cups sifted flour	¼ cup shortening, melted
½ teaspoon salt	¼ cup milk
3 teaspoons baking powder	½ cup orange juice
⅓ cup sugar	1 egg, well beaten
1 teaspoon grated orange peel	½ teaspoon vanilla

Sift together dry ingredients. Add orange peel. Combine remaining ingredients all at once; mix well. Add dry ingredients, stirring just until all is moistened. Pour into greased 9-inch square pan. Sprinkle with topping. Bake in 375° oven for 30 minutes. Serve hot.

Topping: Cream together;

½ cup sugar	1 teaspoon cinnamon
2 tablespoons grated orange peel	1 tablespoon softened butter

MRS. JOHN S. ALLEN

MAMA KELLY'S CHIFFON CAKE

2 cups sifted flour	¾ cup cold water
1½ cups sugar	1 tablespoon vanilla (or almond
3 teaspoons baking powder	flavoring)
1 teaspoon salt	1 cup egg whites
½ cup salad oil	½ teaspoon cream of tartar
7 unbeaten egg yolks	

Measure and sift together into a mixing bowl, the flour, sugar, baking powder and salt. Make a well and add in order the salad oil, egg yolks, cold water, and vanilla. Beat until smooth. Combine in a large mixing bowl, the egg whites and the cream of tartar. Whip until very stiff peaks form. Pour egg yolk mixture slowly and gradually over egg whites, gently folding until blended. Do not beat or stir. Pour into ungreased tube pan immediately. Bake 55 minutes at 325°. Then increase heat to 350° for 10 to 15 minutes. Immediately turn pan upside down until cake is cold.

This is a very low-calorie cake, especially good for diabetics. Diabetics may serve it with fresh peaches or ice-milk. Non-diabetics may use strawberries and whipped cream or seven-minute icing. It is a very fine-grained cake.

MRS. T. PAINE KELLY, JR.

C E N T E N N I A L   C R E A M   C A K E

2 cups sifted cake flour
1 cup sugar
3 teaspoons baking powder
½ teaspoon salt

1 cup heavy cream
1 teaspoon vanilla extract
2 eggs

Sift flour, sugar, baking powder and salt together twice. Pour cream and vanilla into a deep 1-quart bowl; beat cream with electric mixer or rotary beater until just stiff, about 1½ minutes. Add unbeaten eggs and beat just until blended. Add flour mixture and beat (if an electric mixer is used, beat at low speed) until batter is well blended.

Turn into two 8-inch layer pans which have been greased, wax paper-lined and greased again. Bake in a 350° oven 25 to 30 minutes or until top of cake springs back when lightly touched with finger. Cool cake in pan on rack for about 10 minutes. Remove from pan; remove wax paper. When thoroughly cooled, frost with Almond Cream. Decorate with maraschino cherries and almonds. If desired, chill before serving.

ALMOND CREAM:

1 pint heavy cream
3 to 4 tablespoons confectioners
  sugar

½ to 1 teaspoon almond extract

Whip cream, add confectioners sugar and almond extract. Spread between layers and on top and sides of cake.

Mrs. Louis Wisdom

F R E N C H   C R U M B   C A K E

2 cups bread flour
1½ cups sugar
¾ cup Crisco
2 heaping teaspoons double acting
  baking powder

¾ teaspoon salt
2 eggs, well beaten
¾ cup milk
1 teaspoon vanilla
1 tablespoon cinnamon

Mix flour, sugar and Crisco until crumbly. Remove ¾ cup and save for topping. Add baking powder, salt, eggs, milk and vanilla to remaining mixture. Beat well. Put in 2 greased and floured pans (8 x 8 x 2-inch), and sprinkle top with remaining crumbs and cinnamon. Bake at 350° for 25 minutes.

Florence Felters

MRS. H. S. HAMPTON'S COCONUT CAKE

Make a 2-egg cake and bake in two 8-inch cake pans.

FILLING:

Milk of 2 coconuts
½ cup sugar
5 tablespoons cornstarch

Meat of 2 coconuts, shredded
1 recipe 7-minute frosting.

Combine milk, sugar and cornstarch in top of double boiler. Place over hot water and stir constantly until a thick, creamy sauce is formed. This takes about 30 minutes, so pull up a stool and just sit and stir. Remove from heat. Add shredded meat of 1 coconut. Spread half of this satiny mixture on the top of 1 of the cooled cakes. Place second layer on top of first layer, and cover the top of the second layer with remaining satiny mixture. Now frost entire cake (top and sides) with 7-minute frosting, and sprinkle remaining coconut over all. This fabulous cake is worth every minute of that stirring.

CRAZY CAKE

6 tablespoons butter
1½ cups flour (sift before
    measuring)
1 cup sugar
3 tablespoons cocoa

1 teaspoon soda
1 teaspoon salt
1 cup water
1 teaspoon vanilla
1 tablespoon vinegar

Melt butter in 10-inch ungreased pan. Sift dry ingredients into pan. Pour water with vanilla added over top. Swirl in pan with a fork until blended. Pour 1 tablespoon vinegar over top. Swirl with fork. Bake at 350° for 30 minutes.

MRS. GEORGE NETTLES

DATE NUT CAKE

1 pound dates, chopped
1 teaspoon baking soda
1 cup hot water
¼ pound butter

1½ cups brown sugar
2 eggs, separated
2 cups flour
1 cup chopped nuts

Add dates and soda to hot water. Cream butter and sugar, then add egg yolks. Add alternately the flour and date mixture. Add nuts. Fold in stiffly beaten egg whites. Bake in 8 x 12-inch pan at 350° about 35 minutes. Serves 14.

MRS. J. G. SPICOLA

PENNSYLVANIA DUTCH CRUMB CAKE

3 unbaked pie crusts
3 cups flour
1 cup brown sugar
¼ teaspoon salt
½ cup butter and lard mixed

1 tablespoon sugar
1 tablespoon cinnamon
1 cup molasses
1 teaspoon soda
1 cup hot water

Line 3 pie pans with unbaked crusts. Combine flour, brown sugar, salt, butter and lard. Mix this into crumbs. Save out ½ cup crumbs for topping, adding sugar and cinnamon to this. To remaining crumbs, add molasses. Put soda in hot water and add. Place this mixture in pie pans. Sprinkle cinnamon crumbs on top. Bake at 325° until pie dough is brown, 30 to 40 minutes. Cut in fingers and serve.

MRS. SIDNEY J. TAYLOR

DATE NUT LOAF

1 pound dates (chopped)
1 cup flour
1 cup sugar

1 pound pecans (chopped)
3 eggs, beaten

Roll dates in flour. Mix in sugar and pecans. Add beaten eggs. Mix until all ingredients are moist. Pour into loaf pan that has been greased and floured. Bake 1 hour or a little over at 300°.

MRS. WILSON DAVIS

EGGNOG CAKE

5 egg yolks
½ cup rum or whiskey
½ pound butter
1 pound powdered sugar

¼ pound almonds, slivered
and toasted
¼ pound crushed macaroons
1 large angel food cake

Beat egg yolks and add rum. Cream butter. Gradually beat in sugar. Combine with egg yolk mixture. Stir in almonds and macaroons. Chill until of spreading consistency. Fill 2 layers of angel food cake and cover with whipped cream. Decorate with cherries.

MRS. A. B. HULL, JR.

DEVIL'S FOOD CAKE AND FUDGE ICING

½ cup cocoa
1 cup hot water
½ cup butter
1¼ cups sugar
2 eggs, beaten

1½ cups flour
1 teaspoon baking powder
½ teaspoon salt
1 teaspoon vanilla

Put cocoa in hot water. Cream butter and sugar. Add beaten eggs to creamed mixture. Sift dry ingredients and add alternately with cocoa. Add vanilla. Bake 40-50 minutes at 350° in 10 x 10-inch pan.

FUDGE ICING:

2 squares chocolate
⅔ cup milk
2 tablespoons light corn syrup

2 cups sugar
2 tablespoons butter
1 teaspoon vanilla
Dash of salt

Shave chocolate into milk and cook over low flame until chocolate is dissolved. Remove from heat and add syrup and sugar. Cook until sugar is dissolved, stirring constantly; then boil to soft ball stage. Do not stir. Remove from fire and add butter, vanilla, and salt. Cool to lukewarm and beat slightly. Nuts may be added to fudge icing or sprinkled on top if desired.

MRS. FRANK CALDWELL

WHITE FRUIT CAKE I

1½ pounds each candied cherries
   and pineapple
1 pound white citron
½ pound orange and lemon
   mixed (candied peel)
1½ cups brandy
1 pound blanched almonds
   (quartered)

3 tablespoons rose water
4 cups flour (sift before
   measuring)
¾ pound butter
2 cups sugar
8 eggs

Soak fruit in ½ cup brandy, and the almonds in rose water, overnight. Dust fruit in half the flour. Cream butter and sugar and add remaining flour. Add eggs one at a time, beating well after each addition. Add remaining brandy. Mix all ingredients together. Pour into a buttered and floured tube pan, and bake at 200° about 2½ hours.

MRS. HARLAN LOGAN

WHITE FRUIT CAKE II

1 pound butter
1 pound sugar
1 dozen eggs, separated
1 wine glass sherry
1 wine glass brandy
½ teaspoon mace
½ tablespoon cinnamon
4 level teaspoons nutmeg
1 pound flour

1 pound almonds
1 pound pineapple
1 pound white raisins
1 pound brazil nuts
½ pound white cherries
1 quart coconut, fresh grated
2 ounces crystalized ginger
2 pounds citron

Cream butter and sugar well. Add egg yolks, beat well; add sherry and brandy. Sift spices with flour over all fruit and nuts, which have been cut in small pieces. Add to batter, and fold in stiffly beaten egg whites. This recipe makes about 10 pounds and may be divided any way desired. Line pans with brown paper (grease pan and paper). Fill about ⅔ full and weigh. Bake in very slow oven (275°) 30 minutes to the pound.

MRS. C. M. PHIPPS

ORANGE FRUIT CAKE

¾ cup butter (or one stick
   of margarine)
1 cup sugar
3 beaten eggs
1 cup buttermilk
1½ teaspoons baking soda

3 cups unsifted plain flour
1 grated orange
1 teaspoon salt
1 teaspoon vanilla
1 cup chopped pecans
1 cup chopped dates

TOPPING:

1½ cups orange juice
1 grated orange rind

¾ cup sugar

Cream butter and sugar. Add eggs, and beat well. Put buttermilk in 2 to 3 cup container. Add soda to this and stir. Let it fizz and rise. Add flour and buttermilk mixture alternately to batter. Grate whole orange (except seeds) and add to batter. Add salt, vanilla, nuts, and dates. Mix well. Pour into greased angel food cake pan. Cook at 300° for about 1½ hours, or until cake springs back to light touch. Combine topping ingredients in saucepan. Bring to boil and cook 2 to 3 minutes. When cake is done, arrange 2 large pieces of foil crisscrossed, and immediately turn cake out on foil. Pour topping over cake, filling center hole, too. Wrap and let stand overnight. Serves about 20.

Better than regular fruit cake because it's not so rich and heavy.

MRS. BRYANT B. SKINNER

DARK FRUIT CAKE

1½ pounds flour (6 cups sifted)	2 pounds raisins
1 teaspoon cinnamon	2 pounds currants
1 teaspoon nutmeg	1 pound butter
¼ teaspoon cloves	1 pound sugar
⅔ teaspoon allspice	12 eggs
1 teaspoon salt	1 teaspoon soda
2 pounds citron	1 cup molasses
2 pounds dates	⅔ cup whiskey

Divide the flour into two equal parts. To one part add the spices and salt. Cut fruit in very small pieces (do this the day before) and mix with the unspiced flour.

Cream butter and sugar and add eggs which have been beaten slightly. Dissolve soda in a little warm water and add to molasses. Add spiced flour and molasses alternately to the butter-egg mixture; then the whiskey and last the fruit. Beat thoroughly.

Grease 2 tube pans, line with brown paper extending ½ inch along sides of pans, bake at 250° and do not open oven door under 1½ hours. When cake is done it will leave sides of pan slightly and feel firm on top. A straw will come out clean. It takes about 4½ hours to bake and should remain in pan until cold. Remove brown paper, wrap in wax paper and store in covered tin. Will keep several months.

Best when it is two to four weeks old.

MRS. WILLIAM C. BLAKE, JR.

JELLY ROLL

3 eggs	1 teaspoon baking powder
1 cup sugar	¼ teaspoon salt
1 cup sifted cake flour	3 tablespoons water

Beat eggs until light and add sugar. Sift flour, baking powder and salt together several times. Add flour mixture alternately with water to egg mixture. Grease and line cookie sheet with wax paper. Bake at 375° for about 12 minutes, or until done. Turn out on wax paper which has been sprinkled with granulated sugar. Trim crusty edges and spread with favorite jelly. Roll up while warm.

MRS. WILLIAM C. BLAKE, JR.

FUDGE BAR CAKE

2 ounces baking chocolate
  (cut in pieces)
½ cup boiling water
1 cup sifted cake flour
1 cup sugar
1 teaspoon salt

1 teaspoon soda
¼ cup shortening
¼ cup sweet milk plus 1½
  teaspoons vinegar
½ teaspoon vanilla
1 egg, unbeaten

Put chocolate in mixing bowl. Pour boiling water gradually over chocolate and stir until melted. Cool. Sift flour, sugar, salt, and soda into mixing bowl containing chocolate mixture. Drop in shortening. Beat on low speed of electric mixer for 2 minutes or beat 200 strokes by hand. Add milk, vanilla, and egg. Beat another minute on low speed or 100 strokes by hand. Bake in greased 8 x 8 x 2-inch pan in 350° oven for 45 minutes. Ice with Minute Fudge Frosting or Minute Penuche Frosting.

MINUTE FUDGE FROSTING:

1 ounce baking chocolate,
  finely cut
1 cup sugar
⅓ cup milk

¼ cup shortening
¼ teaspoon salt
1 teaspoon vanilla

Place all ingredients, except vanilla, in saucepan. Bring slowly to a full rolling boil, stirring constantly, and boil 1 minute. Add vanilla and beat until thick enough to spread. If frosting becomes too thick add 1 tablespoon cream.

MINUTE PENUCHE FROSTING:

1 cup brown sugar,
  firmly packed
¼ cup milk

¼ cup shortening
¼ teaspoon salt
½ teaspoon vanilla

Cook, using same procedure as in Minute Fudge Frosting.

MRS. ANSLEY WATSON

POUND CAKE

1⅔ cups sugar
½ pound butter
5 large or 6 small eggs (cold)

2 cups cake flour (measure after
  sifting 3 times)
1 teaspoon vanilla
1 tablespoon brandy or bourbon

Cream sugar and butter well. Add whole eggs one at a time, beating until all trace of egg disappears. Add flour gradually. Add flavoring. Pour in angel food pan, well greased and lined with greased paper. Place in cold oven, then set at 350° and bake 1 hour.

MRS. H. L. CROWDER, JR.

MOCHA CREAM CAKE

1 ½ cups sifted flour
1 ½ teaspoons baking powder
¾ teaspoon salt
4 eggs, separated
½ cup water

1 ½ teaspoons grated lemon rind
¾ teaspoon vanilla
1 ½ cups sugar
3 tablespoons lemon juice

Sift together the flour, baking powder and salt. Combine the egg yolks, water, lemon rind and vanilla and beat well. Add gradually sugar and lemon juice. Blend in the dry ingredients carefully. Beat egg whites stiff but not dry and fold into the batter. Pour into 2 greased and wax paper-lined 9-inch cake pans and bake at 350° for 25 minutes. When cool, split the layers, frost and refrigerate for at least 4 hours before serving.

MOCHA CREAM FROSTING:

2 squares unsweetened chocolate
½ cup water
½ cup sugar

½ teaspoon vanilla
2 teaspoons instant coffee
1 pint cream

Melt the chocolate in the water over low heat, stirring constantly. Add the sugar, vanilla and coffee and boil for 3 minutes. When cool stir in cream, whipped stiff.

THE GARDEN SEAT INN
CLEARWATER, FLORIDA

MYSTERY MOCHA CAKE

¾ cup sugar
1 cup sifted all purpose flour
2 teaspoons baking powder
⅛ teaspoon salt
1 square unsweetened chocolate
2 tablespoons butter

½ cup milk
1 teaspoon vanilla
½ cup brown sugar
½ cup sugar
4 tablespoons cocoa
1 cup double-strength cold coffee

Mix and sift first 4 ingredients. Melt chocolate and butter together over hot water and add to first mixture; blend well. Add combined milk and vanilla and mix well. Pour into greased 8 x 8-inch pan. Combine the two sugars and the cocoa and sprinkle over the batter. Pour the coffee over this. Bake at 350° for 40 minutes. Makes a pudding-cake type of dessert, with cake on top and sauce underneath. May be garnished with chopped nuts and/or whipped cream.

MRS. DAVID J. KADYK

LANE CAKE

1 cup butter
2 cups sugar
1 teaspoon vanilla
3 ¼ cups sifted all-purpose flour

3 ½ teaspoons double-acting
    baking powder
¾ teaspoon salt
1 cup milk
8 egg whites

Cream butter and sugar until fluffy. Add vanilla. Sift flour, baking powder and salt together. Add to butter mixture alternately with milk in small amounts. Beat egg whites until they stand in soft glossy peaks, but not dry, and fold into batter. Bake at 375° in four 9-inch round layer pans. Let pans stand on cake racks 5 minutes. Carefully loosen around edges, turn out on racks and cool before frosting.

FROSTING:

1 ½ cups coarsely chopped pecans
1 ½ cups chopped, seeded raisins
1 ½ cups shredded fresh coconut
1 ½ cups quartered, candied
    cherries

12 egg yolks
1 ⅓ cups sugar
½ teaspoon salt
¾ cup butter
½ cup rye or bourbon whiskey

Prepare fruit and nuts. Put egg yolks in top of double boiler and beat slightly with rotary beater. Add sugar, salt and butter. Cook over simmering water stirring constantly until sugar is dissolved, butter melts, and mixture is slightly thickened. Do not overcook or let egg yolks become scrambled in appearance. Mixture should be almost translucent. Remove from heat and add whiskey. Beat mixture 1 minute with rotary beater. Add nuts and fruit and let cool.

Spread frosting between layers and on top and sides of cake. After an hour, if any drips off, spread it back on sides. Cover with cake cover or loosely with foil and store to ripen a few days. Stored this way, cake will keep several weeks.

Mrs. John Whitehurst

LITTLE EVA'S SWEET BREAD CAKE

4 cups flour
4 teaspoons baking powder
1 cup butter
3 cups sugar

4 eggs, separated
1 cup milk
1 teaspoon vanilla
Cinnamon, butter, sugar

Sift flour once, measure, then sift twice more with baking powder. Cream butter and sugar. Beat egg yolks; add to sugar mixture; then add milk and flour. Beat egg whites stiff; fold in. Add vanilla. Bake at 350° 40 to 45 minutes, and just before cake is done, spread with cinnamon, butter, and sugar.

Mrs. Guy King, Jr.

LEMON CHEESE CAKE

1½ cups sugar
½ cup butter
1 teaspoon lemon extract
2½ cups flour

2 teaspoons baking powder
⅔ cup milk
4 egg whites

Cream sugar and butter thoroughly. Add flavoring. Sift flour with baking powder. Add to butter mixture alternately with the milk. Fold in stiffly beaten egg whites. Bake in 2 layers at 350°.

FILLING:

1 cup sugar
½ cup hot water
4 egg yolks

Juice and grated rind of
one lemon

Boil sugar and water to a thick syrup. Beat egg yolks (add a little milk to make them very thin). Pour into boiling syrup, stirring briskly to prevent lumping. Add lemon juice and rind. Cook until it thickens. Spread between layers. Frost with a seven-minute frosting.

MRS. JOHN WHITEHURST

ORANGE CAKE I

1 cup butter
1 pound sugar
6 eggs
4 cups sifted flour

2 heaping teaspoons baking
powder
1 cup milk
6 oranges
1 tablespoon grated orange peel

Cream butter; add sugar gradually, creaming well. Add eggs one at a time, beating well after each addition. Fold in dry ingredients alternately with milk. Makes three 9-inch layers. Bake at 350° for 30 to 35 minutes or until done.

While cake is cooling squeeze the juice from 6 oranges. Do not strain. When cake is cool, lightly pierce the top of each layer with a large-pronged fork. Set aside.

Make a 7-minute white icing. Fold in grated orange peel. Pour ⅓ of juice on bottom layer of cake, let soak for a minute, then ice. Add second layer and repeat, then third layer. Ice whole cake. Icing will turn slightly yellow from orange peel. Chill in refrigerator.

MRS. J. HARDIN KIRBY

ORANGE CAKE II

1 cup sugar	1 cup sour milk
½ cup butter	1 teaspoon vanilla
1 egg	1 cup raisins (or ½ cup raisins
2 cups sifted flour	and ½ cup dates)
1 teaspoon soda	½ cup nuts
⅛ teaspoon salt	Rind of 1 orange

Cream sugar and butter. Add beaten egg. Sift flour, soda, and salt and add alternately with the sour milk. Stir in vanilla. Grind together the raisins (or raisins and dates), nuts, and orange rind. Fold ⅔ of this mixture into cake batter, reserving remainder for icing. Pour batter into greased and floured 8 x 8 x 2-inch pan. Bake at 350° 25 to 30 minutes or until done. Ice top of warm cake and cut in squares.

ICING:

Reserved fruit mixture	Orange juice
2 cups confectioners sugar	

Mix fruit and sugar. Add just enough orange juice to moisten for spreading. Spread on warm cake.

MRS. MARY BROCKMAN

PRUNELLA CAKE

½ cup butter	1 teaspoon baking soda
1½ cups sugar	1 teaspoon each cinnamon,
3 well beaten eggs	allspice, cloves
2¼ cups flour (sifted before	1 cup sour milk
measuring)	1 pound cooked prunes (cook
½ teaspoon salt	covered with grapefruit juice
1 teaspoon baking powder	until tender)

Cream butter and sugar well. Then add eggs. Sift flour, salt, and baking powder, soda and spices. Add alternately to mixture with sour milk. Cut up prunes in rather large pieces and add to mixture. Pour into three 9-inch cake pans and bake 30 to 35 minutes in a 350° oven.

MOCHA FILLING AND ICING:

1 stick butter	1 pound package confectioners
1 heaping tablespoon cocoa	sugar
	4 tablespoons very strong boiling
	coffee

Cream butter well and add cocoa. Sift in sugar a little at a time, then add the coffee, creaming to desired consistency.

MRS. CATHERINE VAUGHN

QUEEN ELIZABETH CAKE

1 teaspoon soda
1 cup boiling water
1 cup dates
1 cup sugar
¼ cup butter
1 egg, beaten

1 teaspoon vanilla
1½ cups sifted plain flour
1 teaspoon baking powder
½ teaspoon salt
½ cup nut meats

Put soda in boiling water and pour over dates. Let stand while mixing the batter. Cream sugar and butter. Add egg, then vanilla. Sift dry ingredients together and gradually add to batter. Add nuts, then date mixture. Mix well. Bake in 9 x 12-inch greased pan at 350° for 35 minutes.

FROSTING:

5 tablespoons brown sugar
5 tablespoons light cream

2 tablespoons butter
Grated coconut or chopped nuts

Combine and boil for 3 minutes. Spread on cake without beating. Sprinkle with grated coconut or nut meats.

This is said to be the cake that Queen Elizabeth makes herself in the palace kitchen. The recipe is sold for 50 cents and the money used for charity.

MRS. JOHN B. SUTTON

SPICE CAKE

2½ cups sifted flour
1 teaspoon baking powder
1 teaspoon salt (scant)
1 teaspoon cloves
1 teaspoon cinnamon
1 teaspoon soda
1 scant cup of shortening
　(half butter and half margarine)

2 cups light brown sugar
2 well beaten eggs
2 egg yolks
1 cup sour milk or buttermilk
Meringue—2 egg whites, 1 cup
　light brown sugar, ½ cup
　nut meats

Sift flour once, measure, add baking powder, soda and salt and spices and sift together 3 times. Cream butter thoroughly, add sugar gradually and cream together until light and fluffy. Add beaten eggs and egg yolks; then flour alternately with milk, a small amount at a time. Beat until smooth. Bake in 9 x 13-inch sheet cake pan which has been well greased and floured. Pour batter into pan and cover with meringue made from folding the brown sugar into stiffly beaten egg whites (beat well while adding sugar). Spread evenly on cake batter and sprinkle with nut meats. Bake at 350° 50 to 60 minutes.

MRS. STEPHEN M. SPARKMAN

SOUR CREAM POUND CAKE

1 cup butter	1/4 teaspoon soda
3 cups sugar	3 cups sifted flour
6 eggs, separated	1/2 pint sour cream

Cream butter and sugar thoroughly. Add egg yolks one at a time. Add soda to flour. Add alternately flour and sour cream to creamed mixture. Beat egg whites stiff and fold in. Bake in large size tube pan, greased and floured, at 300° for 1 1/2 to 2 hours, or until a toothpick inserted in center of cake comes out clean. Should have nice brown crust on top. Let stand 15 minutes before taking out of pan. No flavoring needed. The longer you keep this cake the more moist it gets!

MRS. ROBERT C. BIGBY, JR.

SUNSHINE ISLAND

(Second prize winner, Second All-Florida Orange Dessert Contest)

1/3 cup butter	1 teaspoon salt
1/3 cup Crisco	1/2 cup milk
1 1/2 cups sugar	1/2 cup orange juice
3 eggs	1 cup coconut flakes
2 1/4 cups sifted flour	1 1/2 teaspoon grated orange rind
2 1/2 teaspoons baking powder	

Cream together butter, Crisco and sugar until fluffy. Beat in thoroughly the eggs. Sift together flour, baking powder, salt. Stir in, alternating with milk and orange juice. Add coconut and rind. Bake in greased and floured 9-inch pans for 25 to 30 minutes at 350°. Put cooled layers together with Clear Orange Filling. Frost top and sides with Orange Mountain Icing. Decorate with fresh orange sections (membranes removed) nestled in coconut.

CLEAR ORANGE FILLING:

1 cup sugar	1 cup orange juice
4 tablespoons cornstarch	2 tablespoons grated orange rind
1/2 teaspoon salt	1 1/2 tablespoons lemon juice
2 tablespoons butter	

Mix together in saucepan and bring to rolling boil and boil 1 minute, stirring constantly. Cool.

ORANGE MOUNTAIN ICING:

2 egg whites	1/4 cup orange juice
1 cup sugar	Dash of salt
1/8 teaspoon cream of tartar	2 tablespoons light corn syrup

Combine all ingredients in top of double boiler. Place over boiling water stirring occasionally for about 2 minutes. Then with mixer, on high speed, beat until mixture holds its shape.

MRS. BOB YOUNGER

FEATHER SPONGE CAKE

6 egg yolks	1½ cups cake flour
½ cup orange juice	¼ teaspoon salt
1½ cups sugar	6 egg whites
½ teaspoon vanilla	¾ teaspoon cream of tartar

Beat egg yolks until thick and lemon-colored; add orange juice and continue beating until very thick. Gradually beat in sugar, then vanilla. Fold in flour, sifted with salt, a little at a time. Beat egg whites until foamy; add cream of tartar and beat until they form moist, glossy peaks. Fold into egg yolk mixture. Bake in 10-inch ungreased angel cake pan in slow oven (325°) 1 hour. Invert pan to cool.

MRS. D. A. KAFKA

Cupcakes

WASHINGTON PUFFS

CAKES:

1 cup powdered sugar	2 cups flour
½ cup butter or margarine	2 teaspoons baking powder (Royal)
3 egg yolks, beaten thick	1 cup milk

Cream sugar and butter; add yolks and beat. Sift flour twice, then measure 2 cups; sift again with baking powder. Stir milk and flour mixture into creamed mixture. Bake at once in hot greased iron gem pans (muffin tins) in 350° oven about 25 minutes or until browned on top. Makes 12 cakes.

ORANGE SAUCE:

2 or 3 oranges	1 cup powdered sugar
3 whites of eggs	⅛ teaspoon salt

Squeeze orange juice into a bowl. Beat whites of eggs to stiff froth. Gradually add powdered sugar and salt; lastly fold in the orange juice. Serve immediately over the hot cakes. Stir between servings in order to get both juice and "fluff". The more sauce used, the tastier the dessert, especially since left-over sauce separates.

MRS. CHESTER FERGUSON

CHOCOLATE REFRIGERATOR CUPCAKES

1 stick butter	⅔ cup unsifted flour
1½ 1-ounce squares bitter chocolate	1 teaspoon vanilla
	2 eggs, well beaten
1 cup sugar	1 cup coarsely chopped nuts

Melt butter and chocolate together in double boiler. Mix other ingredients and add chocolate-butter mixture. Place small size paper baking cups in muffin tins. Fill half full—no more. Bake 12 minutes at 350°. This may not look done, but don't overcook. While cakes are cooking prepare icing.

ICING:

2 tablespoons butter	¾ box powdered sugar
1 ounce square bitter chocolate	Cold coffee

Melt butter and chocolate together. Add powdered sugar gradually and enough cold coffee to make mixture smooth. Ice cakes while hot (fill to top of paper cups). Put in refrigerator. Makes 2 dozen. These cupcakes freeze well.

Mrs. W. Braxton Schell

ORANGE CUPCAKES

2⅔ cups flour	⅓ cup evaporated milk
4 teaspoons baking powder	⅔ cup orange juice
¼ teaspoon salt	2 eggs, beaten
1½ cups sugar	½ cup soft butter

Combine and sift dry ingredients. Add milk, orange juice, eggs, and soft butter to dry ingredients. Stir until well mixed. Bake in paper cups at 400° (put paper cups in muffin pans). Ice while warm.

ICING:

1 tablespoon grated orange rind	¼ teaspoon salt
1 tablespoon evaporated milk	2 cups of confectioners sugar
2 tablespoons orange juice	(or just enough to thicken icing to spread on cakes)

Mrs. M. E. Wilson

FRUITCAKE CUPCAKES

⅓ cup Crisco	½ teaspoon ground cloves
1 cup sugar	1 teaspoon baking soda
1 cup sour cream	½ cup chopped nuts (pecans)
2 eggs	½ cup chopped candied cherries
2 cups sifted flour	½ cup chopped candied green
1⅓ teaspoons cinnamon	and yellow pineapple
1½ teaspoons nutmeg	½ cup chopped dates

Cream together Crisco and sugar. Add the sour cream and eggs. Beat well. Combine the remaining ingredients and add gradually. Bake in greased and floured tiny muffin tins in 375° oven for 15 minutes.

MRS. J. R. BORING

Frostings and Fillings

CHOCOLATE FLUFF FROSTING

4 tablespoons butter	2 squares chocolate, melted
1½ cups sifted confectioners sugar	¼ teaspoon salt
1 teaspoon vanilla	2 egg whites

Cream butter, add ¾ cup sugar, blend well. Add vanilla, melted chocolate and salt. Beat egg whites stiff, not dry. Add ¾ cup sugar, a little at a time, beating after each addition. Continue until mixture stands in peaks. Add chocolate mixture, folding enough to blend. This is enough icing for the top and sides of a 9-inch layer cake, but not enough to put between layers too. It was intended to be used in conjunction with the Golden Cream Filling. Increase proportions by one half again if you wish to ice cake completely.

MRS. ONAN WHITEHURST

THREE-MINUTE ICING OR FAST FUDGE

1 cup sugar	¼ stick butter
¼ cup milk	Pinch of salt
¼ cup cocoa	½ teaspoon vanilla

Mix together all ingredients except vanilla. Bring mixture to a boil; cook 3 minutes. Remove from heat. Add vanilla and beat until creamy. This recipe can be doubled.

MRS. GUY A. BURNETT, JR.

GOLDEN CREAM FILLING

½ cup sugar	1½ cups milk
3 tablespoons cake flour	2 egg yolks
¼ teaspoon salt	1 teaspoon vanilla

Combine sugar, cake flour and salt in double boiler. Add milk gradually. Mix thoroughly. Place over boiling water, stirring constantly for 10 minutes. Pour small amount of the sauce over slightly beaten egg yolks. Return to double boiler and cook 2 minutes longer. Add vanilla and cool. Use as a filling for chocolate cakes which you ice with Chocolate Fluff Frosting.

MRS. ONAN WHITEHURST

WARM SAUCE FOR FRUITCAKE

2 cups granulated sugar	1½ tablespoons white vinegar
1½ sticks butter	¼ to ½ cup sherry
2 egg yolks, beaten	

Combine sugar, butter, egg yolks, and vinegar and cook over hot water until sugar is melted. Add sherry or other wine. Keep sauce over hot water until time to serve, or make the day before, store in refrigerator, and heat in top of double boiler just before serving. Makes 4 to 6 servings.

Before serving fruitcake, wrap pieces separately in wax paper and heat in double boiler. Unwrap at serving time and pour warm sauce over cake.

MRS. C. E. MICKLER

FRUIT FILLING
(For 3-layer white or gold cake)

1 cup sugar	½ cup pecans or walnuts, chopped
2 tablespoons flour	
1 cup boiling water	2 tablespoons lemon juice
1 cup dates, chopped	2 tablespoons rum, brandy or sherry (optional)
1 cup figs, chopped	

Mix together sugar and flour. Slowly add boiling water. Cook over medium heat until thick, stirring constantly. Add dates, figs, nuts and lemon juice. Cook over low heat until fruits absorb moisture. Cool. Add rum, brandy or sherry. Spread between 3-layer cake. Ice with seven-minute frosting.

MRS. RALPH POLK, JR.

CHAPTER XVI

Pastry and Pies

In these diet conscious days it must not be forgotten that enjoyable eating can be balm to the spirit. A man who has just topped off a wonderful dinner with a gorgeous slice of pie, radiates peace and contentment, and happy is the wife who is the recipient of his fond admiration. In these days of frozen foods, children will gaze over a serving of homemade pie, big eyed, and marvel, "Gosh, Mom, did you make this?". It cannot be denied that such treats will be remembered long after a calorie count is forgotten. Let us forget the vitamins now and then, and feed the soul.

Pie Crust

PIE CRUST

1 cup sifted flour
1 teaspoon baking powder
1 tablespoon sugar

⅛ teaspoon salt
⅓ cup shortening
1 tablespoon cold water

Sift together dry ingredients. Cut in shortening until mixture is crumbly. Sprinkle water over and mix well until mixture forms a ball. Sprinkle ball with flour; turn out on wax paper and roll.

MRS. KARL WHITAKER

FLAKY PIE CRUST

2 cups flour
1 teaspoon salt

¼ cup cold water
⅔ cup vegetable shortening

Sift and measure flour. Sift again with the salt. Take out ⅓ cup flour and salt and mix with cold water. Cut shortening into the flour and salt, then add the paste. Mix until it forms a soft ball. This may be rolled out at once on a lightly floured board, but the results are better if the dough has been wrapped in wax paper and chilled thoroughly first. Yields 2 crusts.

MRS. E. C. DePURY

HOT WATER PIE CRUST

½ cup boiling water
1 cup plus 1 tablespoon lard
½ teaspoon salt

3 cups pastry flour
½ teaspoon baking powder

Pour boiling water over lard and salt. Stir until dissolved. Sift in the flour and baking powder. Stir well until it forms a smooth ball. Chill. Better the second day. Roll and bake as with any crust.

MRS. E. W. BERRIMAN

CHOCOLATE CRUMB CRUST

1½ cups chocolate snap crumbs, rolled fine

½ cup butter or margarine

Mix crumbs and butter. Press into pie plate. Bake 10 minutes at 350°.

MRS. JOHN A. LEWIS

ORANGE PECAN PIE CRUST

2 cups sifted flour
Rind of ½ orange, ground fine

¼ cup chopped pecans
½ cup oil
¼ cup orange juice

Mix flour, ground orange rind and nuts well. Combine the oil and orange juice and beat with fork until thoroughly creamy. Pour in mixture and blend well. Roll out on wax paper, well floured as dough is moist. Makes two 9-inch shells. Bake 10 minutes at 400° or until lightly browned.

KITCHEN CORNER

GRAHAM CRACKER CRUST

16 large graham crackers
¼ cup sugar
1 tablespoon flour

1 teaspoon cinnamon
4 tablespoons melted butter

Crumble graham crackers. Add sugar, flour, cinnamon and melted butter. Mix all and pat into a 9-inch pie plate. Chill well.

MRS. EMORY PORTAS

Baked Pies

APPLE CRUNCH PIE WITH CINNAMON ICE CREAM

6 juicy sour apples
1 cup flour

1 cup brown sugar
¼ pound margarine

Pare, core and slice apples, and put in pie plate. Mix flour and brown sugar, then add margarine and mix until crumbly. Sprinkle this mixture over apples and bake at 350° for about 30 minutes or until apples are done. Serve warm with Cinnamon Ice Cream.

CINNAMON ICE CREAM:

½ pint whipping cream
2 tablespoons sugar
1 heaping teaspoon cinnamon

1 quart vanilla ice cream
1 tablespoon red-hot cinnamon
candy (optional)

Whip the cream, add sugar and cinnamon. Soften ice cream, add cinnamon mixture and whip. If desired, add cinnamon candy. Freeze. Serves 8.

MRS. SHIRLEY R. HANSON

BUTTERSCOTCH PIE

2 cups milk
4 tablespoons cornstarch
1 cup dark brown sugar
3 egg yolks

4 tablespoons melted butter
¼ teaspoon salt
1 teaspoon vanilla

Scald the milk in top of double boiler. Meanwhile mix cornstarch and brown sugar. Stir in well-beaten egg yolks. Add hot milk gradually, then butter and salt. Return to top of double boiler and cook over hot water until thick, stirring constantly. Cool. Add vanilla. Pour into baked pastry shells. Top with meringue.

MERINGUE:

3 egg whites
6 tablespoons sugar

½ teaspoon vanilla
Pinch of salt

Beat egg whites stiff but not dry. Add sugar 2 tablespoons at a time, beating well. Add salt and vanilla. Spread over pie, sealing edges. Brown in slow oven (325°) for about 15 minutes.

MRS. KARL WHITAKER

APPLE CUSTARD PIE

Line a pie pan with pastry. Fill with raw apples, cut in thin slices. Pour the following custard mixture on top of apples:

2 egg yolks	1 cup milk
1/2 cup sugar	2 tablespoons butter
1 tablespoon flour	

Cream egg yolks with sugar and flour. Add milk and butter. Lattice the top with strips of pastry. Bake in 425° oven for 10 minutes, then reduce heat to 350° and bake for 20 to 25 minutes. When done put meringue (made from the 2 egg whites and 2 tablespoons sugar) inside each lattice. Sprinkle meringue with chopped nuts. Return to oven and brown meringue.

MRS. WILSON COLLINS

APPLE TART PIE

Make your favorite pie shell and pierce the bottom with a fork. Make the edge a bit fancy, as there is no top or stripping to the pie. Do not bake it first.

3 tart apples	1/2 cup milk
2/3 cup sugar	Butter
1/2 teaspoon salt	Cinnamon

Peel apples. From the side of each apple slice 1 large round piece. (One apple gives 4 pieces.) Place these flat side down in the bottom of the pie pan on the pastry. Arrange them in a decorative manner. Pour over the apples a mixture of the sugar, salt, and milk. Dot with butter, sprinkle with cinnamon, and bake until custard firms, about 350° oven for 35 minutes. Cool and serve. Serves 4. You will find this apple pie quite different.

It is nice to make 2 different kinds of apple pie at one time. This way the rest of the apple may be used. Otherwise cook the remaining pieces with 1 1/2 cups of sugar and a cup of water in an open pot over a medium heat. When liquid cooks down, add 2 drops of red coloring to apples and serve hot or cold. Wonderful with pork.

MRS. RICHARD D. FIELD

GETTIE'S APPLE PECAN PIE

1 unbaked 9-inch pie shell
4 cups chopped cooking apples
1 cup sugar
2 tablespoons flour

4 tablespoons butter, cut into
  small pieces
1 cup chopped pecans
1 teaspoon cinnamon

Mix sugar and flour together. Mix lightly with apples, then mix in butter, chopped pecans and cinnamon. Fill pie shell and bake at 400° for 30 minutes. Serve hot. Top with ice cream or whipped cream.

MRS. EDWIN K. NELSON, JR.

CALAMONDIN PIE

3 egg yolks
½ cup sugar
¼ cup calamondin juice
3 egg whites

⅛ teaspoon salt
½ cup sugar
Baked pie shell

Beat egg yolks until lemon colored. Add ½ cup sugar and juice and cook in double boiler until thick, stirring constantly. Remove from heat and cool. Add 2 or 3 drops of red food coloring to custard to get rich orange color.

While custard cools beat egg whites and salt 2 minutes on high speed. Add sugar slowly and continue beating another half minute. Fold into custard. Fill a baked pie shell and bake in slow oven (325°) until slightly browned, about 15 minutes.

MRS. G. PIERCE WOOD, JR.

TENNESSEE CHESS PIE

1 unbaked 9 inch pie shell
5 egg yolks
1 cup sugar
⅛ teaspoon salt

⅓ cup melted butter
3 tablespoons heavy cream
1 teaspoon vanilla

Beat egg yolks until fluffy, adding sugar and salt gradually. Add butter, cream and vanilla and beat well. Turn into unbaked pie shell and bake at 325° for 40 minutes.

MRS. CHARLES SWEAT

CREAM CHEESE PIE

1 pound cream cheese	1 cup sour cream
3 eggs	3 tablespoons sugar
⅔ cup sugar	1 teaspoon vanilla
½ teaspoon vanilla	Slivered Brazil nuts

Cream the cheese, eggs, ⅔ cup sugar, and vanilla in an electric mixer; beat until smooth and thick. Pour into buttered 9-inch pie plate. Bake at 350° for 25 minutes. Cool 20 minutes. While mixture is cooling, beat sour cream, 3 tablespoons sugar, and vanilla with a spoon. Pour mixture over top of pie. Return to 350° and bake 10 minutes. Cool before serving and sprinkle slivered Brazil nuts on top. (Can refrigerate day or so.) Serves 6 or 8.

MRS. FRED L. WOLF

FIG PIE

1 No. 2½ can of Kadota figs, undrained	1 tablespoon lemon juice
3 tablespoons sugar	1 to 1½ teaspoons powdered ginger
1 tablespoon butter	

Put mixture in unbaked pie shell and bake 10 minutes at 450° then at 350° for 25 to 30 minutes or until done. If desired, mixture can be thickened with 1 tablespoon flour or cornstarch and put in baked pie shell. When still warm serve with slightly sweetened whipped cream.

MISS CAROL KELLER

FUDGE PIE

9-inch unbaked pastry shell	2 cups sugar
⅓ cup margarine	¼ teaspoon salt
3 squares unsweetened chocolate	1 teaspoon vanilla
4 eggs	⅔ cup chopped pecans

Melt margarine and chocolate together and cool slightly. Beat eggs, add sugar, salt and vanilla, blending well. Add chocolate mixture and pecans. Mix thoroughly and pour into unbaked pastry shell. Bake at 350° for 40 minutes or until top is crusty and filling is set, though soft.

MRS. CARLTON C. CONE

CHOCOLATE CREAM PIE

3 squares unsweetened chocolate,
  cut in pieces
2½ cups cold milk
4 tablespoons flour
1 cup sugar
½ teaspoon salt

4 egg yolks, slightly beaten
2 tablespoons butter
2 teaspoons vanilla
1 baked 9-inch pie shell
8 tablespoons sugar
4 egg whites, stiffly beaten

Add chocolate to milk and heat in double boiler. When chocolate is melted, beat with rotary beater 1 minute, or until mixture is smooth and blended. Combine flour, sugar and salt. Add to egg yolks. Pour small amount of chocolate mixture over egg mixture, stirring vigorously. Return to double boiler and cook until thickened, stirring constantly. Add butter and vanilla. Cool. Pour into pie shell and cover with meringue made by folding sugar into egg whites. Bake in slow oven (300°) 12 minutes, or until a delicate brown.

MRS. STEPHEN M. SPARKMAN

GRAHAM ANGEL PIE

12 plain graham crackers
3 eggs
1 cup sugar

1 teaspoon baking powder
1 teaspoon vanilla
½ cup chopped pecans (sprinkled
  on top)

Roll crackers to fine crumbs. Add eggs and beat well. Add remainder of ingredients in order given. Bake in greased pie pan at 350° for 20 minutes. Cut wedges and serve with whipped cream or ice cream. Top with a cherry. Serves 6.

MRS. JACK WALL EVANS

GUAVA PIE

2 tablespoons flour
⅔ cup sugar
½ teaspoon cinnamon
⅛ teaspoon salt

4 cups peeled, seeded and
  sliced guavas
1 teaspoon lemon juice
2 tablespoons butter

Mix flour, sugar, cinnamon and salt. Line pie plate with your favorite pastry. Add guavas and flour mixture. Sprinkle with lemon juice and dot with butter. Cover with pastry. Cut gashes in pastry for steam to escape. Bake 10 minutes at 450°, then lower heat to 350° and bake 30 minutes.

FLORIDA DEPARTMENT OF AGRICULTURE

LEMON MERINGUE PIE

1 cup sugar	3 egg yolks
3 tablespoons flour	¼ cup lemon juice
3 tablespoons cornstarch	½ teaspoon grated lemon rind
¼ teaspoon salt	1 tablespoon butter
2 cups boiling water	1 baked pie shell

Blend dry ingredients in top of double boiler. Add water, blend and cook until mixture is thick. Continue to cook for 10 minutes. Remove from heat. Beat yolks slightly and pour small amount of custard on yolks. Add this to mixture and return to double boiler. Cook slowly for 2 minutes. Add lemon juice, grated rind and butter. Remove from heat and pour into baked pie shell.

MERINGUE:

3 egg whites	⅛ teaspoon cream of tartar
3 tablespoons sugar	

Beat egg whites; add sugar and cream of tartar gradually. Beat until stiff peaks form. Pour meringue on top of pie and place in hot oven until brown. Cool pie before serving. Serves 6.

MRS. J. E. HARRIS

VARIATION: Meringue for Lemon Pie

2 egg whites	½ tablespoon lemon juice
2 tablespoons confectioners sugar	

Beat egg whites until stiff but not dry, then beat in sugar gradually until smooth and creamy. Add lemon juice. Spread evenly on pie (being sure it touches sides of pan); bake in 300° oven for 15 minutes.

MRS. E. C. DePURY

LEMON PIE

2 eggs	1 lemon, juice and rind
1 cup of sugar	1 cup water
⅛ teaspoon salt	2 tablespoons butter, melted
⅓ cup of flour	1 unbaked pastry shell

Beat eggs, add blended sugar, salt, flour and lemon rind. Add lemon juice and water, then melted butter. Pour into unbaked pastry shell. Bake at 400° for 45 minutes. Brown on top shelf of oven.

MRS. GEOFFREY W. STEPHENS

HEAVENLY PIE

MERINGUE:

4 egg whites

1 cup sugar

1 teaspoon vinegar

Whip egg whites until stiff, and gradually beat in ½ cup sugar. Add vinegar, and fold in remaining ½ cup sugar. Spread flat in greased 9 or 10-inch pie pan, bringing the mixture a bit above the edge of the pan. Bake 30 minutes in 300° oven. Turn off and let cool in oven.

CUSTARD:

6 egg yolks

¾ cup sugar

6 tablespoons orange juice

½ teaspoon lemon juice

Pinch of salt

1 cup whipped cream

Chopped nuts

Combine egg yolks, sugar, orange juice, lemon juice, and salt, and cook in double boiler until thick. Cool. Spread meringue with ½ cup whipped cream, then put on custard layer. Top with other ½ cup whipped cream and sprinkle with chopped nuts. Will keep in refrigerator. Avoid serving too cold.

MRS. FRANK W. STANTON, JR.

PECAN PIE

3 eggs

½ cup sugar

½ teaspoon salt

4 teaspoons melted butter

1 cup light corn syrup

1 teaspoon vanilla

1¼ cups pecan halves

1 uncooked 9-inch pie shell

Beat eggs well; blend in sugar and salt; add butter, syrup, vanilla, and pecans. Pour into uncooked pastry shell. Place in middle or lower part of oven. Bake 15 minutes at 450°, then 30 minutes at 350°.

MRS. H. PHILLIP HAMPTON

MRS. NEWLAND'S CYPRESS GARDENS PECAN PIE

1 cup chopped pecans

3 eggs, beaten

1 cup dark brown sugar

1 cup light corn syrup

¼ teaspoon salt

3 tablespoons milk

1 teaspoon vanilla

1 unbaked pastry shell

Place pecans in bottom of unbaked pie shell. Blend together remaining ingredients. Pour the mixture into the pie shell and bake at 450° for 10 minutes. Then reduce oven heat to 325° for approximately 40 minutes.

CYPRESS GARDENS, WINTER HAVEN, FLORIDA

MYSTERY PIE

CUSTARD:

2 cups milk
2 tablespoons cornstarch
3 egg yolks

1 teaspoon vinegar
½ teaspoon salt

Combine ingredients in top of double boiler; beat well. Cook until thick or it coats the spoon, stirring constantly to prevent sticking.

CRUST:

1 package unsweetened zweiback
½ cup sugar

2 teaspoons cinnamon
½ cup melted butter

Put zweiback through food chopper; add sugar and cinnamon; mix well and reserve ½ cup for future use. To remainder of mixture, add butter and mix well. Press firmly into bottom and sides of 10-inch pie plate.

MERINGUE:

3 egg whites

6 tablespoons sugar

Beat egg whites until stiff. Add sugar and beat again. Pour custard into crust; top with meringue; sprinkle reserved crumb mixture over all. Bake ½ hour in slow oven (250° to 275°). Serves 6 to 8.

Mrs. J. E. McElmurray

PUMPKIN PIE

1 pie shell, unbaked
1¾ cups canned pumpkin
⅓ cup sugar
½ teaspoon salt
1 teaspoon cinnamon
½ teaspoon ginger

2 eggs
1 cup milk (small can evaporated
    milk plus enough plain milk to
    make 1 cup)
½ cup white corn syrup

Line a 9-inch pie plate with pastry having a fluted edge. Simmer pumpkin over low heat, stirring frequently, for 10 minutes. (As the pumpkin heats it dries out a little.) Remove from heat. Stir in next 4 ingredients. Beat eggs just until frothy. Combine with milk and corn syrup. Turn this egg mixture into pumpkin mixture and beat with beater until just blended. Turn into unbaked pie shell. Bake in 450° oven for 15 minutes, then in 300° oven for 40 minutes, or until a silver knife comes out clean. Serve pie topped with whipped cream.

Mrs. E. C. DePury

SWEET POTATO PIE

3 small sweet potatoes   1 ¼ cups sugar
¼ pound butter   ½ teaspoon allspice
1 cup milk   1 unbaked pie shell
2 eggs, slightly beaten

Grate raw sweet potatoes. Melt butter and add other ingredients. Stir in grated potatoes. Pour into pie shell. Bake 10 minutes at 425° then 50 minutes at 325° or until custard is set in the middle. Cool on rack to prevent soggy crust. The raw sweet potatoes make an entirely different flavored and textured pie. As a variation sprinkle top thinly with mixture of brown sugar, cinnamon and melted butter before baking.

MRS. A. M. CROWELL, JR.

PRIZE PEACH COBBLER

¾ cup flour   ¾ cup milk
Less than ⅛ teaspoon salt   ½ cup butter or margarine
2 teaspoons baking powder   2 cups fresh sliced peaches
1 cup sugar   1 cup sugar

Sift flour, salt and baking powder. Mix with 1 cup sugar; slowly stir in milk to make batter. Melt butter in 8 x 8 x 2-inch baking pan. Pour batter over melted butter. Do not stir. Carefully spoon over this the peaches and sugar, mixed thoroughly. Bake 1 hour at 350°. Serves 6. Delicious hot or cold. Serve with cream if desired.

MRS. JULIAN LANE

DEEP DISH PEACH AND APRICOT PIE

1 can peach pie mix   Nutmeg to flavor
1 can apricots (seed them)   ½ cup flour
  with juice   ½ cup sugar
⅓ cup honey   ½ cup milk
¾ stick of butter or margarine 1 teaspoon baking powder

Combine peach pie mix, apricots, honey, butter and nutmeg in a deep casserole. Combine flour, sugar, milk, and baking powder. Mix well and pour over pie in casserole. Bake at 350° for 1 hour. Serve with vanilla ice cream.

MRS. A. W. McCORMICK

CHESS CAKES

Make rich pie crust and fit into gem pans; then make filling as follows:

1 cup melted butter	4 egg yolks, beaten
1 cup sugar	1 teaspoon vanilla extract
1 cup dates, chopped not too fine	

Mix all together. Fill crusts and bake in 350° oven until brown on top and crust is done (45 to 55 minutes).

Make meringue with:

4 egg whites	1 teaspoon vanilla
6 tablespoons sugar	

Spread on top of cakes and brown in oven.

Mrs. Ray C. Brown

GUAVA TURNOVERS

1½ cups sifted flour	½ teaspoon salt
½ cup shortening	Guava paste (available at Spanish
¼ cup boiling water	restaurants and markets)

Sift flower into mixing bowl. Add shortening, then boiling water and salt. Mix with spoon until well blended. Roll out thin and cut into circles 4 inches across (use large size glass as cutter). Slice guava paste ¼ inch thick and place one slice on half of each circle. Fold other half over, pinch edges with fork to seal and make attractive pattern on tart. Place on ungreased cookie sheet and bake in 325° oven for 15 or 20 minutes. After this length of time if guava paste is bubbly but pastry has not browned, turn oven to broil for a minute or two and leave oven door ajar until tarts are golden brown. Do not bake at higher temperature as guava paste burns easily.

Mrs. Alton B. Coggin

CURRANT TARTS

⅓ cup butter	⅔ cup of currants
⅔ cup brown sugar	8 pastry shells unbaked
1 egg, slightly beaten	Whipped cream

Cream butter, add brown sugar and egg. Add currants which have been rinsed and well drained. Pour into unbaked pastry shells and bake at 350° for about 35 minutes. Top with whipped cream. Serves 8.

Mrs. T. N. Henderson, Sr.

GEM-DANDIES

1 stick of butter or margarine   1 3-ounce package cream cheese
1 cup flour

Combine above ingredients and press into very small muffin pans (gem pans), making miniature pastry shells. Fill with the following mixture:

½ cup sugar   2 tablespoons lemon juice
¼ teaspoon salt   1 teaspoon grated lemon rind
2 tablespoons soft bread crumbs   2 tablespoons currants, chopped
  (made from bread crusts)   2 tablespoons walnuts or pecans
1 egg

Bake in 375° oven for 20 to 25 minutes, until edges are browned. Serves 16.

MRS. PRESTON GARRETT

GOLDEN TASSIES

2 3-ounce packages cream cheese   2 cups sifted all-purpose flour
2 sticks margarine   ¾ cup chopped pecans

Allow cream cheese and margarine to come to room temperature; thoroughly blend with a wooden spoon or at lowest speed on mixer. Add flour. Mix well, chill in refrigerator for 2 or 3 hours. Roll into 1-inch balls and press each into tiny muffin tins, forming shells. Sprinkle a few chopped pecans into bottom of each shell (approximately ½ teaspoon).

FILLING:

2 eggs, slightly beaten   2 tablespoons melted butter
1½ cups light brown sugar,   ⅛ teaspoon salt
  firmly packed   1 teaspoon vanilla

Mix eggs, sugar, melted butter, salt and vanilla. Spoon this sticky mixture into shells, filling about ⅔ to ¾ full. Sprinkle a few chopped pecans over tops and bake in 350° oven 15 to 17 minutes, then reduce temperature to 250° for 10 minutes or until set. Makes 48 tassies. Can be frozen for future use. These are like miniature pecan pies.

MRS. GRADY LESTER

Refrigerator and Frozen Pies

BLACK BOTTOM PIE

CRUST:

14 crisp ginger snaps   5 tablespoons butter, melted

Roll cookies into fine crumbs. Add butter and mix well. Press in 9-inch pie pan and bake 10 minutes at 300°. While crust is cooling make filling.

BASIC CUSTARD:

2 cups milk   1 tablespoon plus ¾ teaspoon
½ cup sugar   cornstarch
                     4 egg yolks, well beaten

Scald milk; combine sugar and cornstarch. Add scalded milk slowly to beaten egg yolks, then stir in sugar and cornstarch. Cook in double boiler, stirring occasionally, for about 20 minutes or until custard coats spoon. Remove from heat. Take out 1 cup of the custard and use for making chocolate filling.

CHOCOLATE CUSTARD:

1½ squares baking chocolate,   1 teaspoon vanilla
   melted

Add melted chocolate and vanilla to 1 cup custard. Beat well. When cool, pour into crust and chill. Top with rum filling.

RUM FILLING:

1 tablespoon gelatin   ½ teaspoon cream of tartar
¼ cup cold water   ½ cup sugar
4 egg whites   1 teaspoon rum extract

While remaining custard is still hot, stir in gelatin which has been softened in cold water, then dissolved over hot water. Beat egg whites until frothy; add cream of tartar and beat in sugar until mixture holds soft peaks. While egg white mixture is still smooth and soft fold into custard and blend in rum flavoring.

As soon as chocolate custard is set cover it with the fluffy rum custard. Chill until set. Cover with slightly sweetened whipped cream and sprinkle with shaved chocolate curls.

MRS. GUY BURNETT

BROWNIE PIE

¾ cup chocolate wafer crumbs
¾ cup sugar
½ cup chopped pecans
3 egg whites

TOPPING:
½ pint whipping cream
2 tablespoons sugar

Roll wafers into fine crumbs. Mix with sugar and nuts. Fold crumb mixture into stiffly beaten egg whites. Pour into buttered 8-inch pie pan and push up on sides. Bake in preheated oven for 30 minutes at 325°. Let cool thoroughly before adding topping.

Whip cream with sugar. Spread on top of cooled pie and chill for 3 to 4 hours.

MRS. PETE HEARN

FROSTED CHERRY PIE

1 16-ounce can tart cherries, drained and juice reserved
¾ cup sugar
3½ tablespoons cornstarch
¼ cup water
1 teaspoon almond flavoring

9-inch baked pie shell
6 large graham crackers
2 tablespoons butter, melted
2 cups dairy sour cream
¼ cup sugar
½ teaspoon vanilla

Mix cherry juice, sugar, cornstarch, and water. Cook, stirring constantly, until thick and clear. Cool. Add flavoring and cherries. Turn mixture into pie shell. Roll crackers until very fine. Mix with butter and sprinkle over cherries. Mix sour cream, sugar, and vanilla. Spread over crumbs. Bake at 350° for 7 minutes. Chill for several hours. Serves 6 to 8.

MRS. JOHN R. CULBREATH

CHOCOLATE BAR PIE

20 regular size marshmallows
4 small chocolate almond bars
⅔ cup milk

1 cup whipping cream, whipped
Baked pie shell or crumb crust, (8-inch)

Combine marshmallows, chocolate bars and milk in top of double boiler. Heat over hot, not boiling, water until melted. Cool. Fold whipped cream into cooled mixture. Pour into baked pie shell or crumb crust and chill at least 4 hours. Serves 6.

MRS. JOHN R. CULBREATH

CHOCOLATE MERINGUE PIE

2 egg whites
½ cup granulated sugar

½ teaspoon vinegar (scant)
½ teaspoon vanilla (scant)

Beat egg whites stiff; gradually add ⅔ of sugar, beating continually. Stir in remaining sugar with fork and fold in vanilla and vinegar. Spread this meringue mixture into well buttered pie pan. Bake in slow oven (275°) for 1 hour. Cool thoroughly.

FILLING:

¾ cup semi-sweet chocolate
  bits (scant)
3 tablespoons hot water

1 cup whipping cream, whipped
  stiff

Melt chocolate bits in water over hot water. Cool. Fold in whipped cream and spread evenly over cooled meringue shell. If desired ½ cup whipping cream, beaten stiff, may be spread over top. Chill in refrigerator for 1 hour. May be made in advance and kept in the refrigerator. It serves 6.

MRS. SAM M. GIBBONS

"GIRDLE-BUSTER" PIE

1 recipe graham cracker crust
1 quart coffee ice cream
1 can or jar of any commercial
  fudge sauce (not chocolate,
  it is too thin)

½ cup chopped pecans, walnuts
  or almonds

Soften and beat coffee ice cream. Pour into graham cracker crust and freeze. When firm spread chocolate fudge sauce over top and sprinkle with nuts. Keep frozen until served. Serves 6 to 8.

MRS. JOHN R. CULBREATH

STRAWBERRY PIE

1 quart strawberries
1 cup sugar
2 tablespoons cornstarch

1 baked pastry shell
1 cup whipping cream

Mash 1 pint of strawberries until juice is well extracted, bring to a boil, add sugar mixed with cornstarch, and cook until clear and thick. Place 1 pint of whole berries in the baked pastry shell. Pour over these the hot cooked berries, then place in refrigerator until very cold. Top with sweetened whipped cream before serving.

MRS. J. C. COUNCIL

LIME CHIFFON PIE

1 envelope plain gelatin
¼ cup cold water
3 tablespoons sugar
1 cup light corn syrup
6 tablespoons Florida lime juice

1 teaspoon lime rind, grated
½ teaspoon salt
4 eggs separated
1 9-inch pie shell, baked
(graham cracker crust may be
substituted)

Soften gelatin in cold water. Combine sugar, ½ cup corn syrup, lime juice, grated rind and salt in top of double boiler. Beat egg yolks and fold into lime juice mixture. Cook over hot water until slightly thickened. Beat egg whites until stiff. Gradually beat in remaining corn syrup until mixture is "marshmallowy". Fold egg whites into gelatin mixture. Pile mixture lightly into baked pie shell and chill. Serves 6.

MRS. CLAUDE D. LOGAN, JR.

FLORIDA ORANGE GROVE PIE
(Grand Prize Winner, Second All-Florida Orange Dessert Contest)

4 egg whites
¼ teaspoon cream of tartar
1½ cups granulated sugar
5 tablespoons finely crushed
walnuts
5 egg yolks

2 tablespoons lemon juice
3 tablespoons grated orange rind
⅛ teaspoon salt
1 pint heavy cream
5 Florida oranges

MERINGUE:

Heat oven to 275°. Beat egg whites until foamy, add cream of tartar and beat to stiff peaks. Gradually add 1 cup sugar and continue beating to very stiff peaks. Spread over a 9-inch pie plate which has been greased thoroughly, just to the edge. Sprinkle edge with finely chopped walnuts. Bake 1 hour. Cool.

FILLING:

Beat egg yolks slightly and add ½ cup sugar, lemon juice, grated orange rind and salt. Cook over boiling water, stirring constantly until thick, about 10 minutes. Fold in 2 oranges which have been peeled and diced. Cool and fold in 1 cup whipped cream. Pour this mixture into center of meringue and smooth over. Chill 12 hours or longer in refrigerator.

Just before serving, top with mounds of whipped cream (1 cup), leaving room for center to be filled with orange sections. Top cream with grated orange rind and decorate around center edge with orange slices.

MRS. MYRTLE I. RISDALL

APRICOT CHIFFON PIE

1 ¼ cups dried apricots
1 ¼ cups water
6 tablespoons sugar
Dash salt
1 envelope unflavored gelatin

¼ cup cold water
½ cup boiling water
2 tablespoons lemon juice
1 cup evaporated milk,
    chilled icy cold
9-inch graham cracker pie shell

Wash apricots. Add to 1 ¼ cups water. Cover and simmer till tender, about 15 minutes. Drain and reserve liquid. Mash apricots with fork or potato masher. Stir in any liquid that is left from cooking apricots. Add sugar and salt. Cool. Soften gelatin in ¼ cup cold water. Dissolve in the boiling water. Cool slightly, then stir into the apricot mixture. Add lemon juice to chilled milk. Whip till very stiff. Fold the whipped milk into cold apricot mixture quickly but thoroughly. Turn into shell. Chill slightly. May be frozen. Serves 6 to 8.

MRS. BERNARD WILSON

CALAMONDIN CHIFFON PIE

1 9-inch pie shell, baked
1 envelope unflavored gelatin
¼ cup water
3 eggs, separated

1 cup sugar
¾ cup calamondin juice
⅛ teaspoon salt
Whipping cream, ½ pint

Soften gelatin in water; set aside. Beat egg yolks until lemon colored. Add ½ cup sugar, juice, and salt. Mix well and cook in top of double boiler, stirring constantly until mixture coats spoon, about 10 minutes. Add gelatin, stir and cook 2 or 3 minutes longer. Remove from heat, cool thoroughly. Beat egg whites stiff, gradually add remaining sugar. Fold into well cooled custard. Pour into pie shell. Chill until firm. Top with whipped cream and serve.

MRS. W. F. HIMES

RUM CREAM PIE

3 egg yolks
½ cup sugar
1 ½ teaspoons gelatin
½ cup cold water

1 cup heavy cream, whipped
¼ cup dark Jamaican rum
1 9-inch baked pastry shell
Bittersweet chocolate, shaved

Beat egg yolks until lemon colored. Add the sugar while still beating. Soften gelatin in water. Put gelatin mixture over low heat and, stirring constantly, let it come to a boil. Pour this over egg mixture, stirring briskly. Fold in whipped cream. Add rum. Cool but do not let set. When cool pour into pie shell and chill. When filling has set sprinkle top of pie generously with shaved chocolate. Serves 6.

MRS. BERNARD WILSON

LUSCIOUS LIME PIE

1 tablespoon plain gelatin	1 teaspoon grated lime rind
½ cup sugar	Few drops green food coloring
¼ teaspoon salt	½ cup sugar
4 eggs, separated	1 cup cream, whipped
½ cup lime juice	1 9-inch pie shell, baked, or
¼ cup water	cracker crumb shell

Mix gelatin, ½ cup sugar, and salt in saucepan. Beat egg yolks well, add lime juice and water. Stir into gelatin mixture. Cook over low heat, stirring constantly, just until mixture comes to a boil. Remove from heat, stir in grated rind and coloring. Chill, stirring occasionally, until mixture mounds slightly when dropped from spoon. Beat egg whites until soft peaks form. Gradually add ½ cup sugar, beating until stiff. Fold into chilled gelatin mixture. Fold in whipped cream, (some cream may be reserved for topping if desired). Pour into prepared crust. Chill until firm.

MRS. JOHN S. ALLEN

NESSELRODE PIE

1 tablespoon gelatin	1½ teaspoons rum flavoring or
¼ cup cold water	1 tablespoon white rum
2 cups light cream	1 cup whipping cream, whipped
2 eggs separated	Unsweetened chocolate shavings
Pinch of salt	1 9-inch baked pie shell
¼ cup plus 6 tablespoons sugar	

Soak gelatin in cold water for 5 minutes. Scald cream in top of double boiler. Beat egg yolks with fork, stir in salt and ¼ cup sugar. Add scalded cream slowly to egg yolks while stirring constantly. Return mixture to double boiler and cook over boiling water, stirring constantly, until smooth and slightly thickened (about 5 minutes). Remove from heat; add gelatin and stir until dissolved. Chill until it begins to thicken.

Beat egg whites until stiff and gradually add remaining 6 tablespoons sugar; continue beating until very stiff. Add flavoring to chilled custard and fold in egg white mixture. Fold in whipped cream, reserving enough to garnish top of pie; use pastry tube or spread as you would meringue. Pour into baked pastry shell and sprinkle chocolate shavings over top. Chill thoroughly. Well drained chopped maraschino cherries and chopped pecans may be folded into the mixture, if desired.

If the pie is made the day before serving, the whipped cream garnish and chocolate shavings should be added just prior to serving. This pie may be wrapped and frozen. It is suggested that frozen pie be garnished after thawing. For a larger pie make 1½ times the recipe.

MISS SARAH NORRIS

SHERRY CHIFFON PIE

1 tablespoon gelatin	⅓ teaspoon salt
⅓ cup cold water	1 baked 9-inch pie shell
4 eggs, separated	(or graham cracker crust)
1 cup sugar	½ pint whipped cream
⅔ cup sherry	2 teaspoons powdered sugar

Soak gelatin in water 5 minutes. Beat yolks with ½ cup sugar until light. Add sherry. Cook in double boiler stirring constantly until consistency of custard. Stir in gelatin and cool. Beat egg whites until stiff. Add ½ cup sugar and salt. Combine with custard, fill pie shell, and chill until firm (about 3 hours). Cover with whipped cream to which the powdered sugar has been added. Serves 6 to 8.

MRS. ROBERT A. FOSTER

FLORIDA SUN-KING ORANGE PIE
(Third prize winner, Second All-Florida Orange Dessert Contest)

1 package unflavored gelatin	⅓ cup sugar
1 cup fresh orange juice	¾ cup grated fresh coconut
3 eggs, separated	1 cup peeled and diced oranges
½ cup sugar	(remove seeds)
Grated rind of ½ lemon and	1 baked 9-inch pie shell
1 orange	½ pint whipping cream
⅛ teaspoon salt	1 tablespoon sugar

Peel and grate enough fresh coconut, or use grated fresh frozen coconut, to make ¾ cupful. Grate rind of ½ lemon and 1 orange. Juice oranges for 1 cupful. Peel and dice oranges for 1 cupful, being careful to remove all skins and seeds. Refrigerate coconut and diced orange until needed.

Combine gelatin and ½ cup orange juice. Put in top of double boiler beaten egg yolks, ½ cup sugar, and ½ cup orange juice. Cook over boiling water, stirring constantly, until thick. Remove from heat. Add gelatin mixture and grated rinds. Chill until it begins to congeal. Put into large bowl of electric mixer egg whites and salt. Beat on speed No. 10 until stiff. Gradually add ⅓ cup sugar. Continue beating only until blended. On speed No. 2, fold in the gelatin mixture. Now, with rubber spatula or perforated spoon, fold in ½ cup coconut and diced oranges. Pour into previously baked, cooled pie crust. Chill until ready to serve. Put into small electric mixer bowl ½ pint whipping cream. Beat until stiff, but not dry, gradually adding 1 tablespoon sugar. Spread over top of the pie, sprinkle with remaining coconut, and garnish with dainty orange slices.

MRS. C. B. CLAYTON

BRANDY COFFEE PIE

1½ cups macaroon or vanilla
   wafer crumbs
¼ cup soft butter (approximately)
1 teaspoon almond extract
2 egg whites
¼ cup sugar

1 pint heavy cream, whipped
1 teaspoon instant coffee
1 teaspoon boiling water
3 to 4 tablespoons brandy to taste
Toasted almonds, ground fine

Mix crumbs with butter. Use just enough butter to hold crumbs together. Add almond extract. Press into 9-inch pie plate. Chill until firm.

Beat egg whites stiff. Add sugar. Fold egg whites into whipped cream. Dissolve coffee in boiling water and let cool. Add to cream mixture with brandy. Turn into crumb shell. Cover top with ground almonds. Freeze and serve frozen.

MRS. JOHN HUNNICUTT

BAKED ALASKA PIE

1 baked pastry shell
1 quart vanilla ice cream

1 package frozen strawberries
1 packet meringue mix

Soften ice cream, whip and spread in baked pie shell. When ice cream is frozen again, spread slightly thawed strawberries over top of pie. Return to freezer. Just before serving, prepare meringue and spread carefully over frozen pie sealing all edges. Brown quickly in very hot oven and serve immediately. Serves 6 to 8.

MRS. JOHN R. CULBREATH

FROZEN EGGNOG PIE

¾ pound vanilla wafers,
   crushed
1 egg, separated
¼ cup sugar
3 tablespoons bourbon

½ pint heavy cream
1 4-ounce bottle maraschino
   cherries, drained
½ cup nuts

Grease pie pan; line with about ¾ of the vanilla wafer crumbs. Beat egg yolk well. Combine sugar and bourbon and add slowly, beating well, to egg yolk. Whip cream; fold in bourbon mixture. Beat egg white until stiff, fold into mixture. Add half of cherries and all of nuts. Pour into crumb-lined tray; sprinkle remaining crumbs over top; decorate with rest of cherries cut in half. Freeze several hours. Serves 6. Red or green cherries (or a combination of both) may be used.

MRS. MARSHALL C. FERRELL

FRENCH GLACÉ STRAWBERRY PIE

FLAKY PASTRY:

1 cup sifted Gold Medal flour
½ teaspoon salt

⅓ cup shortening
2 tablespoons cold water
Butter

Mix flour and salt. Cut in shortening with pastry blender. Sprinkle with cold water and mix thoroughly. Shape into ball. Roll out ⅛ inch thick. Dot with bits of firm, not hard, butter. Fold over and roll again. Repeat butter procedure. Roll out dough and fit into 9-inch pie plate. Trim edges leaving ½ inch overhanging rim of pan. Fold this extra pastry under and make fluted edge. Prick pastry to prevent puffing. Bake at 475° (very hot oven) for 8 minutes. Cool completely.

STRAWBERRY GLACÉ FILLING:

1 quart strawberries
1 3-ounce package cream cheese

1 cup sugar
3 tablespoons cornstarch

Wash, cap, and drain strawberries. Soften cream cheese to spreading consistency. Cover bottom of crust with the cream cheese, then place on the cheese about half of the whole berries, using the choicest. Mash and strain remaining berries until juice is extracted. There should be 1½ cups of juice. Add a little water to make this if necessary.

Mix cornstarch and sugar. Stir in a small amount of the measured juice to make a smooth paste. Heat remainder of juice to boiling. Stir in sugar-cornstarch paste. Over low heat bring again to boiling and boil ONE minute, stirring constantly. Cool thoroughly. Pour over berries in pie shell. Chill 2 hours or more. Just before serving decorate with whipped cream and whole berries. This may be prepared a day ahead. Fresh peaches may be substituted for strawberries. Use about 1½ pounds of peaches—3½ cups sliced. Add a few drops of lemon juice to sliced peaches.

MRS. FRANK C. CALDWELL

CHAPTER XVII

Cookies

One of the first words in a baby's vocabulary is "cookie". Later, when he comes home from school in the afternoon, he will head straight for the cookie jar. Letters from camp will spell out a need for these treats, although the spelling may be somewhat strange. Teenage party refreshments will consist largely of cookies. Sophisticated college students will pen letters home asking in exalted language for money and, cookies. The bride's first little party for her girlhood friends will feature cookies. All through the adult years people will relish a snack of cookies and milk before bedtime. There is no escaping it, cookies are essential to a happy home life.

Who doesn't have fond memories of coming home on a chill winter day to a kitchen warm and fragrant with the delicious smell of baking cookies? Who can forget the welcome pause on a hot summer day for crisp cookies served with iced tea or tall glasses of chilled milk? It doesn't matter that a day's baking is gone almost before it is out of the oven. It's a way of life we must cherish.

PECAN DREAMS

1st LAYER:

½ cup butter
¼ cup powdered sugar

1 cup cake flour less
2 tablespoons for 2nd layer

2nd LAYER:

2 eggs
1½ cups brown sugar

2 tablespoons flour
½ teaspoon baking powder
1 cup pecans, broken

Mix butter, sugar, cake flour until thoroughly blended. Put in 11 x 15-inch pan. Beat eggs lightly. Add brown sugar, flour, and baking powder sifted together. Mix until smooth. Add nuts. Spread on top of first layer. Bake at 375° 30 to 40 minutes. Cut in squares.

MRS. HAL HOLTSINGER

BROWNIES

4 1-ounce squares unsweetened chocolate
1 stick margarine
2 cups sugar

4 well beaten eggs
1 cup sifted all-purpose flour
1 cup chopped pecans
1 teaspoon vanilla

Melt chocolate and margarine over hot water and blend. Gradually add sugar, then eggs and beat well. Add flour gradually, mixing just until it disappears. Add nuts and vanilla. Pour into two 8 x 8 x 2-inch pans which have been greased and paper-lined. Cook 25 to 30 minutes at 350°. Cut each pan into 16 squares. Let stand 5 minutes before turning out to cool. Makes 32.

MRS. FRANK BENTLEY, JR.

CRESCENTS

1¾ sticks butter
2 cups flour sifted 6 times
6 tablespoons powdered sugar

1 teaspoon vanilla
1 cup nuts, chopped

Cream butter, add other ingredients, and mix thoroughly. Shape with fingers in crescents 1 inch thick and about 3 inches long. Arrange on buttered cookie sheet. Bake 35 minutes in slow oven, 300°. Cool. Roll in confectioners sugar. Makes 36.

MRS. HARLAN LOGAN

CHOCOLATE DROP OATMEAL COOKIES

½ cup shortening
½ cup brown sugar
½ cup granulated sugar
1 egg
1 teaspoon vanilla

½ teaspoon salt
½ teaspoon soda
1½ cups uncooked oatmeal
½ cup semi-sweet chocolate bits
¾ cup enriched flour

Cream shortening and sugars. Add egg and vanilla and beat well. Add sifted dry ingredients, then oatmeal and chocolate bits. Mix well. Drop by teaspoonfuls on greased cookie sheet. Bake in moderate oven for 10 minutes. Yields 4 dozen.

MRS. W. E. BLAKE

SOUR CREAM OATMEAL COOKIES

1 cup butter or margarine	½ teaspoon baking powder
1½ cups sugar	2 cups flour
2 cups uncooked old fashion oatmeal	2 teaspoons cinnamon
1 teaspoon soda	1 cup nuts, chopped
1 cup sour cream	1 cup raisins, chopped

Mix in order given. Add a little more flour if dough is too soft. Drop onto greased cookie sheet and bake at 350° 15 to 18 minutes.

MRS. A. C. MADDEN

PECAN DATE BARS

½ cup butter or margarine	1½ cups flour
1 cup sugar	1½ teaspoons baking powder
2 eggs	1 package pitted dates, cut fine
¼ cup milk	1 cup chopped pecans

Cream butter and sugar, add beaten eggs and milk. To this mixture add the flour, baking powder, dates and nuts. Beat well, and pour into two 10 x 6-inch well-greased pans. Bake in slow oven, (325°) until firm. Cut in bars and roll in powdered sugar.

MISS MABEL MABRY

SESAME SEED WAFERS

1 stick margarine	¼ teaspoon salt
2 cups brown sugar	½ teaspoon baking powder
1 egg	1 teaspoon vanilla
1 cup plain flour	⅔ to ¾ cup sesame seed, toasted

Cream margarine and sugar. Add egg, flour, salt and baking powder. Add vanilla and sesame seed. Drop about ½ teaspoon on greased cookie sheet. Bake at 325° 8 to 10 minutes. Allow to cool about 1 minute before removing from sheet. Yields over 100 wafers. Wafers burn easily, so watch closely.

MRS. JOHN CORCORAN, JR.

SCOTCH BAKES

1 cup butter	¼ teaspoon soda
½ cup brown sugar, well packed	2 cups flour

Cream butter, sugar and soda together until well blended. Stir in 1 cup flour, then knead in the second cup of flour. When well blended roll out to ¼ inch thickness. Cut with cookie cutter (the size of a fifty cent piece). Cook on ungreased cookie sheet in a 325° oven for 20 minutes.

MRS. J. ADAMS BRUCE

ALMOND SHORTBREAD

½ pound butter	1 cup blanched almonds,
1 cup sugar	ground or chopped
1 egg (separated)	2¼ cups flour

Combine butter, sugar and beaten egg yolk. Add nuts and flour. Mix thoroughly. Pat shortbread in lightly greased 9 x 13-inch pan until smooth and about ½ inch thick. Pour egg white over shortbread, pour off excess (this glazes). Bake in moderate 350° oven for 25 to 30 minutes until light brown. Cut in 1½-inch squares, let stand 10 minutes before removing from pan. For best results, mix by hand rather than electric mixer. Makes 48 to 54 squares.

MRS. R. S. CLARKE

CHOCOLATE CHIP NUT BARS

⅓ cup butter	½ teaspoon baking powder
1 cup brown sugar	½ teaspoon salt
1 egg slightly beaten	⅛ teaspoon soda
1 teaspoon vanilla	1 package chocolate chips
1 cup sifted cake flour	1 cup chopped pecans

Cream butter and sugar well. Add egg and vanilla. Beat well. Sift together flour, baking powder, salt and soda. Sift 4 times. Fold into butter mixture. Add chocolate chips and nuts. Bake in 350° oven for 20 to 25 minutes in a 9-inch square pan which has been greased and lined with wax paper. Allow cake to cool before cutting into squares.

MRS. ONAN WHITEHURST

SNICKENDOODLES

1 cup shortening	½ teaspoon salt
1½ cups sugar	1 teaspoon baking powder
2 eggs	For rolling:
2¾ cups sifted flour	2 tablespoons sugar
2 teaspoons cream of tartar	2 tablespoons cinnamon

Mix shortening, sugar and eggs. Sift dry ingredients together and gradually blend into sugar mixture. Roll into balls the size of walnuts. Roll balls in sugar and cinnamon mixture. Place on ungreased cookie sheet. Bake 7 to 10 minutes at 400°. Makes 4 dozen.

Mrs. Hillery D. Jones

BROWN MYSTERY COOKIES

1 cup sugar	1 pinch of salt
1¼ cups chopped pecans	4 egg whites, stiffly beaten
1⅓ cups rolled graham crackers	1 teaspoon vanilla
1 teaspoon baking powder	

Mix first 5 ingredients. Fold in egg whites and add vanilla. Bake about 25 minutes in 350° oven in 7 x 11-inch pan. While warm, cut into square or diagonal shapes. Makes 21 cookies.

Mrs. Paul H. Jacobs

MRS. JAMERSON'S CHOCOLATE FUDGIES

½ stick butter	15-ounce can condensed milk
12-ounce package semi-sweet	1 cup flour
chocolate drops	8-ounce package pecans, broken
1 teaspoon vanilla	

Melt in top of double boiler the butter and chocolate. Add vanilla and remove from heat. Stir in milk and flour and add nuts. Using an iced tea spoon, spoon small amounts onto cookie sheet and bake at 350° 7 minutes only. Will be soft until cool. Makes 2 large cookie sheets.

Mrs. A. L. Brady

COCOA-NUT BALL COOKIES

½ cup butter	2 tablespoons cocoa
¼ cup sugar	½ teaspoon salt
1 teaspoon vanilla	¾ cup chopped nuts
1 cup sifted flour	Confectioners sugar

Cream together butter, sugar and vanilla. Stir in flour, cocoa and salt. Mix well. Add nut meats. Shape into small 1-inch balls. Place on ungreased cookie sheet. Bake in 350° oven for 15 minutes. Cool and roll in confectioners sugar. Yield: 3 dozen.

MRS. ROBERT MAURAIS

CHINESE CHEWS

¾ cup flour	1 cup pecans, chopped
1 cup sugar	2 eggs, beaten
1 teaspoon baking powder	½ cup butter (1 stick)
1 cup dates, chopped	

Sift together flour, sugar and baking powder; mix well. Add chopped dates and nuts; then add beaten eggs. Melt butter, mix with all ingredients. Bake in well-greased 7 x 10-inch pan about 30 minutes in 350° oven. Cool slightly. Take out of pan by teaspoonful, shape into balls or fingers and roll in confectioners sugar. These may be made several days ahead. Keep in tightly closed jar.

MRS. JACK GRIFFIN

CREAM CHEESE COOKIES

½ pound butter or margarine	2 tablespoons sugar
6 ounces cream cheese	Thick jam
2 cups flour	Powdered sugar
2 teaspoons baking powder	

Cream butter and cheese until light. Add flour, baking powder and sugar. Mix smooth. Roll out about ¼ inch thick on floured pastry cloth and cut with 1½-inch cookie cutter. Make a slight depression in the center and fill with ½ teaspoon jam. Bake on ungreased cookie sheet for about 10 minutes at 350°. Cool and sift powdered sugar over the cookies. Makes about 60 cookies.

MRS. J. C. COUNCIL

GLAZED COOKIES

1 cup butter	1 egg yolk
1 cup sugar	¼ teaspoon vanilla
¾ teaspoon salt	1¾ cups plain flour
½ teaspoon cinnamon	

Cream butter and sugar. Mix in other ingredients thoroughly and spread evenly in ungreased 12 x 17-inch pan. Spread and glaze.

GLAZE:

1 egg white	⅓ cup sugar
1 tablespoon cold water	½ teaspoon cinnamon

Combine ingredients and beat lightly.

After spreading batter with glaze, sprinkle with ½ cup nuts. Bake 30 minutes at 275° to 300°. When done, dip knife in iced water and cut immediately in finger lengths. Remove from pan to cool. Store in tightly covered container.

MRS. WARREN RENDALL

LEBKUCHEN

8 cups sifted cake flour	2 cups brown sugar
½ teaspoon soda	¼ cup water
1½ teaspoons cinnamon	2 eggs slightly beaten
¼ teaspoon ground cloves	1½ cups orange peel, shredded
¼ teaspoon ground nutmeg	1½ cups candied citron, shredded
1⅓ cups strained honey (1 pound)	2 cups slivered almonds

Sift flour, then measure. Add soda and spices and sift together 3 times. Boil honey, sugar, and water 5 minutes. Cool. Add flour mixture, eggs, fruit, and almonds. Work into loaf and place in refrigerator. Let ripen 2 or 3 days. Roll on slightly floured board to ¼ inch thickness. Cut in 1 x 3-inch strips. Bake on greased sheets at 350° 15 minutes. When cool, cover with Transparent Icing and decorate as desired with candied fruits. Lebkuchen should be ripened in cake tins at least 1 day before they are served. I have stored them up to a year. Makes 10 dozen.

TRANSPARENT ICING:

2 cups confectioners sugar	1 teaspoon vanilla
3 tablespoons boiling water	

Combine sugar and water. Add vanilla and beat thoroughly. Drop from teaspoon on to Lebkuchen. If icing becomes too hard, add tiny bit of hot water.

MRS. J. WALLY GRAY

DATE BARS

½ stick butter
   (or oleo), melted
1 cup sugar
3 eggs, beaten until
   thick and creamy
1 cup flour

½ teaspoon baking powder
Pinch of salt (*very* sparing)
1 cup dates, finely cut
1 cup nuts, chopped
Confectioners sugar for dusting

Line 14 x 18-inch pan with wax paper. Mix first 8 ingredients in the order given. Spread mixture in pan. Bake 15 to 20 minutes in 350° oven. While still warm, cut in finger-shaped pieces and roll in the Confectioners sugar. Yield 40 bars.

MRS. DEPURY MORGAN

FLORIDA COOKIES

½ cup butter
1 cup sugar
Rind of 2 oranges, grated
1 egg

½ cup orange juice
3 cups sifted flour
½ teaspoon cinnamon
4 teaspoons baking powder

Cream together butter, sugar, and orange rind. Gradually add lightly beaten egg, orange juice, flour, cinnamon and baking powder. When dough is thoroughly mixed drop from a teaspoon onto an ungreased cookie sheet. Bake in 325° oven 10 to 12 minutes until light brown. Yields approximately 6 dozen cookies.

MRS. JOSEPH A. SAVARESE, JR.

JELLY ROLL COOKIES

1 stick butter
1 stick margarine
2 3-ounce packages of cream
   cheese
2 cups sifted flour

1 12-ounce jar of guava jelly
   (good idea to have second jar
   on hand in case you need extra)
¼ pound of chopped pecans

Cream together butter, margarine and cream cheese. Mix in flour 1 cup at a time. Set in refrigerator for 2½ to 3 hours. Divide dough into 2 parts and roll out each. Spread jelly on top of dough generously but not too heavily. Sprinkle nuts on top of jelly. Roll up dough (each roll is usually about a foot long). Place in greased pan. Refrigerate over night. Preheat oven to 375°. Slice cookies and place on greased cookie sheet. Cook 10 to 15 minutes or until golden brown. Makes 3 to 4 dozen.

MRS. WILLIAM L. HARPER

ICEBOX COOKIES

1 cup Crisco	4 cups sifted flour
1 cup brown sugar	1 teaspoon salt
1 cup white sugar	1 teaspoon soda dissolved in
2 eggs	2 tablespoons boiling water
1 teaspoon vanilla	1 cup chopped nuts

Cream shortening and sugar until smooth. Add eggs one at a time, beating 1 minute after each. Add vanilla, then flour and salt gradually. Add soda dissolved in the boiling water. Mix on slow speed until smooth. Remove beaters and add chopped nuts, using a spoon for this. Grease a bread pan thickly with shortening, put the dough in the pan, pushing it down evenly so it will be firm. Cover with wax paper and chill in the refrigerator. Slice thin and cut slices in half. Bake on a lightly greased cookie sheet at 375° for 10 to 12 minutes. This makes 100 cookies.

MRS. E. C. DePURY

LONDON STICKS

1 teaspoon sugar	Calamondin marmalade
1¾ cups flour	1 cup pecans
1 stick butter	1 cup sugar
4 egg separated	Confectioners sugar

Heat oven to 350°. Add 1 teaspoon sugar to flour and sift. Cut in butter as for pastry. Add egg yolks to pastry mixture. Using hands, work into a smooth dough. This will be very stiff. On a cookie sheet shape the dough into a 12-inch square about ¼ inch thick. Spread thin layer of marmalade over square. Grate nuts very fine, using hand nut grater. Beat egg whites until stiff. Add 1 cup sugar gradually as for meringue. Fold in nuts. Spread meringue over pastry and jelly. Lower heat to 275°. Bake until light brown on top—about 30 to 45 minutes. Sift confectioners sugar over top and cut at once into 1½-inch squares with a sharp knife. Be sure to cut through to bottom of sheet. They are very tart.

CALAMONDIN MARMALADE:

Wash and scald fruit with soda and boiling water. Seed and chop fruit. Put into pan and barely cover with water. Boil until tender. Measure 1 cup fruit to 1 cup of sugar. Boil together 10 minutes, then pour into sterilized glasses. Let cool and top with melted paraffin. Four cups of cooked fruit and sugar will make approximately 6 to 8 small jars of marmalade. If calamondin marmalade is not available a very tart red currant jelly may be used.

MRS. TELKY MEDOCK

PECAN CRISPIES

½ cup Crisco   2½ cups flour
½ cup margarine   ½ teaspoon salt
2½ cups brown sugar   ½ teaspoon soda
2 well beaten eggs   1 cup chopped pecans

Cream shortening, margarine and sugar. Add eggs and beat well. Add sifted dry ingredients, then nuts. Drop from teaspoon about 2 inches apart onto a greased cookie sheet. Bake in a moderate oven (350°) 10 to 12 minutes.

MRS. H. E. BRUCE

COCONUT DREAM BARS

1 cup flour   ½ cup brown sugar
½ cup melted butter

Mix together, press into a 8 x 8 x 2-inch ungreased pan and bake until light brown, 12 to 15 minutes at 350°. Allow to cool while preparing the following:

1 cup brown sugar   ½ teaspoon salt
2 eggs   1 teaspoon baking powder
1 teaspoon vanilla   1½ cups shredded coconut
2 tablespoons flour   1 cup pecans

Beat sugar and eggs, add vanilla, then flour, salt and baking powder. Mix in coconut and nuts, spread evenly over the baked crust and bake in a moderate oven (350°) for 20 to 25 minutes. Cool slightly before cutting into small squares. Makes 25 squares.

MRS. CHARLES G. MULLEN, JR.

OLD-FASHIONED MOLASSES COOKIES

1 cup white sugar   ½ cup milk or coffee
1 cup shortening   4 heaping cups flour
1 cup molasses   3 teaspoons soda
2 eggs or 3 yolks   1 teaspoon salt

Mix together sugar, shortening, molasses, eggs, and milk or coffee. Combine flour, soda, and salt and add to mixture. Drop by teaspoons on ungreased baking sheet and bake at 350° for 10 minutes. Yield over 8 dozen.

MRS. PERRY R. WILSON

WILLIE'S COOKIES

1 ⅓ sticks of butter
1 cup nuts
2 cups brown sugar
2 eggs, beaten

1 cup flour
¼ teaspoon baking powder
Powdered sugar

Melt butter, add nuts and mix well. Add brown sugar, eggs, flour, and baking powder last. Bake in 8-inch square pan lined with oiled paper. Cook in 300° oven about 45 minutes. Cut while hot into small squares and roll in powdered sugar. Makes 24 to 32 cookies.

MRS. C. E. HOLTSINGER

YUMMIE SQUARES

1 ½ cups cake flour (sifted once before measuring)
1 teaspoon salt
1 teaspoon baking powder
½ cup margarine or butter

1 cup sugar
2 eggs, well beaten
1 teaspoon vanilla
¼ teaspoon almond extract

FROSTING:

2 egg whites
2 cups brown sugar

1 cup chopped nuts

Sift together first 3 ingredients. Work shortening until creamy; add sugar, and cream again; add eggs and beat until light. Mix in flour. Add vanilla and almond extract. Spread in 12 x 12-inch aluminum pan. Next beat egg whites until stiff. Gradually beat in brown sugar until stiff. Fold in nuts. Spread this on first layer. Bake in a 375° oven for about 25 minutes. Remove from oven and cut in squares while still hot. Makes about 3 dozen 2-inch squares.

MRS. J. REX FARRIOR

MARMALADE COOKIES

1 ½ cups flour
¼ teaspoon soda
¼ teaspoon salt
¼ cup shortening

1 egg, beaten
½ cup sugar
½ cup orange marmalade
Nuts, if desired

Sift flour, soda and salt together. Cream shortening; add egg, sugar, dry ingredients, then marmalade. Drop from teaspoon onto greased cookie sheet. Bake at 350° for 12 minutes. Makes 3 dozen.

MRS. JOHN LEWIS

TEA WAGON CAKE

1 stick butter	Salt, less than ⅛ teaspoon
1 cup granulated sugar	1 teaspoon vanilla
2 eggs, separated	1 cup brown sugar, packed firmly
1½ cups sifted flour	1 cup pecans, broken coarsely
1 teaspoon baking powder	

Cream butter; gradually add granulated sugar, beat until light and fluffy. Beat egg yolks well, add to butter-sugar mixture. Sift together dry ingredients, and add "by hand" to mixture. Add vanilla. Spread evenly over bottom of greased 8 or 9-inch square pan, pushing and patting it smooth and into the corners with fingers.

Beat egg whites stiff, gradually add brown sugar (be sure there are no lumps), beating until smooth. Spread this over uncooked dough. Sprinkle with broken pecans; press nuts lightly into meringue. Bake at 300° for 30 to 40 minutes. Cut into small squares while warm, let cool in pan. (Meringue cracks, and it is a bit difficult to cut; dipping knife in warm water helps.) Cut larger squares and top with ice cream for dessert.

MRS. J. P. HINES

NUTMEG COOKIES

2 sticks butter or margarine	4 teaspoons baking powder
1 cup sugar	1 nutmeg, freshly grated
2 eggs	½ teaspoon salt
3½ cups flour	2 teaspoons vanilla

Soften butter; cream with sugar. Add beaten eggs. Sift flour twice with baking powder; add nutmeg and salt. Add to egg mixture, then add vanilla. Roll out on floured board and cut with fancy Christmas cutters and decorate. Bake on ungreased cookie sheets at 375° for 10 minutes. Dough may be made early and allowed to stand in the refrigerator for a day or so. Makes approximately 4 dozen.

MRS. WILLIAM C. GILMORE, JR.

CHAPTER XVIII

Candy

In Florida at Christmas time, it's easy to visualize the first Christmas. The cool night skies seem close enough to touch, and the stars have a crystal brilliance, illuminating the heavens, imparting a faint, pale glow to earth. A traveler would have no difficulty in following a star on nights such as these.

In the houses, large and small, there is preparation for the feast. Presents are made and wrapped to commemorate the first gifts in Bethlehem. Families draw together in peace, and ties of friendship are renewed. Then it is that we gather bright boxes, painted and gilded cardboard containers, decorative jars and bottles to pack our Christmas candies. Then it is we distribute our feelings of affection and goodwill in gay wrappings of tinsel and paper, the friendly thoughts of Christmas which endure throughout the year.

ALMOND ROCA

1 cup sugar	½ cup butter
¼ cup water	½ cup blanched almonds
1 tablespoon corn syrup	½ pound chocolate bar

Put first 5 ingredients into a skillet, cook to a hard crack stage, or until almonds are toasted a light brown, stirring constantly. Pour into pan to cool and spread with melted chocolate while candy is still hot. Cool and break into pieces.

MRS. G. B. HOWELL, JR.

APRICOT CANDIES

1 pound dried apricots	Grated peel of 1 orange
2 cups sugar	½ to ¾ cup chopped nuts
Juice of 1 orange	Powdered sugar

Grind apricots; combine with sugar, orange juice and grated peel. Boil 10 minutes. Stir in nuts; cool just enough to handle. Shape into small balls and roll in sifted powdered sugar.

MRS. NORMAN STALLINGS

C A R A M E L   C A N D Y

3 cups sugar
1 cup sweet milk
1 stick margarine

Pinch of salt
1 teaspoon vanilla
1 cup (or more) of nuts

In a deep boiler, mix 2 cups sugar and milk and cook. In an iron skillet melt 1 cup sugar stirring constantly to keep from burning. Pour browned sugar into deep boiler mixture, stirring constantly. Cook until it reaches the soft-ball stage in cold water or 230° on a candy thermometer. Add margarine, salt, vanilla, and nuts. Beat well and cool. Add 1 tablespoon cold water during final stage if candy begins to get too hard.

MRS. W. H. MONCRIEF

C H R I S T M A S   B O U R B O N   B A L L S

1 6-ounce package chocolate chips
2 tablespoons white corn syrup
½ cup bourbon

2½ cups vanilla wafers, crushed fine
1 cup nuts (chopped fine)
½ cup powdered sugar

Melt chocolate over warm water. Remove from stove, add syrup and bourbon and mix well. Add vanilla wafers and nuts. Mix with hands and let stand 20 minutes. Make into balls, then roll in powdered sugar.

MRS. A. L. BRADY

C H R I S T M A S   F O N D A N T

1 egg white
1 tablespoon cold water
3 tablespoons cream
1½ teaspoons vanilla

1 pound confectioners sugar
½ teaspoon red food coloring
½ teaspoon green food coloring
Dates, raisins or nuts

Beat first 4 ingredients until well blended. Add very slowly sifted confectioners sugar. Knead and work until mixture is smooth. Take ½ of mixture and place in another bowl. Add red food coloring to one bowl of mixture and green food coloring to the other bowl. Mix well and make a roll of each batch. Wrap in wax paper and put in cool place for 1 hour. Slice roll in thin slices and press on top of each a piece of date, raisin or nut meat.

MRS. J. E. HARRIS

MUMSIE'S OPERA FUDGE

3½ pounds sugar by weight   Cream of tarter, the size of a
  (or approximately 7 cups)   hazelnut (approximately
1 quart coffee cream   1 teaspoon)
                             4 cups nuts, coarsely broken
                             4 to 6 tablespoons vanilla

Put first 3 ingredients in a large pot. (This mixture will increase in size about 3 times, maybe more, when you are boiling it.) Stir with a large spoon until completely liquified. Place over high heat and boil until candy thermometer reads 232°; then pour on a large marble slab or something similar. Allow to cool for about 15 to 20 minutes. Sprinkle the nuts and vanilla over it.

Take a spatula and a large knife and work this mixture, continually trying to pile it up in a mound. After about 15 minutes of working and mixing it will suddenly get firm and form a mound about the size of a pound cake, probably 4 inches thick and 12 inches in diameter. Cover candy with a dry towel then place a damp towel on top of the dry towel for about 45 minutes. Slice into size desired. Place on a plate and allow to stand at least overnight until it becomes a little crisp on the outside. Place in cans or jars for storage.

W. F. EDWARDS

PEANUT BUTTER FUDGE

2 cups sugar   ½ teaspoon salt
1 cup milk   3 heaping tablespoons peanut butter

Bring sugar, milk, and salt to soft ball stage, stirring occasionally. Put pan in cold water and beat in peanut butter. Beat until stiff. Drop on wax paper or turn onto buttered plate and cut into pieces.

MRS. G. B. HOWELL, JR.

MAPLE CREAMS

1 cup maple sugar or syrup   ½ cup milk
½ tablespoon butter

Place all ingredients in saucepan. Bring to boil and cook, stirring frequently, until a drop in cold water will form a soft ball. Remove from fire and beat until creamy. Pour in buttered pan. When cool, cut in squares.

MRS. H. L. CROWDER

FUDGE

3 tablespoons butter   ¾ cup coffee cream
3 cups sugar   3 ounces unsweetened chocolate
½ teaspoon salt   1 teaspoon vanilla
3 teaspoons light corn syrup   1 cup broken pecans
1 teaspoon vinegar

Melt butter in heavy pan. Add sugar, salt, syrup, vinegar, cream and chocolate. Cook, stirring constantly, until sugar is dissolved. Cook to soft ball stage (234°). Cool to luke warm. Add vanilla and pecans and beat until thick. Turn fudge into buttered 9 x 9 x 2-inch pan. When candy is cold cut into squares. Yields 36 pieces.

MRS. CHARLES SKOW

CANDIED GRAPEFRUIT PEEL

5 grapefruit halves   2 cups sugar
2 cups water

Cut fruit in strips with scissors. Put in large kettle and cover with cold water; bring to boil and drain. Do this 3 times. Drain well the third time and add fruit to 2 cups water and sugar. Cook, stirring often, until only 1 tablespoon of syrup remains. Then cool candied peel on a rack and roll in granulated sugar. Place on racks to dry. Store in box.

MRS. VIOLET STOWEL

PRALINES I

2 cups white sugar   1 scant teaspoon salt
1 cup brown sugar   1 teaspoon vanilla
¾ cup water   1 cup chopped pecans
1 tablespoon white corn syrup

Combine sugar, water, syrup and salt. Cook until soft ball forms when dropped in water or candy thermometer shows 236°. Add vanilla and remove from heat. Cool for 5 minutes. Add pecans and beat until liquid clouds. Drop from a tablespoon on wax paper. Leave until firm. If mixture hardens in pot, place in hot water to soften. Yields 18 pralines.

EUGENE KNIGHT

PRALINES II

3 dozen coarsely broken pecans	1 cup sweet milk
3 cups white granulated sugar	1 tablespoon butter

Grease generously large counter-top area of porcelain, tile, or formica. Place broken pecans (equivalent of one pecan to pile) close together in piles about 2 inches apart. In saucepan, mix 2 cups sugar and 1 cup milk. While this is coming to boil, melt 1 cup sugar in iron skillet.

Important: Do not let melted sugar in skillet get too dark. This determines color, taste, and ease of mixing.

Very slowly pour the melted sugar into rapidly boiling milk and sugar mixture, stirring constantly. If lumps form, stir and mash them out. Boil mixture until it reaches soft ball stage in cold water, or reaches 236° on a candy thermometer. Remove from heat. Add butter and beat until creamy and thick. Drop from a spoon over piles of nuts, and allow to harden. If the mixture gets too stiff while spooning out soften over a pan of boiling water.

MRS. EDWIN M. JONES, III

EASY PRALINES

2 cups sugar	½ teaspoon soda
1 cup milk or cream	1 teaspoon vanilla
2 tablespoons butter	2 cups nuts

Mix sugar, milk, butter, and soda in a saucepan and cook to the soft ball stage. The soda turns the sugar to a caramel taste and color as it cooks. Remove from stove, let cool a few minutes, add vanilla, then beat. Before the mixture begins to stiffen, add nuts and spoon on wax paper or foil.

MRS. W. F. MCLANE

AUNT HELEN'S PEANUT CANDY

1 package confectioners sugar	2 heaping tablespoons
3 tablespoons cream	peanut butter

Save ½ cup sugar to knead and work mixture after combining all ingredients. When mixture becomes creamy, roll in wax paper and put into refrigerator overnight. Slice off as needed. Garnish with nuts.

MRS. W. FRANK HOBBS

SUGARED WALNUTS

1 cup brown sugar
½ cup white sugar
½ cup sour cream

1 teaspoon vanilla
2½ cups walnut meats

Combine brown and white sugars and sour cream. Cook to soft-ball stage. Add vanilla and beat until thick. Add walnuts, stirring until well-coated, and turn onto greased platter. Separate into individual pieces. Cinnamon may be added if desired.

MRS. CLAUDE LOGAN, JR.

APRICOT-COCONUT BALLS

1 cup dried apricots
1 cup flaked coconut
¾ cup chopped nuts
1 teaspoon lemon rind

1 tablespoon lemon juice
1 tablespoon orange juice
Confectioners sugar

Heat apricots over boiling water 10 minutes; then put apricots, coconut, and nuts through food grinder. Knead mixture with lemon rind and juices. Add enough confectioners sugar to make firm mixture. Form into balls.

MRS. CLARE McMINN

DING BATS

1½ cups dates
1 cup sugar
¼ cup butter
1 egg, beaten
¼ cup water

1½ cups Rice Krispies
1 teaspoon vanilla
½ cup nuts
1 3½-ounce can coconut

Combine dates, sugar, butter, and egg, and stir. Add water; cook for 10 minutes. Add Rice Krispies, vanilla, and nuts. Cool and drop from a teaspoon into bowl of coconut; roll into small balls. Store in airtight container. Will keep for weeks. Very pretty for special occasions when the coconut is tinted. Yield: 6 dozen.

MRS. RUFUS JAMERSON

CHAPTER XIX

Fruit

A Florida citrus grove is a wondrous place to visit. Row on row there can be trees alternately in bloom, bearing the first tiny green fruit, or alight with the sharp clear colors of fully ripened fruit. A citrus tree is a ball of glossy green foliage; the dark, thickly-leaved branches sweep the ground, presenting their fruit as a gift to the passer-by. Although oranges, grapefruit, and tangerines are plentiful all year round, their biting sweetness recalls to mind the bright chill of Florida winter; azure skies dimpled with tiny white clouds, plumes of smoke motionless in the still air, tall black pines, wisped with Spanish moss, edging a hunter's field. Florida is many things, but its winter is a tang tempered with sweetness.

GLAZED APPLES

4 cups sugar
1 cup water
Red coloring (enough to make apples a deep red)

3 tablespoons red hots, (cinnamon candies)
12 small apples, cored and peeled

Combine all ingredients and cook slowly until apples are tender.

Mrs. Earl H. McRae

FLORIDA SHERBET AMBROSIA

Cut 3 medium grapefruit or large oranges in half. Carefully remove the sections and set them aside. Remove all the membrane from each fruit half and line the entire inside of the shells with tangerine or orange sherbet about ½ inch thick leaving a small cavity in the center. Freeze until firm, then smooth over the sherbet with a spatula to make it even. It takes about a quart of sherbet to line 6 grapefruit halves. When the sherbet and shells are thoroughly firm (about 2 hours) fill the centers with a mixture of 2 cups orange or grapefruit sections, 1 cup sliced strawberries and ⅓ cup shredded coconut. Top each half of fruit with shaved Brazil nuts and garnish with mint.

Mrs. Leon Whitehurst

GRAPES AU RHUM

2 pounds seedless (small white)   ¾ cup rum
   grapes   ½ pint sour cream
Brown sugar

Sprinkle grapes lightly with sugar (in layers). Pour rum over all and refrigerate for several hours. Drain juice and mix gently with sour cream. Serve in chilled dessert dishes.

MRS. NELSON MASON

BRANDIED GRAPEFRUIT

3 grapefruit   6 ounces brandy
1 pound 2 ounces brown sugar

Cut 3 selected grapefruit in half and well segment each half grapefruit in its shell. Spread 1 ounce of light brown sugar on top of each half grapefruit. Pour 1 ounce of good quality brandy over each, and allow to stand for ½ hour. Bake in moderate oven (350°) for 20 minutes. Then add 2 ounces light brown sugar to each half grapefruit and glaze under broiler. Serve hot. Serves 6.

STRAWBERRIES ROMANOFF

2 quarts fresh strawberries   1 cup heavy cream, whipped
Sugar   6 tablespoons Cointreau
1 pint vanilla ice cream   Juice of one lemon

Early in the day, wash and cap strawberries. Sugar to taste. Chill. At serving time, soften and beat ice cream, then fold in whipped cream, Cointreau, and lemon juice. Pour over very cold strawberries. Blend quickly and lightly so as not to bruise the berries. (This is effective done at the table.) Serve at once. Serves 12.

MRS. BRIGHTMAN J. SKINNER, JR.

SHERRIED GRAPEFRUIT HALVES

After you have sectioned a grapefruit half, pour in just enough sherry wine to cover level with the tops of the section. Sugar to taste and serve chilled.

LEISURE HOUSE, TAMPA ELECTRIC COMPANY

VIENNESE DESSERT

1½ cups bananas, bite-size pieces
1½ cups oranges, bite-size pieces
1 cup chopped English walnuts

1 cup miniature marshmallows
2 ounces Cointreau

Combine bananas, oranges, walnuts and marshmallows. Place in shallow baking dish, cover with Cointreau and let stand for 2 hours in refrigerator. When ready to serve, pile in orange cups and top with whipped cream. Makes 6 servings.

MRS. BEN I. SIMMONS

FROZEN FRUIT COMPOTE

2 packages frozen sliced peaches
2 packages frozen raspberries
1 large can Bing cherries, pitted

4 tablespoons brandy
2 tablespoons sugar (or to taste)

Place peaches, raspberries, and Bing cherries together in a large bowl. When almost defrosted add brandy and sugar and stir well. Serves 6.

MRS. WILLIAM SAVAGE

GUAVA SHELLS

Wash guavas, remove blossom and stem ends, peel, halve, and scoop out seeds with a spoon. Put fruit in a kettle and sprinkle sugar over it (about ¾ cup of sugar to 1 cup of fruit). Let stand until juicy enough to cook over very low heat. Cook until fruit is tender, about ¾ to 1 hour. Pack in sterilized jars. Delicious for dessert with slices of cream cheese.

MRS. S. M. SPARKMAN, JR.

CHAPTER XX

Jellies

In this abundant region, no meal is complete without homemade jellies or jams. The yield of decorative fruit trees in the backyard will furnish a family's supply. Shiny yellow guavas, rose-tinted and seeded on the inside, make a clear amber-hued jelly which shimmers like honey on buttered hot biscuits. Tiny orange kumquats become a bitter-sweet marmalade fit for a king. Luscious winter strawberries make preserves so delicious one is tempted to eat them with a spoon. Fortunate is the family which has a preserving kettle and a cook who loves to use it.

GUAVA JELLY

STEP I: The Juice

Select guavas in good condition. Any type guava may be used, including catley. The secret of making guava jelly is in the making of the juice. It must be strong so don't use too much water. Wash fruit well, remove blossom end, and slice. Put in large heavy pot and barely cover with water. Cook until fruit is soft. Strain through a clean cloth. I find an old pillow slip best. Hang bag and let it drip into a large container overnight or until all the juice is out.

STEP II: The Jelly

1 cup guava juice	3 teaspoons lemon or lime juice
1 cup sugar	

Put ingredients into a deep pot which will allow for boiling up. Boil briskly until mixture begins to jell or when it flakes from spoon. This takes 8 to 10 minutes. Pour into sterilized jars and cover at once with melted paraffin. Continue cooking jelly in small amounts until guava juice is used up. It is very important to cook a small amount at a time. The larger the amounts the longer it must be cooked, making the jelly darker and inferior in quality. You *cannot* cook jelly and do anything else at the same time. You must watch the pot—and this one does boil.

MRS. W. FRANK HOBBS

CALAMONDIN CONSERVE

1 quart (at least) calamondins   Water
5 pounds (approximately) sugar

Wash fruit, cut in half, remove seeds and stem. Grind or chop coarsely. Measure 1 cup water to 1 cup of juice and pulp. Cook about 15 minutes. Stir to prevent sticking. Remove from heat. Measure 1 cup of mixture to 1 cup sugar. Bring to boil and cook for 20 minutes, stirring every few minutes. Do not cook more than 4 or 5 cups at a time as it readily boils over. Pour into jars and seal or allow to cool and then seal with paraffin.

MRS. WILLIAM C. GILMORE, JR.

KUMQUAT MARMALADE

2 pounds kumquats   1½ quarts water
1 lemon   4 cups sugar

Wash and dry kumquats. Slice thinly in rings. Remove seeds. Thinly slice lemon. Add cold water and let stand 12 hours. Then heat to boiling point, and cook over low flame until peel is clear and tender. Let stand 24 hours. Add sugar and cook very slowly until marmalade thickens to consistency of jelly. Stir occasionally to prevent scorching. Pack, seal and store in sterilized jars. Makes 3 pints. Serve with fowl, or with toast for breakfast. Very simple to make, as you do one part each day for three days.

MRS. J. CLIFFORD MACDONALD

SURINAM CHERRY JELLY

Wash cherries. Remove stems and blossom ends. Place cherries in a saucepan. Add water until it can be seen through the top layer of cherries. The fruit must not float in water. Cover the pan and simmer until cherries are soft (25 or 30 minutes). Strain the juice through a flannel or heavy muslin jelly bag. Measure the juice, and place it in a deep kettle that will allow for the boiling up of the liquid. Cook no more than 4 cups of juice at a time. Boil juice rapidly for 5 minutes. Skim, if necessary. Add ½ cup sugar to each cup of juice. Stir until sugar is dissolved. Continue to boil the juice rapidly, without stirring it, until it has reached the "sheeting stage" or 220° to 222°. Pour the jelly into hot sterilized glasses and seal immediately.

MRS. CLIFFORD ULMER

STRAWBERRY PRESERVES

1 pound strawberries   ¼ pound sugar

Wash, cap and place large firm fruit in pot, add sugar, and gently melt to form a syrup. Let this stand overnight. In the morning boil 3 to 5 minutes, but do not boil hard enough to allow berries to disintegrate. Cover and let stand until fruit is plump and mixture is cool. Later simmer slowly until preserves are of the thickness you desire. Pack and seal.

MRS. W. FRANK HOBBS

GUAVA PASTE

4 cups guava pulp   2 cups sugar

Sieve guava pulp to remove seeds, then measure. (Pulp from making jelly or from fresh guavas may be used.) Cook pulp until it begins to thicken, add sugar and continue cooking until the mixture follows a wooden spatula around the pan. Cook quickly for a clear paste, being careful not to burn. Mold paste and wrap in heavy wax paper. It is better to make paste only as needed. Serve squares of guava paste on soda crackers spread with cream cheese for a delicious and light dessert.

MRS. MITCHELL DASHER

ANGOSTURA JELLY

2½ cups sugar   1 6-ounce can lemonade
1¼ cups water   concentrate
½ bottle liquid fruit pectin   ¼ cup Angostura bitters

Combine sugar and water in saucepan. Bring to full rolling boil, stirring constantly. Boil hard for 1 minute; remove from heat. Stir in pectin; add lemonade concentrate and bitters. Mix well; skim very quickly and pour into sterilized jars. Cover at once with ⅛-inch layer of melted paraffin. Makes about 8 small glasses. Delicious with meats and perfect for Christmas giving.

MRS. LOUIS SAXTON

MANGO BUTTER

6 cups mangos, chopped fine
2 cups water
2 tablespoons lime juice
2½ cups sugar

½ teaspoon each ground cloves
and allspice
½ teaspoon each ground cinnamon
and nutmeg

Cook mangos with water and lime juice until tender. Put through a sieve to remove strings. Add sugar and spices and cook until the consistency of butter.

Mrs. Clifford Ulmer

APRICOT JAM

1 pound dried apricots
3 pints water

3 pounds sugar
4 tablespocns lemon juice

Wash the fruit, then soak in the water overnight. The next day add the sugar and lemon juice to the apricots and water and bring to a boil on the stove. Simmer slowly for about 2 hours. Skim off any foam which forms. Stir occasionally. Pack in sterilized jars and seal with melted paraffin.

Mrs. Rogers Morgan

Peaceful Florida West Coast Lake Scene

CHAPTER XXI

Pickles and Relishes

The smooth white highways of this peninsula run on and on through fragrant citrus groves, brown-carpeted piney woods, tangled hardwood forests. Broad sweeps of savanna stretch for miles, their feathery grasses dotted here and there with spiky clumps of palmettos and sudden, fairy rings of cypress trees, the tall silent guardians of Florida's hidden treasure, her lakes. Just north of Tampa, the land is honeycombed with lakes. Here city dwellers build simple weekend and summer retreats. Each property has a few citrus trees, assorted livestock, and a fertile patch plowed for a kitchen garden. Here the days are long, and the pace is leisurely. Here there is time for pickling, canning, preserving, for churning, baking, and the making of smooth homemade ice cream.

Close by the water's edge is the garden patch, its deep sandy loam shielded by the lake's screen of myrtle, laurel, and huckleberry growing wild among cypresses, oaks, and pines. Before the sun breaks over the sheltering trees, the harvester fills her basket with firm, perfect vegetables. Before the day is done, the kitchen shelves are lined with sparkling jars of crisp spicy relishes and pickles. Meals at the long wooden tables in these country kitchens make one realize what the early Florida pioneers were struggling for, and why.

CUCUMBER AND ONION PICKLES

6 cucumbers	¾ cup mayonnaise
6 onions	2 tablespoons vinegar
Salt	

Thinly slice cucumbers and onions, a layer of each into colander. Salt each layer. Put colander over bowl or pan, cover and put in refrigerator to drain for at least 2 hours. Remove and shake off any excess salt water. Mix mayonnaise and vinegar together. Put cucumbers and onions in a bowl and pour the mayonnaise mixture over them. Turn mixture gently until just mixed. Pack in jar and keep refrigerated. Makes 2 pints.

MRS. WILLIAM C. GILMORE, JR.

GARLIC PICKLES

5 pounds of sour pickles
5 pounds of sugar
1 box of pickling spice

1 clove of garlic
1 cup of tarragon vinegar

Slice pickles thin. Put in a crock, big bowl or large jar and cover with sugar, pickling spice, garlic, and vinegar. Stir well every day for 4 or 5 days. Put in sterilized jars. Chill before serving. Makes 7 pints.

MRS. H. L. CROWDER, JR.

ICE PICKLES

4 quarts cucumbers, sliced thin
1 gallon lime water
3 pints vinegar
4 pounds sugar (8 cups)

½ teaspoon salt
½ teaspoon cinnamon
½ teaspoon cloves
½ teaspoon allspice

Dissolve a tube of lime in 1 gallon of water. Let cucumbers stand 24 hours in lime water. Rinse 3 times and drain on cloth. Mix vinegar, sugar and seasonings together. Put cucumbers in this solution and soak 12 hours. Heat to boiling point. Put in jars and seal. Chill before serving.

MRS. G. PIERCE WOOD, JR.

MANGO CHUTNEY

1 quart sliced green mangoes
2 or 3 green peppers, chopped
1 large onion, chopped
2 hot peppers, cut very fine,
  (remove seeds unless very
  hot flavor is desired)
1 clove of garlic, sliced
1 tablespoon salt
1 cup grapefruit juice
1 cup cider vinegar

1 pound brown sugar
1 pound seedless raisins
1 tablespoon white mustard seed
2 teaspoons each of allspice,
  cinnamon and cloves
1 3-ounce package sliced almonds
  (optional)
1 or 2 tablespoons finely chopped
  crystalized ginger (optional)

Combine first 6 ingredients. Let stand for 1 hour. Drain. Heat the grapefruit juice, vinegar, sugar, raisins, mustard seed and spices. Add mango mixture. Boil 30 minutes (if pressure cooker is used, cook 15 minutes). Seal while hot. Yields 4 pints.

RICHARD E. KNIGHT

OLIVE OIL PICKLES

4 pounds cucumbers, sliced
2 pounds onions, peeled and
  sliced

5 sweet red peppers, cut in rings
Handful of salt

Mix the above ingredients, toss well, and let stand 24 hours. Pour 1 cup of cold water over to rinse, and drain well.

2 pounds brown sugar
1 quart vinegar (or a little less)
1 tablespoon turmeric
2 tablespoons white mustard seed

2 tablespoons celery seed
3 tablespoons horseradish
8 tablespoons olive oil

Mix first 6 ingredients well, bring to boil, and boil 5 minutes. Cool well, then add olive oil. Pour over drained vegetables, put in scalded jars and seal.

MRS. WALTER BARRET

PICKLED ONION SLICES

5 or 6 large white onions
2 cups iced water
2 cups white vinegar

¼ cup salt
1 heaping tablespoon sugar
1 tablespoon dill weed

Slice onions and soak in iced water to crispen. Boil vinegar, salt, sugar and dill weed and steep ½ hour. Meanwhile scald jars, and place drained onion rings in them. Strain liquid through cheese cloth and pour over onions. Makes 3 or 4 jars.

MRS. J. BROWN FARRIOR

PEAR RELISH I

1 peck pears (13½ pounds
  hard green cooking pears)
5 medium onions
6 medium bell peppers (3 red if
  available and 3 green)

2 tablespoons mixed whole spices
2 pounds sugar
1 tablespoon turmeric
1 tablespoon salt
4 cups vinegar

Peel and grind pears in food chopper with onions. Grind peppers in separate container. Drain juice from peppers. Combine all ingredients and cook on medium heat for 30 minutes. Seal in ½ pint or pint jars while hot. Yields about 12 pints.

MRS. H. L. CROWDER

GREEN TOMATO CRISPS

It is best to use small green tomatoes that will slice small enough to slip easily into jars.

Soak 7 pounds of green tomatoes, sliced, in 2 gallons of lime water for 24 hours. (Use 3 cups builders hydrated lime to 2 gallons of water to make lime water.) Starting around lunch time works out fine. Use a big crockery bowl if possible. Drain, then soak for 4 hours in fresh water, draining and changing the water every hour. Drain the last time on a kitchen towel. Replace tomatoes in crockery bowl.

Make a syrup of:

5 pounds of sugar
3 pints of apple cider vinegar

1 teaspoon each of powdered
cloves, ginger, celery seed,
mace, and cinnamon

Bring the syrup to a boil. Pour over tomatoes and let stand overnight. In morning boil for 1 hour and seal in jars.

MRS. MARIANNE E. STRAUSS

WATERMELON PICKLES I

4 quarts watermelon rind
2 quarts cold water

2 tablespoons lime

Trim dark green skin and pink meat from watermelon rind. Cut in 1-inch cubes or with a small biscuit cutter. Soak overnight in the lime water. In the morning give rind a cold water bath. Drain.

1 gallon water

1 tablespoon alum

Cover rind with water and alum. Bring to boil and cook 10 or 15 minutes. Give another cold water bath. Cover with fresh water and cook until it can be pierced with a fork. Drain.

1 quart vinegar
2 cups water
6 cups sugar

½ teaspoon oil of cloves
½ teaspoon oil of cinnamon

Bring these ingredients to a boil. Pour over the rind and let stand overnight. The next morning drain syrup, reheat and pour over rind, and again let stand overnight. The third morning, thoroughly heat rind and syrup together and seal in sterilized jars. If liquid cooks away, add more water as needed. Makes 6 pints of beautiful, light-colored pickle.

MRS. W. FRANK HOBBS

GREEN TOMATO RELISH

1 quart green tomatoes	1 small cabbage
1 quart ripe tomatoes	2 cucumbers
2 bunches celery	1 pound brown sugar
2 sweet peppers (preferably red for color)	1 teaspoon mustard seed
	1 teaspoon black pepper
2 large onions	1 quart vinegar

Chop tomatoes, celery, peppers, onions, cabbage, and cucumbers all together; add ½ cup of salt and let stand 2 hours. Drain off all excess liquid. In large pot mix sugar, mustard seed, pepper, and vinegar. Heat and when sugar dissolves, add chopped vegetables. Bring to slow boil and fill sterilized jars. Chill before serving. Makes 7 pint jars. Delicious on ham or lamb sandwiches. It is important to *chop* vegetables rather than grind them.

MRS. GUY KING

MISS MEL ROBERTSON'S GREEN TOMATO PICKLES (SWEET)

1 peck green tomatoes	2 tablespoons whole cloves
6 large onions	2 tablespoons white mustard seed
½ cup salt	2 tablespoons whole allspice
2 quarts water	1 tablespoon Cayenne pepper
4 quarts vinegar	2 tablespoons cinnamon
2 pounds brown sugar	

Slice tomatoes and onions. Sprinkle with salt and let stand overnight. In the morning drain well. Put them into a porcelain kettle (modern aluminum best) with the water and 1 quart of vinegar. Boil 15 minutes; drain them dry. In the kettle combine the remaining 3 quarts of vinegar, sugar and spices. Boil slowly for 1 hour, taking care not to burn. When cold put in stone crock and cover.

GARDEN SPECIAL

1 quart chopped onions	4 quarts peeled, chopped tomatoes
1 quart chopped celery	3 tablespoons salt
6 green peppers, chopped	2 tablespoons sugar
1 quart water	

Combine onion, celery, and pepper. Add water and cook 20 minutes. Add tomatoes, salt and sugar. Bring to a boil and cook until thick. Put in hot sterilized jars and seal.

MRS. GEOFFREY W. STEPHENS

WATERMELON PICKLES II

5 pounds watermelon rind
2 quarts water

2 tablespoons slaked lime
  (get at hardware store)

Remove the green peel and the pink meat. Cut rind in ¾-inch cubes. Soak overnight in water and lime. Rinse, soak in clear water for 2 hours.

1½ quarts vinegar
4 pounds sugar

2 teaspoons salt
⅓ cup pickling spice (in bag)

Combine vinegar, sugar, salt and pickling spice and bring to a hard boil. Add rind and cook slowly for 45 minutes or until rind is tender. Fill sterilized pint jars and seal. Makes 7 or 8 pints.

Mrs. M. E. Wilson

ORANGE-LIME RELISH

2 large oranges
1 lime
2 tablespoons wine vinegar

1 to 2 tablespoons sugar
1 tablespoon instant minced
  onion

Peel oranges over bowl to catch any juice; cut into medium-thick slices. Slice lime very thin. Combine remaining ingredients; pour over fruit. Chill for several hours. Makes 4 to 5 servings.

Kitchen Corner

PICKLED SPICED BEETS

1 can red beets (approxi-
  mately 1 pound
½ cup sugar
½ teaspoon dry mustard
¼ teaspoon cinnamon

6 whole cloves
1 bay leaf
2 slices onion
1 cup vinegar

Combine all ingredients. Bring to a boil; lower heat and simmer about 5 minutes. Chill thoroughly. Remove beets; drain well to serve. Serves 5 or 6.

Mrs. J. Wally Gray

PEAR RELISH II

Coarsely grind together:

1 gallon pears	14 green peppers
½ gallon white onions	4 hot peppers

Add 2 cups of salt to the mixture, let stand overnight.

Drain and rinse in 3 changes of water. Drain dry.

Syrup:

2 quarts vinegar	2 tablespoons turmeric
4 cups sugar	2 tablespoons mustard seed

Cook syrup 5 minutes, add to ground mixture. Bring to the simmering point and cook for 5 minutes. Pour in hot sterilized jars and seal. Yields 20 pints.

MRS. WILLIAM C. GILMORE, JR.

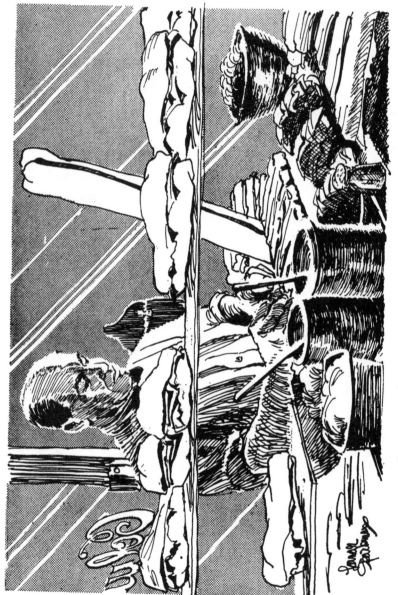

Creating Cuban Sandwiches at Columbia Restaurant

CHAPTER XXII

Sandwiches and Spreads

No Florida cookbook would be complete without a section on sandwiches. In a climate such as this, where people live outdoors as much as in, someone is always packing a lunch or a picnic, or preparing for a backyard supper. We build every sort of sandwich, ranging from the gigantic Dagwood to the lowly peanut butter and jelly, but Cuban sandwiches are the outstanding favorite, by far.

Aside from the fact that the Cuban sandwich is utterly delicious and completely satisfying, it may be refrigerated, frozen, or packed in a lunch box without risk of spoilage or loss of flavor. It may be made at home or bought, neatly wrapped, on the way to an outing. In the Spanish restaurants, it has been standard practice for years to make Cuban sandwiches at a long counter in the front of the coffee shop where passers-by can gaze through the windows at the fascinating sight. The long loaves of bread are stacked like cordwood beside rosy baked hams, succulent roasts of pork, gigantic rolls of Italian salami, great chunks of Swiss cheese and huge jars of frosty dill pickles. The sandwichmaker's long knife flashes brightly through bread, through meat and cheese, through pickles. In the wink of an eye, the slices of bread are dressed with mustard, layered with slice after slice of meat and cheese, blessed with thin-sliced pickles, then closed and wrapped in gleaming white paper. If there is one food that means home to a Tampan, this, the magnificent Cuban sandwich, is it.

CUBAN SANDWICH

1½ loaves Cuban bread	¼ pound thinly sliced Swiss cheese
Mustard and butter	¼ pound Italian salami,
¾ pound baked ham, thinly sliced	thinly sliced
½ pound barbecued or roast pork	Lengthwise slices of dill pickle

Cut Cuban bread in 6 pieces 8 inches long. Split lengthwise and spread mustard on 1 piece, and butter on the other. Divide ham, pork, Swiss cheese, salami and pickle among the 6 sandwiches, arranging in layers on the bread. Wrap each sandwich in a paper napkin and secure with a toothpick. Flavor is improved by warming in the oven before serving. Serves 6.

SILVER RING CAFE, TAMPA, FLORIDA

CHATTERBOX OPEN-FACED SANDWICH

Rye or whole wheat bread slices
Lettuce leaves
Sliced chicken or turkey
Swiss cheese

Crisp bacon slices
Sliced tomato
Hard-boiled eggs
Thousand Island Dressing

Have all ingredients icy cold. On each slice of bread place, in this order, lettuce, chicken or turkey, cheese, bacon, slice of tomato, and 1 hard-boiled egg, sliced. Cover each sandwich with Thousand Island Dressing.

THOUSAND ISLAND DRESSING:

1 pint mayonnaise
½ small onion, chopped very fine
¼ cup chopped green olives
1½ tablespoons capers
½ cup chili sauce

3 tablespoons chopped parsley
3 tablespoons green pepper,
   chopped fine
¼ cup dill pickles (not garlic)
   chopped or put through blender

Mix and let the flavors blend for several hours before serving.

THE CHATTERBOX, ST. PETERSBURG, FLORIDA

HAM-WICHES

⅓ cup butter, melted
2 tablespoons prepared mustard
1 small chopped onion
1 tablespoon poppy seeds

6 hamburger buns
6 slices ham
6 slices Swiss or American cheese

Combine butter, mustard, onion and poppy seeds. Spread on inside of hamburger buns. Place 1 slice ham and 1 slice of cheese on each bun. Spread sauce on top of buns. Heat in oven on cookie sheet 15 minutes at 350°. Serves 6.

MRS. FRED L. WOLF

ONION SANDWICHES

1 large Bermuda onion
Vinegar, salt and pepper
2 ice cubes

Sandwich bread
Homemade mayonnaise

Slice onion in thin slices, then chop each slice fine. Soak in vinegar, salt and pepper to taste, and ice cubes. While onion is soaking, trim crusts from bread and spread with homemade mayonnaise. Drain onion well in strainer. Use about 1 heaping teaspoonful for each sandwich. After sandwiches are made, cut into fingers, triangles or whatever shape you desire.

MRS. DEVEREUX BACON, JR.

PEPPER-NUT SPREAD

1 cup pecan nut meats
1 bell pepper, cleaned and
   chopped coarsely

½ cup American cheese
Mayonnaise to moisten

Put first 3 ingredients through fine blade of food grinder. Add just enough mayonnaise to bind ingredients together for easy spreading. This may be used as a filling for sandwiches or in canapés.

This recipe originated in 1883 at the home of Captain W. B. Bonacker, founder of Lakeland, Florida, where it was used for tea sandwiches.

JACK BONACKER WILSON

PIMIENTO CHEESE SPREAD

1 pound medium Cheddar cheese,
   grated
1½ ounce jar pimiento chopped
   (reserve about 1 tablespoon
   of oil)
2 heaping tablespoons mayonnaise
   (more if necessary)

2 dashes vinegar
Pinch of dry mustard
1 teaspoon scraped onion
¼ teaspoon Worcestershire
1 teaspoon salt
½ teaspoon pepper

Mix by hand until smooth and well blended. Allow to blend in refrigerator for several hours before serving. Use for sandwiches, toasted cheese sandwiches, or stuffed celery.

MRS. HARLAN LOGAN

TOASTED CRABMEAT SANDWICHES

¾ cup fresh mushrooms,
   chopped fine
2 tablespoons butter
6 slices tomato (⅓ inch thick)
6 slices bread, crust removed

1 egg, beaten
½ pound flaked crabmeat
¼ teaspoon salt
¾ cup grated sharp cheese

Sauté mushrooms in butter about 5 minutes. Place slice of tomato on each slice of bread. Spoon 2 tablespoons mushrooms over each. Mix egg, crabmeat, and salt. Put a portion over mushrooms; sprinkle 2 tablespoons cheese over each. Place under broiler until cheese melts.

MRS. J. BROWN FARRIOR

OPEN-FACED SHRIMP SANDWICHES

½ pound soft or semi-soft sharp
   Cheddar cheese
¼ pound butter or margarine
¼ cup finely minced onion
1 teaspoon Worcestershire sauce
¼ cup lemon juice

½ teaspoon paprika
1 pound shrimp, cooked and
   deveined
12 frankfurter rolls
A little extra soft butter

Have cheese (if soft type) and butter at room temperature. If cheese is semi-soft, grate it coarsely. There should be 2 cups lightly packed. Stir cheese, butter, onion, Worcestershire sauce, lemon juice, and paprika together. Stir in finely chopped shrimp. Scoop out rolls, fill, and dot with butter. Place on foil in broiling pan. Broil about 4 inches from heat until bubbly and lightly browned (about 3 to 5 minutes). Can use 2 dozen small finger rolls, scooped, filled and heated as canapés.

Mrs. T. A. Bell, Jr.

TUNA SOUFFLÉ SANDWICHES

8 slices bread
1 cup flaked tuna (7 ounce can)
¼ cup chopped celery
¼ cup chopped green pepper
½ cup shredded Cheddar cheese

1½ cups milk
3 eggs, beaten
1 teaspoon salt
⅛ teaspoon paprika

Trim crusts from bread. Place 4 slices in greased 8-inch square baking dish. Combine tuna, celery, and green pepper and spread over bread. Sprinkle cheese over all. Top with remaining slices of bread. Combine milk, eggs, and salt, mixing well. This much can be done several hours ahead and set aside. When ready to bake (45 minutes before mealtime), pour milk mixture over bread. Sprinkle with paprika. Bake in slow oven (325°) 40 minutes. Serves 4.

Mrs. A. M. Crowell, Jr.

AVOCADO SANDWICH SPREAD

Mash meat from avocado and sprinkle with lime juice to keep from darkening. Mix with salt, finely chopped onion, lots of crisp crumbled bacon and enough mayonnaise to bind. Spread on buttered whole wheat or rye bread.

Mrs. James W. Gray, Jr.

TOMATO PIQUANTS

2 eggs	1 teaspoon prepared mustard or
1 pound grated American cheese	½ teaspoon dry mustard
2 tablespoons mayonnaise	Dash of Tabasco
1 teaspoon onion juice	6 slices toast
1 tablespoon Worcestershire sauce	2 fresh tomatoes
	12 slices bacon

Beat eggs, add cheese, mayonnaise, onion juice, Worcestershire sauce, mustard, and Tabasco, making a soft paste. To each slice of toast, add a slice of tomato, cover with cheese paste, and place under broiler until slightly browned. Top with 2 slices previously cooked bacon and serve hot. Serves 6.

MRS. ROBERT A. FOSTER

CONEY ISLAND RED HOTS

1 tablespoon cooking oil	Dash of Worcestershire sauce
1 medium onion, chopped	Weiners
1 pound ground beef	Weiner buns, split and toasted
1 No. 303 can tomatoes, sieved	Mustard
Dash of Tabasco (optional)	Chopped onion
Salt and pepper, to taste	Chopped dill pickle (optional)

In a frying pan sauté the onion in oil until clear. Add meat and brown well, then add tomatoes, Tabasco, salt and pepper and Worcestershire sauce. Simmer for ½ hour or until the sauce is no longer soupy. Place boiled weiners on buns which have been spread with mustard, ladle sauce over the weiners and top with chopped onion and pickle.

MRS. ROGERS MORGAN

TOASTED SARDINE SANDWICHES

Mash 1 can of imported sardines. Mix with 1 tablespoon mayonnaise, the juice of ½ lemon, a dash each of Tabasco and Worcestershire sauce, and 1 hard-boiled egg, chopped fine. Spread between slices of bread, butter the outside and toast under the broiler until golden brown.

MRS. GUY KING, JR.

Index

THE JUNIOR LEAGUE OF TAMPA

Women Building a Better Community

The Junior League of Tampa is an organization of 1,700 women committed to promoting voluntarism, developing the potential of women, and improving communities through effective action and leadership of trained volunteers.

Since 1926, the volunteers in our organization have shared their time, talents, and treasures with the Tampa community. We have been proud to support many local nonprofit organizations and community projects through volunteer hours and money raised through fund-raisers, including the sale of our cookbooks. Our community investment to date totals over $5 million.

The Junior League of Tampa cookbooks have always served as a legacy, an investment of time and tradition, handed from one generation to another, from our community to yours. But more than that, The Junior League of Tampa cookbooks are an investment in the foundation of the community.

Our proud history of cookbook publishing dates back fifty years to the first printing of *The Gasparilla Cookbook* in November 1961. Since that time, we published *A Taste of Tampa* (1978; out of print) and *Tampa Treasures* (1992) and most recently created the first-ever Junior League cookbook series, now a four-volume set known as The Junior League of Tampa Culinary Collection. The Culinary Collection includes:

The Life of the Party (2002)
EveryDay Feasts (2004)
Savor the Seasons (2006)
Capture the Coast (2010)

To learn more about The Junior League of Tampa, visit www.jltampa.org.

FRP.INC

FRP creates successful connections between organizations and individuals through custom books.

 Favorite Recipes® Press

Favorite Recipes Press, an imprint of FRP, Inc., located in Nashville, Tennessee, is one of the nation's best-known and most-respected cookbook companies. Favorite Recipes Press began by publishing cookbooks for its parent company, Southwestern/Great American, in 1961. FRP, Inc., is now a wholly owned subsidiary of the Southwestern/Great American family of companies, and under the Favorite Recipes Press imprint has produced hundreds of custom cookbook titles for nonprofit organizations, companies, and individuals.

Other FRP, Inc., imprints include

BECKON BOOKS   The Booksmith Group   **Community**Classics®
                      A DIVISION OF FRP

Additional titles published by FRP, Inc., are

Favorite Recipes of Home Economics Teachers

| Cooking Up a Classic Christmas | Recipes Worth Sharing | More Recipes Worth Sharing | The Hunter's Table | The Vintner's Table |

Junior Leagues In the Kitchen with Kids: Everyday Recipes & Activities for Healthy Living

Almost Homemade

The Illustrated Encyclopedia of American Cooking

To learn more about custom books, visit our Web site, www.frpbooks.com.

Classic JUNIOR LEAGUE® COOKBOOK COLLECTION

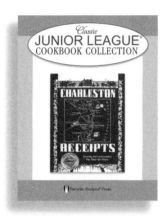

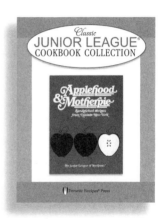

This collection includes six of the most well known and respected Junior League cookbooks of all time; combined there are more than 2,000 pages with 4,000 regionally inspired, tried-and-true recipes. Collectively, over 2,000,000 copies of these cookbooks have sold over a span of 60 years.

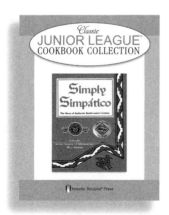

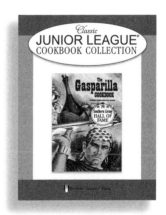